Temple Bar

A HISTORY

Temple Bar

A HISTORY

MAURICE CURTIS

The
History
Press
Ireland

Front cover illustration: The Ha'penny Bridge and the Merchant's Arch entrance to Temple Bar. (Courtesy of Psyberartist, Wikimedia Commons)
Back cover illustation: The Wood Quay end of Temple Bar in the late 1960s. (Courtesy of Gemma Jackson)

First published 2016

The History Press Ireland
50 City Quay
Dublin 2
Ireland
www.thehistorypress.ie

The History Press Ireland is a member of Publishing Ireland,
the Irish book publishers' association.

British Library Cataloguing in Publication Data.
A catalogue record for this book is available from the British Library.

ISBN 978 1 84588 896 1

Typesetting and origination by The History Press

CONTENTS

ACKNOWLEDGEMENTS

There were many individuals and organisations that helped with this book, including *Archiseek (www.archiseek.com)*, Dublin Decoded, Donal Fallon and his history blog, *Come Here to Me!* (www.comeheretome.com), Sean Murphy of the Centre for Irish Genealogical Studies and Historical Studies, Dublin City Archives (in particular Dr Máire Kennedy), Pearse Street and Dolphin's Barn Public Libraries, the Irish Georgian Society, the Royal Society of Antiquaries of Ireland, the National Archives, the National Library of Ireland, the National Gallery of Ireland and the Irish Architectural Archive. Other organisations also helped, including Dublin City Council, Temple Bar Trust, Temple Bar Properties and the Irish Landmark Trust (thanks especially to Miriam and Brendan Conway). A special thanks to Pat Liddy, whose knowledge of Temple Bar is inspiring. Willie and Teresa Ahern of the Palace Bar were most helpful with stories and images. Thanks to Christopher Morash of Trinity College Dublin (TCD) for information on the Smock Alley Theatre and theatre life in old Dublin. Olivia Kelly and Frank McNally of *The Irish Times* were similarly enlightening on the same topic. The former *Irish Times* columnist and Temple Bar resident Frank McDonald was an absolutely indispensable mine of information – a veritable walking encyclopaedia on all things Temple Bar. No journalist or individual campaigned (and continues to campaign) as strongly for the area as Frank McDonald, a constant opponent of bad planning in Dublin. He reported on Dublin City Council meetings on the matter and gave space to alternative voices, such as An Táisce, which believed the area had a future if properly preserved and encouraged. Thanks also to Lisa Cassidy of *Built Dublin* (www.builtdublin.com), Dublin City Architects, Turtle Bunbury and the Kildare Local History Society. Arnold Horner, Angrett Simms and Joseph Brady of the UCD School of Geography,

Planning and the Environment were also helpful in this respect. And also in UCD, Professor Mary Daly of the History Department, has always been a guiding light. I would also like to acknowledge Gerry Mac Gann and his mobile Gilbert Library collection, raconteur Noel 'Valdez' Bailey, archaeologist Linzi Simpson, architectural historian Christine Casey, Group '91 architects and in particular Shane O'Toole. Colette Adanan and Colm Mac Con Iomaire pointed me in the right direction when it came to researching Dublin's coffee houses. I am also thankful to Bewleys for information on coffee history. Historian Patrick Geogheghan of TCD provided information on Buck Whaley. Thanks to Valerie Shanley of the *Irish Independent* and Joe Jackson of *The Irish Times* for information on Margaret Leeson. Patrick Freyne, also of *The Irish Times*, was knowledgeable on the subject of brewing. John Lee of Old Dublin Town and architect James Kelly provided much information on Read's of Parliament Street. For the history of Dublin newspapers, I thank Hugh Oram and also my late cousin Vincent Kinane of TCD, who gave me newspaper and bibliographic information. The assistance of those at the Irish Architectural Archive, who offered me photographs, advice and architectural history, was indispensable. A special thanks go to David Dickson, Peter Pearson, Niall McCullough, Colm Lennon, John Montague and Dermot O'Gráda for their sterling work on numerous aspects of Dublin's history. I am also grateful to the Temple Bar Residents' Association and the many organisations, cultural centres and businesses of Temple Bar for their determination to make this unique area prosper, thrive and also be eminently residential. Finally, I would like to offer a big thanks to Ronan Colgan and Beth Amphlett of The History Press Ireland for their encouragement, patience and guidance.

INTRODUCTION

Temple Bar is one of the most iconic parts of Dublin and is well known nationally and internationally as the 'cultural quarter' of the capital. A mixed-use area of 28 acres in the centre of Dublin city, it is one of Dublin's most visited districts. It is bustling with colourful pubs, cafés, restaurants, galleries, cinemas, theatres, resource centres, old family businesses, mainstream and craft shops, all crowded together along the busy, cobbled streets. It is also home to a couple of thousand residents and sees hundreds of thousands of visitors annually.

Since the last decade of the twentieth century, Temple Bar has transformed from a derelict area into a thriving, dynamic space. Today's Temple Bar can boast of many new arts venues and there are around fifty cultural organisations based in Temple Bar, with scores of artists and creative professionals making it their base. It is an area of national importance, with a significant architectural, cultural, civic and historic character. The street pattern and the old street names have survived the upheavals that have shaken Dublin and Ireland since medieval times and give a good insight into the history of the area.

The area is bounded by the Liffey to the north, Dame Street to the south, Westmoreland Street to the east and Fishamble Street to the west. The close proximity of Temple Bar to City Hall (formerly the Royal Exchange), the Irish Parliament House (now Bank of Ireland), the old custom house on Essex Quay and Dublin Castle, the centre of colonial administration in the city, ensured the centrality and importance of Temple Bar in Dublin's civic, political and commercial life. As a result, the area's history is full of references to culture, trade, design, craft, publishing, the performing arts, coffee houses and politics, all of which is garnished with a dash of mayhem, magic and mystery.

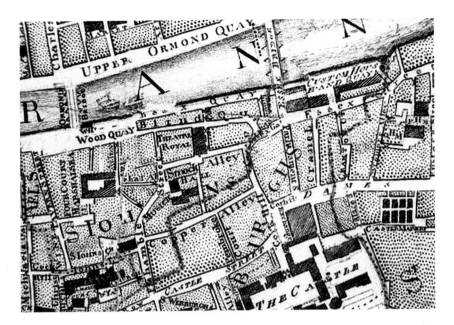

Early eighteenth-century map showing Custom House Quay area. (Courtesy of IHI)

From the early 1600s, Sir William Temple, the first provost of Trinity College Dublin, was the owner of some of the land in the area, which still bears his name. The Temple Bar area as we know it today originated in the old medieval city of Dublin and expanded eastwards from the early 1600s onwards. Over the following two centuries, it became a flourishing centre of trade, crafts and commerce, as well as social and political life. It also became the primary residential, commercial, political and dockland area of Dublin during the seventeenth and eighteenth centuries.[1]

Temple Bar is also filled with many triumphs of architectural design. The area is a feast of modern, original and highly stylish buildings integrating into the existing fabric. Renewal has embraced the old and the new and extended the life of Temple Bar for future generations. Every street and alleyway contains buildings of interest. The oldest houses are early- to mid-eighteenth-century buildings on Eustace and Fownes Street. There are also some interesting examples of eighteenth- and nineteenth-century brick-built warehouses, e.g. the Gaiety School of Acting building on Essex Street West, beside the theatre, and on Temple Lane South, Crown Alley and Cecilia Street. Temple Bar has furthermore become something of a showpiece for contemporary Irish architecture. The Wooden Building, the Green Building, Spranger's Yard, Temple Bar Gallery and Studios,

Curved Street and Meeting House Square, and the Ark are all significant buildings or spaces. This mix of old and new is part of what makes Temple Bar such an attractive and distinctive area.

Some of the most important names in Irish history have strong links to Temple Bar, including Oliver Cromwell, the Temple family, Richard and Robert Boyle, Jonathan Swift, George Faulkner, George Frederick Handel, Thomas Cooley, James Gandon, the Duke of Wellington, Richard Brinsley Sheridan, Margaret Leeson, Daniel O'Connell, Henry Grattan, Delia Larkin, the Sham Squire, Lord Edward Fitzgerald, George Berkeley, William of Orange, Molly Malone, Dorcas Kelly, James Joyce, Maria Edgeworth, Oliver Goldsmith, Thomas Moore, W.B. Yeats, Peg Woffington, Spranger Barry, Walter Osborne, Buck Whaley, 'copper-faced Jack', Harry Kernoff, Phil Lynott, Rory Gallagher, Aldo Rossi, Esther Vonhomrigh (Swift's Vanessa), James Clarence Mangan, Joseph Sheridan Le Fanu, Bram Stoker, Wolfe Tone, Jeremiah O'Donovan Rossa, Arthur Griffith, Kevin Barry, Éamonn Ceannt, Seán MacBride and Robert Smyllie.

From the Vikings to the Victorians, practically every era of Irish history is represented in Temple Bar. The story of Temple Bar then is the story of Dublin, of Ireland – a story of tragedy and triumph, through times of oppression and prosperity, culminating in the vibrant centre we have in Dublin today. Temple Bar was and remains to this day a mirror that reflects the vicissitudes of time and the forces that have shaped us. It is also the story of the rise, decline and rebirth of one of Ireland's architectural treasures.

1

MONKS OF THE TEMPLE – EARLY HISTORY

The growth and development of Temple Bar should be seen in the context of the wider history of medieval Dublin and Ireland. There is archaeological evidence to suggest that the area was first inhabited by Gaelic clans and subsequently by marauding Vikings in the tenth century. The western end of Temple Bar lies in part of the old city that was a Viking town. The remains of Isolde's Tower, part of the thirteenth-century city wall, in Exchange Street Lower, indicate the importance of this part of the town.

To the east of this old city, outside the walls, the Augustinians built a monastery, the Holy Trinity Friary, in the late thirteenth century, in the area of modern-day Cecilia and Crow streets, with lands stretching along the banks of the River Liffey. The historic name of the district was not Temple Bar but St Andrew's Parish, an eastern suburb of medieval (Anglo-Norman) Dublin, located outside the city walls. The old name survives in the form of St Andrew's church, just off Dame Street.

FROM THE VIKINGS TO THE NORMANS

The Normans came to Dublin by invitation – an overture by Dermot MacMurrough, exiled King of Leinster. MacMurrough hoped to win back his kingdom, lost in a dispute with the High King of Ireland. His arrangement with Richard de Clare, the legendary Strongbow, was one of many reciprocal military actions between the Irish, the Welsh and the English at a time when lords and kings were jostling for power. Dublin town fell to the Normans in 1170. The Vikings fled to Oxmanstown on the north bank of the Liffey. Strongbow married Dermot's daughter Aoife and exerted control over the city of Dublin to such an extent that his king, the Norman Henry II, came to Dublin in 1172 to check Strongbow's power. In 1185, Henry declared his son John Lord of Ireland. John unexpectedly inherited the kingship and thus the Lordship of Ireland was tied to the English throne. From then onwards, Dublin started to take on its medieval shape with the building of Dublin Castle (1204–1230) on the site of an old Gaelic (subsequently Viking) fortification, the establishment of a proper administration structure, and the building of churches and monasteries. As early as 1192, Dublin Corporation was established and trade guilds encouraged. Over the succeeding generations, commerce improved and Dublin became a small city, necessitating the improvement of water and drainage, roads and houses and public buildings. The ruling Normans were used to greater convenience in their daily lives and set about laying water pipes as early as 1244. By 1245, a supply of water ran from the River Poddle to their grand stone castle on the hill. The tidal nature of the River Liffey at this point means it was undrinkable, so for generations Dublin residents resorted to alternatives – ale, wine and whiskey, hence Winetavern Street on the periphery of Temple Bar.[1]

The old defences were strengthened with the building of better walls and gates and towers. The only surviving old gate of Dublin (and of the thirteenth century) is on Cook Street, adjacent to the two St Audoen's churches, with the old walls and battlements accessible from St Audoen's Park on High Street. The remnants of Isolde's Tower, one of the towers guarding the city, are still visible on Lower Exchange Street, which itself follows the direction of the old walls of Dublin.[2]

FROM THE MONKS TO THE REFORMATION

On the eve of the mid-sixteenth-century Reformation, the area now known as Temple Bar was sufficiently populous, albeit barely, to be served by a church, St Andrew's. In addition to this church and the Thingmount, an old centre for administering justice, one of the most important features of Temple Bar was the open area known as Hoggen Green, now College Green. St Mary de Hogges Abbey was near this (on the site of present-day Bank of Ireland) and the Augustinian Holy Trinity Friary was halfway between this and the walls of the medieval city. Today, part of the thirteenth-century friary is visible within an apartment-restaurant complex called 'The Friary' in Temple Bar. The friary was founded about 1282 and its site is believed to be marked by the conjunction of Temple Lane, Temple Bar, Fownes Street Upper and Cecilia Street. The site has been partially excavated and is listed on the National Monuments Service database. Those excavations revealed around seventy burials from between the late twelfth century to the fourteenth century, remains of the friary on the east side of Cecilia House and, in 1996, excavations exposed a section of wall with a relieving arch and a corner tower.

Overall, three religious orders occupied more than half of the lands that now make up Temple Bar (the rest is the old city and the area consisting of land reclaimed from the rivers Poddle and Liffey and the surrounding marshland). The lands of the Augustinians and the nuns of St Mary de Hogges would subsequently be the basis for the newer, developed part of Temple Bar stretching from Parliament Street to Westmoreland Street. There was also an order of nuns on the lands presently occupied by Trinity College Dublin.

'STICKY FINGERS' BRABAZON

The Tudor conquest of Ireland from the mid-sixteenth century onwards spelt a new era for Dublin, with the city enjoying a renewed prominence as the centre of the colonists' administrative rule in Ireland. These new colonists needed to be housed and rewarded for their services to the Crown. The suppression and confiscation of the monasteries during the English Reformation, from the mid-1530s, onwards facilitated this.

King Henry VIII (1491–1547), who became king in 1509, ordered that all churches, abbeys and monasteries were henceforth to be under his control. 60 per cent of Irish monasteries and friaries remained undisturbed in the Gaelic and Gaelicised parts of Ireland. Temple Bar, being in the Pale and under direct English influence and control, was not so lucky. If fact, the dissolution had an enormous impact on all of Dublin due to the concentration of cathedrals, churches, monastic houses and lands in the immediate vicinity of the city. The confiscated land was transferred to the English Crown via Dublin Corporation. The speed of land transfer was remarkable – many medieval estates and monasteries were transferred wholesale to private hands or to Dublin Corporation itself.

St Mary de Hogges went to the Crown. In 1591, the old monastery of All Saints was recommissioned as Trinity College Dublin. Cary's Hospital was built on some of the open land at Hoggen (College) Green in 1595 and consisted of a large mansion, garden and a plantation by the seashore. This subsequently changed hands and was renamed Chichester House. It became the seat of the Irish parliament in the early seventeenth century. Finally, St Augustine's Monastery was granted to the Sir Walter Tyrell, who came from a wealthy merchant family also involved in politics. One of his descendants, William Crow, later acquired the land. The Crow family soon built a number of large mansions and sublet plots of land.

Therefore, it is clear that the early history of the development of Temple Bar may be traced back to Dublin's monastic settlement and the dissolution of monasteries in 1541 which began a new era in the eastward expansion and development of Dublin.[3]

Henry VIII gave the monastery of St Thomas Abbey (on Thomas Street in the Liberties) and the land around it to his vice treasurer in Ireland at the time, William Brabazon, who had been sent to Ireland in 1533. William Brabazon's influence and control over government finances at the time of the Reformation had an enormous impact on the subsequent history of Temple Bar (and Ireland). It was he who oversaw the quick transfer of confiscated property to the treasury. Vice treasurer and three times Lord Justice, he was described by historian Hiram Morgan as the prototype New Englishman – 'a hard man with sticky fingers'. Brabazon and other officials such as Lord Deputies Grey and St Leger profited by renting out confiscated land at rates far below market values and leaving thousands of pounds of rent arrears uncollected. This fraudulent activity was not uncovered until three years after his death. When the widespread corruption was brought to light in 1556, St Leger was dismissed, tried and fined £5,000.[4]

REBELLION AND THE GUNPOWDER EXPLOSION

Another important factor in the eastward expansion of Temple Bar was Queen Elizabeth I's determination to make Dublin a Protestant city. She established Trinity College in 1592 (on confiscated monastic lands) as a solely Protestant university and ordered that the Catholic St Patrick's and Christ Church cathedrals be converted into Protestant cathedrals. This move to Protestantise Dublin and extend the conquest, however, coincided with the great gunpowder explosion in Dublin in 1597. The background to the explosion was the English war against the Irish chieftains, the O'Neills and the O'Donnells, who had been successfully waging a campaign during the Nine Years' War. English soldiers and supplies were arriving in Dublin port (by Wood and Essex quays) and, by accident or design, a number of barrels of gunpowder exploded dramatically in the heart of the old city, near Dublin Castle, killing over 100 people and destroying half of the small city. The buildings on Cook Street, Fishamble Street, Bridge Street, High Street and St Michael's Lane suffered the most damage. This and the enormous cost of rebuilding led some merchants to decide to move eastwards, a move that was key to the growth and development of Temple Bar.[5]

2

CROMWELL, THE CROW'S NEST AND FAMILIES OF FORTUNE

From the middle to the late sixteenth century, a concerted effort was made to bring the whole country under the English system of government and the control of a parliament in Dublin. This culminated in the defeat of the Irish armies by those of Queen Elizabeth I at the Battle of Kinsale in 1601, which was followed by the 'Flight of the Earls' a few years later, when Ireland's remaining major chieftains, including the O'Neills and the O'Donnells, left for the European continent. The plantation of Ireland, starting with King Henry VIII's Tudor plantation, continued with the Elizabethan and Cromwellian plantations after the defeat of the Irish armies. These plantations built on the confiscations and forfeitures already begun with under Henry in the mid-1500s and continued with ever-greater severity the adverse possession of Irish property and land.

NOT QUITE FOOTBALL – CHICHESTER

One of the most important figures during the plantations was Sir Arthur Chichester (1563–1627), who commanded English forces in Ulster during the Nine Years' War (1594–1603) and adopted a notorious 'scorched earth policy' in the belief that a winter's famine would do more damage to the Irish forces than a million swords. Following the Treaty of Mellifont (ending the war) in 1605, he became Lord Deputy of Ireland with his residence at Chichester House on College Green, where the legal documents for the Plantation of Ulster were signed in 1612. He oversaw the plantation with great vigour as his brother

Sir John Chichester had been defeated by the MacDonnells in the Battle of Carrickfergus in 1597. To compound matters, after the Irish victory, Chichester's head had been chopped off and used as a football by the MacDonnell clan.

The planning and orchestration of the Ulster Plantation was directed from Chichester House in Temple Bar and from William Crow's mansion on Crow Street, known as 'the Crow's Nest'. Over the following decades, some of the worst excesses of this State policy reached a crescendo, notably in the 1640s and '50s. During the religious wars that wracked Ireland in those years, starting with the 1641 Rebellion, the new English Protestant authorities issued orders expelling all Catholics from the city limits and Dublin became dominated by Protestants. Until about 1800 this power and influence was essentially unchallenged, although towards the end of the eighteenth century voices in Grattan's Irish parliament were heard to question this Protestant dominance of all things Irish.

Chichester House was subsequently the site of the Irish parliament. To this day, two important tapestries hang in the House of Lords building on College Green celebrating the new planters' victories in the Siege of Derry (1688–89) and the Battle of the Boyne (1690). They are also a legacy of the ruthlessness of Arthur Chichester's Plantation of Ulster, which speeded up the process of colonisation, and a monument to the allegiance of the members of the Irish parliament (known as 'undertakers') in the eighteenth century.[1]

Trinity College and the former Houses of the Irish Parliament, College Green, c. 1900. (Lawrence Collection, courtesy of National Library of Ireland (NLI) Commons Collection)

FROM BRABAZON TO TEMPLE

A number of names stand out in the consolidation of English influence and control of Dublin and in particular the growth and development of the Temple Bar area. Besides William Brabazon, who meticulously and avariciously oversaw the implementation of Henry VIII's policy (dispossession of the monasteries and the forfeiture of lands), names such as Crow, Temple, Boyle, Eustace, Annesley and Fownes were very important in the new regime's governance. This was reflected in their acquisition of land and property in the expanding eastern suburb extending from and including the old city. A 1627 inquiry showed a garden and house lately built by William Crow, adjoining Dame Street and a lane leading to the River Liffey (variously called Hoggen Lane, Dirty Lane and finally Temple Lane). This was close to the site of the original Augustinian monastery. The grounds of the monastery were taken for several houses built for Sir George Wentworth, Christopher Wandesford and the Crow, Eustace, Temple, Fownes and Annesley families.[2]

Dame Street from George's Street junction, 1952. (Courtesy of IHI)

They were quick to avail of (and compound) the social, political and financial upheaval that Dublin and the rest of Ireland was undergoing. They were essentially exploitative pioneers in a merchant-based aristocracy, intent on owning and controlling as much of the land as possible. Once the land was forfeited by the monks or whichever Irish had originally legally owned it, it was automatically transferred to the ownership of Dublin Corporation, which leased out plots for a number of years to the new colonists. The Corporation, for instance, received from the Temple family an annual rent of £40 for part of the former monastic lands, on what is now called Temple Lane South, and for land behind the mansion's garden, now part of Temple Bar.[3]

Consequently, within the enclave once owned by the Augustinian friars, there developed, in what was to become the Temple Bar of today, a grid plan of streets and alleys around the sites being acquired by individual colonists to build substantial houses and gardens. The names of those early carpetbaggers, the prominent families living in the Dame Street-Temple Bar area from the early seventeenth century, are still remembered in the area's street names.[4]

TEMPLE TIMES AND TEMPLE'S BARR

In 1599, Sir William Temple (1555–1627), a renowned teacher and philosopher, entered the service of the Lord Deputy of Ireland. He had come to Ireland in that year as secretary to Robert Devereux, the Earl of Essex. Ten years later, he was made provost of Trinity College Dublin and Master Chancery in Ireland. Temple built his house and gardens on the corner of Temple Lane and the street now called Temple Bar. The site included some reclaimed land, which had formed part of the riverbank ('barr') of the Liffey estuary. In the seventeenth century, 'barr' (later shortened to 'bar') usually meant a raised estuary sandbank often used for walking on. Thus, the River Liffey embankment beside the Temple family's plot became known as Temple's Barr or simply Temple Bar. In 1656, Sir William Temple's son, Sir John Temple, acquired additional land, the reclamation of which was made possible by the building of a new sea wall, which enclosed the extended property. The shoreline was gradually extended and enclosed over subsequent generations, having originally run along the present thoroughfare that extends from Essex Street, the Temple Bar street and Fleet Street. North of that line land was reclaimed from either the River Liffey or River Poddle.

Sir William Temple (1555-1627). (Courtesy of IHI)

TEMPLE AND CROMWELL

The 1641 Rebellion was essentially the Irish chieftain class rising up against the colonists, beneficiaries of earlier plantations. However, John Temple, before he acquired additional land, wrote a history of the 1641 Rebellion with a strongly partisan and sectarian slant. The book had a huge influence on Oliver Cromwell's invasion of Ireland later in the decade. *The Irish Rebellion, True and Impartial History* (1644), reprinted as *History of the Irish Rebellion* (1646), was an exaggeration of the 'massacres', accompanied by sensationalist woodcuts depicting the Irish massacring thousands of settlers. This intentionally inflamed Protestant indignation against the native Irish, identifying English rule with God's will and depicting the Irish Catholics as ingrates. This book contributed hugely to the severity of the Cromwellian campaign of 1649–52. In later years, the book was burnt by the public hangman on the orders of the short-lived Jacobite parliament in Dublin in 1689. It was reprinted many times over the ensuing centuries and helped confirm the colonists' sense of entitlement.

Interestingly, Copper Alley in Temple Bar played a role in the 1641 Rebellion. Prior to the planned seizure of Dublin Castle by the Irish, 'the conspirators arrived within the city, and having that day [22 October 1641] met at the Lion Tavern, near Copper-alley, ordered their affairs together, drank health's upon their knees to the happy success of the next morning's work'.[5]

The heightened ferocity and brutality of the 1641 Rebellion in John Temple's book may be partly responsible for Oliver Cromwell's order that the Irish go 'to Hell or Connaught' when he came in 1649. Two individuals based in Temple Bar, William Crow and William Petty, were instrumental in the Cromwellian Plantation that followed the defeat of the Irish.

WILLIAM CROW AND THE DOWN SURVEY

In 1597, Walter Tyrell's heirs transferred their land in Temple Bar to William Crow, an important official in the Court of Common Pleas in Ireland. Subsequently, several large houses and accompanying gardens were built on his lands, near what is today Crow Street. One of these houses was the mansion of Crow himself, which over the first decades of the seventeenth century became known as the Crow's Nest. The office of one of the most important officials in Ireland at the time was in this mansion. This was the office of the 'Survey of the Forfeited Irish Lands', which was in the hands of the meticulous Dr William Petty. Petty (1623-87), a doctor by training, had left England in 1652 to become a physician-general to Cromwell's army in Ireland. In the space of thirteen months in 1654/5, he completed for the government the most important survey of Irish lands ever undertaken.[6]

PETTY'S SURVEY AND THE CROW'S NEST

Cromwell had borrowed huge sums of money from London merchants when he was planning the re-conquest of the country. He did this under the 1642 Act for Adventurers, which established the necessity of the re-conquest of Ireland and the financing of such a re-conquest: 1,500 wealthy investors were to be rewarded by having their money converted into parcels of land from the 2.5 million acres to be confiscated. Their investments essentially funded the suppression of the Irish rebels. However, only one third of the required £1 million was actually raised and following his victory, Cromwell had to repay his enormous loans and pay his soldiers. Some 32,000 officers,

William Petty, author of the Down Survey, was based at the Crow's Nest, Temple Bar. (Courtesy of GCI)

soldiers, followers, adventurers, settlers and creditors of every kind and class had to be paid. Cromwell's solution was to pass anti-Catholic Penal Laws against the vast majority of the population of Ireland and, most importantly, confiscate huge tracts of their land. He did the latter with the help of his brutal policy, 'To Hell or Connaught!', the legality of which was underpinned by the Act for Adventurers. 'Adventurers' was a cryptic word in an age of exploration and exploitation.[7]

Having found it necessary to pay the troops with land taken from the defeated Irish, Cromwell needed a land survey. The appointed supervisor proved inept and in 1654 Petty volunteered to carry out the survey in thirteen months. His proposal was accepted and he employed about a thousand (strong and sturdy) men for the task. Petty, working from the Crow's Nest, was responsible for the calculation, confiscation and transfer of Irish land ownership to the victors. In March 1656, he completed the survey on schedule. Although it was an incredible achievement, there were errors of underestimation of 10–15 per cent, which correspondingly lessened his pay.

According to historian Maurice Craig, 'Petty seems to have been a man entirely devoid of sentiment or any imaginative attachment to the land in which most of his work was done. Petty looked on Ireland with the cold eye of the sophister, economist and calculator. He saw it merely as a description of square measurement. He was contemptuous of the Irish past and all forms of Irish autonomy were to him anathema.'[8] Petty noted dispassionately that the upheaval (involving banishment, transportation or hanging) included 6,000 Irish children (of Irish soldiers), who were transported as slaves to the West Indies, the process easily facilitated by the Bristol sugar merchants, beneficiaries of the sugar plantations.

POWER, PLUNDER AND POSSESSION

Petty's survey was referred to as the 'Down Survey'. He noted down with 'such exactness', his findings, that there was no estate or property which was not distinctly marked and mapped. He presented his completed work on 5 million acres to the Exchequer in 1657 (about half the country, which consisted of the forfeited and expropriated land). From that date, Petty's survey and the accompanying Books of Distribution were regarded by the government as the legal record of the titles on which half the land of Ireland was held (i.e. under new ownership). Following this survey, the distribution of forfeited lands was administered under the direction of Petty, with the help of forty clerks, effectively working around the clock. By January 1654, the 1,500 adventurers (investors) began planning for their share of the land, which made up nearly 1 million acres. Interestingly, despite the exactness of Petty's work, the lots for the forfeited lands appear to have been drawn out of a hat and disputes regularly occurred over the profitable or barren tracts assigned to the various claimants. Despite that, and most importantly, the outcome of Petty's Down Survey and the subsequent distribution of the forfeited land, implemented with brutal efficiency, was that Irish Catholic landowners were left with just over 20 per cent of the land, compared with 59 per cent in 1641. The new English colonial landed class, mainly Cromwellian and Protestant, along with those of the earlier plantations (in Ulster and Munster), now effectively owned and administered the country.[9]

Cromwell subsequently honoured Petty for his work and Petty's payment for his survey enabled him to buy cheaply forfeited and mortgaged lands, thus acquiring considerable property, which he continued to augment throughout his life. This included 50,000 acres in County Kerry. Having acquired his wealth from other men's misfortunes, Petty endured hostility and litigation for the rest of his life. In 1667, he married Elizabeth Fenton, the widow of Sir Maurice Fenton. The Fentons had connections in Temple Bar; they had a house on Copper Alley.[10]

FROM BOYLE'S LAW TO CORK HOUSE

Even before he came to Ireland, William Petty had known Richard Boyle (1566–1643), later to become the First Earl of Cork. Today Cork Hill is a reminder of one of the most influential and ruthless of the Temple Bar families of fortune that had such a resounding impact not only on the early development of Temple Bar, but on Ireland itself. Richard Boyle was the most successful of the New English colonists of the seventeenth century. Oliver Cromwell was an admirer of Boyle, saying once that if there had been more people like Boyle his task in Ireland in later years would have been unnecessary.[11]

Boyle was a fortune-seeker who came to Ireland in 1588 after being unable to afford to complete his legal studies in England. His was a rags-to-riches story of a man who understood the power of self-invention (he had achieved entry into official circles using forged introductions). By a stroke of luck, he was appointed Deputy Escheator of Crown Lands, which involved overseeing the legal transfer of lands to the Crown from those who had died without heirs. With the help of forgery, he exploited the legal uncertainties of land titles and built a substantial estate by coercing landholders and defrauding the Crown in the campaign against concealed lands.

His marriage to Catherine Fenton brought him respectability. Moreover, marrying the Limerick heiress, whose mother was Lady Alice Fenton (whose family had made its fortune from copper mining, with Copper Alley in Temple Bar called after her), was a politically astute and opportunistic move. Consequently, he became an important figure in the continuing English colonisation of Ireland in the sixteenth and seventeenth centuries as he rapidly acquired large tracts of land. He bought Sir Walter Raleigh's Munster plantation at a knock-down price. This was part of his strategy of acquiring land by availing of the prior investment of others. Boyle was soon to be the richest man in Ireland, with a rent roll of £20,000. Even in those times of forfeiture and embezzlement of Irish land, such speed was unusual, but he did so with a single-minded ruthlessness by encouraging the settlement of

The Father of Modern Chemistry, Robert Boyle (1627-1691), son of Richard Boyle of Cork House, Cork Hill, c. 1689. Boyle's Law, relating to the pressure and volume of gases, was one of his contributions to science. (Courtesy of Humphreys)

Protestants and by suppressing the Irish clans and transferring them to the wilds of Kerry. This wealth brought him status and power.[12]

Boyle's subsequent life was spent consolidating his fortune. Part of that fortune was spent building his house on Cork Hill (on the site of what is now City Hall), on the edge of Temple Bar. He had acquired the medieval church of St Marie de la Dam, which had been confiscated during the Reformation, and built a mansion on the site, known as Cork House because he was the Earl of Cork. Lismore Castle in Waterford was his primary residence and Cork House was his Dublin home. He was the wealthiest man in Ireland or England by the time of his death in 1643. The enormous family tomb (the Boyle Monument) erected in St Patrick's Cathedral, Dublin, is a measure of the man – and this was just one of five monuments he commissioned for himself during his lifetime. Boyle erected this huge monument in 1632. His biographer Nicholas Canny confessed he would be loath to sit down at the same table with him and called him 'the upstart Earl'. Historian Ken Nicholls described him as 'a most repellent character but an extraordinary able one'. Historian R.F. Foster, in his *Modern Ireland*, calls him an 'epitome of Elizabethan adventurer-colonist in Ireland'.[13]

Some of his sons played an important role in the rebellion (Irish Confederate Wars) of the 1640s and '50s, fighting for English and Protestant interests in Ireland. One of the sons, Robert Boyle (1627–1691), is considered the father of modern chemistry, and the Royal Dublin Show (RDS) continues to award

Eustace Street from Millennium Bridge. (Courtesy of Psyberartist, Wikimedia Commons)

the Boyle Medal for scientific excellence. Interestingly, Robert's scientific and meticulous approach was of particular help to William Petty in the 1650s when he was dissecting Ireland and transferring the forfeited lands to adventurers, soldiers, speculators and officials.

FROM THE NORMANS TO MAURICE EUSTACE

Another individual with property in Temple Bar was Sir Maurice Eustace (*c.* 1590–1665), an Irish politician, barrister and judge. He spent the last years of his career as Lord Chancellor of Ireland, an office for which he felt himself to be unfit and in which he was generally agreed to be a failure. Eustace was descended from the old Norman family of Fitz Eustache. In 1639, he became Speaker of the Irish House of Commons and a few years later, in 1642, he was appointed by Charles I to negotiate with the Catholic Confederation in Kilkenny, which had assumed control of much of the country. In the 1660s, he was rewarded for his efforts to advance the Protestant religion when he was made Lord Chancellor and given a substantial amount of property in Dublin and Drogheda. His name was given to Eustace Street in Dublin city centre, where his town house, Damask, stood. No trace of Damask survives today, but it is known to have been one of the largest houses in Dublin and both the house and the gardens were much admired by Jonathan Swift.[14]

FROM ANNESLEY TO EARLDOM

Anglesea Street commemorates another prominent resident of the area, Arthur Annesley (1614–1686), created Earl of Anglesea in 1661 for services rendered in Ireland (effectively overseeing the continuation of Cromwell's policy). He was born in Fishamble Street. He filled the office of vice treasurer from 1660 until 1667, served on the committee responsible for carrying out the settlement of Ireland and on the committee for Irish affairs, while later, in 1671 and 1672, he was a leading member of various commissions appointed to investigate the working of the Acts of Settlement. He amassed a large fortune in Ireland, including allotted lands given to him by Cromwell. This earl was great-grandfather of James Annesley, the principal figure in the famous Anglesea peerage case who died in 1760.[15]

29 Anglesea Street. (Courtesy of UCD Digital Library)

THE QUAY MEN – CRAMPTON AND ASTON

Bookseller, property speculator and former Lord Mayor (*c.* 1758), Philip Crampton knew the Temple Bar area well, having built Crampton Quay on reclaimed land on the southern shoreline of the River Liffey, and his involvement in the construction of Parliament Street gives an indication of his importance in the successful development of the street and the wider area

The corner of Essex Street in the early 1970s. (Courtesy of IHI)

Capel Street, Dublin, Tuesday 28 June 1960. (Photographer James P. O'Dea, courtesy of NLI Commons Collection)

of Temple Bar. He was a major landowner in Temple Bar; Crampton Lane, Quay, Court and Buildings are named after him.[16]

Henry Aston was another prominent landowner in the area. The Temple Bar Square and Crown Alley area, on which the old Telephone Exchange is located, was part of his property, as was reclaimed land along the River Liffey (Aston Quay).

ARTHUR CAPEL AND LAVISH GIFTS

Today, Capel Street and Essex Street are reminders of a former English official who was the government's representative in Ireland. Some argue that Arthur

Capel, 1st Earl of Essex (1631–1683), was a contrast to the aforementioned avaricious families of fortune, which greedily encouraged the violence of the brutal and vicious forfeitures and confiscations outlined above. Essex was made Privy Councillor and Lord Lieutenant of Ireland in 1672. Although he was seen to be tolerant and had an independent approach to his job, he still hated Catholics.

He quickly showed an aptitude for understanding accounts, which was to lead to all kinds of challenges, including conflicts with Lord Ranelagh, who was put in charge of Irish taxes on condition of his supplying the requirements of the Crown up to 1675 and whose accounts Essex refused to pass. It has been suggested that his experience of the role was a principled struggle which was ultimately to lead to his recall – it was also an early sign of how out of step Essex's integrity levels (if that was the case) were with those of his contemporaries. He strongly opposed the lavish gifts of forfeited estates to court favourites and mistresses. He prevented the granting of Phoenix Park to the Duchess of Cleveland. Finally, the intrigues of his enemies at home and Charles's continual demands for money, which Ranelagh undertook to satisfy, brought about Essex's recall in April 1677.[17]

3

RECLAMATION
AND EXPANSION

Temple Bar expanded gradually eastward during the sixteenth and seventeenth centuries. This was due to a number of factors. Firstly, as previously stated, there was the transfer of monastic lands to private ownership, as in the cases of the above-mentioned families. This was followed by the infilling of this land and the construction of houses and public buildings along adjacent thoroughfares. Secondly, the reclamation of land bordering the River Liffey shoreline and the building of Dublin's quays further extended the amount of land that could be used for economic development. Moreover, the process of building the quays made reclamation easier and consolidated the size and extent of the area.

In 1610, the cartographer John Speed produced the first recognisable map of Dublin, which shows how the Temple Bar area looked in the early seventeenth century: it was not the uniform area we have today but a triangular area evenly divided with a barrier of river inlets, mud flats and marshland in the vicinity of where the Rivers Poddle and Liffey met. The Poddle, descending from the Dublin Mountains, entered the Liffey estuary by means of tidal sub-estuaries, which formed shifting shoals and bars. It ran overground and across Dame Street, weaving through the mud flats to the Liffey. Speed's map shows that no part of the River Liffey was embanked or walled at this time. The river is shown flowing swiftly by the walls of the old city, which nestled on the south bank. East and west of the walls, bays, inlets and strands shape the landscape. The Liffey is busy with trading vessels, some anchored at 'The Bridge', which boasts a defensive gateway, controlling access to the city. The great Christ Church Bay, once a Viking haven, is now reclaimed land, supporting a riverfront portion of Dublin's walls. Where the newer part of Temple Bar is now located (outside the old city walls and gates, from Parliament Street to Westmoreland Street) approximately half (northwards of Essex Street/Temple Bar/Fleet Street) was covered by the River Liffey in 1610. The main buildings shown on the map are Trinity College, the Augustinian monastery, the hospital, the bridewell (from St Brigid's Well), Dame Street and Dame's Gate, St Andrew's church, and George's Lane (now George's Street).[1]

The subsequent building of the embankment of the river, begun not too long afterwards and gathering apace over the subsequent 200 years, involved much land reclamation, which resulted in additional development land, as well as improved access to Temple Bar. In particular, the large inlets and mudflats that divided the area were reclaimed, adding substantially to the development value and cohesion of the area.[2]

Of great importance in this reclamation process was the channelling, culverting and controlling of the area where the River Poddle flowed into the River Liffey. Crucial work took place in the early years of the seventeenth century, culminating in the triangular area of the Poddle outflow between the city wall and an old custom house being successfully reclaimed (the Poddle-Liffey confluence was a fan-shaped area stretching from what is now Parliament Street to Eustace Street).[3] This development was significant for historical geographer Nuala Burke, who noted that 'by enclosing the Poddle-Liffey confluence ... the major physical obstacle to coherent eastward expansion was overcome, and the reclamation of this tiny area was to prove influential, out of all proportion to its size, in determining the form and character of subsequent urban development on both north and south banks of the Liffey'. Nowadays, the iron grating visible along the walls of Wellington Quay marks where the Poddle joins the Liffey.[4]

THE AGE OF EXPANSION

Further land reclamation then took place. As earlier noted, the line of Essex Street, Temple Bar and Fleet Street generally marked the original line of the seashore. The area north of that was underwater at high tide and belonged to Dublin Corporation, according to tradition. Entrepreneurs recognised the usefulness of the land in the water shallows. In the early 1600s, part of it was leased and enclosed by a stone wall at the low tide mark. From 1660, Dublin Corporation leased out the length of the Liffey from the countryside to the sea for development, effectively making waste space economically useful. Much of the land was leased to private individuals acting as sub-landlords, who in turn offered plots for development.[5]

In 1707, more of the seashore was leased for the construction of a new custom house and quay to replace an old building on Merchant/Wood Quay. This was located on Wellington Quay (then called Custom House Quay). This was linked to Dame Street by Crane Lane, which followed the bank of the River Poddle.[6]

This major land reclamation in the Temple Bar area from the seventeenth century onwards was to be the catalyst for an era of great activity and development. The latter decades of this century were 'a period of heroic growth' for Dublin. It was then that Dublin's modern appearance took shape. It was a time for a new monarch, new money, new inhabitants, including thousands of Huguenots, and new ideas about Dublin.[7]

There was a lull in the mid-1600s because of the Cromwellian wars, but with the Restoration of Charles II in 1660 (whose reign lasted until 1685, though the Restoration era refers to the period up to and including 1715), Dublin was to see an improvement in its hitherto mixed fortunes as the growth and expansion of the city resumed. There was an explosion of the economy, the population and construction. Dublin became the permanent seat of parliament, government, trade and society. Temple Bar was at the hub of this change.[8]

The man responsible for facilitating this success was James Butler, Duke of Ormonde, who, with the Restoration of Charles II, returned in 1662 to govern as Lord Lieutenant of Ireland. Previously he had fought with the Royalists against Cromwell in the Irish Confederate Wars and, after Cromwell's victory, had fled to Europe. He persuaded a generation of entrepreneurs to build in a more enlightened manner.[9]

The ambitious Ormonde put the River Liffey at the heart of Dublin by methodically directing the expansion of the city eastwards and also on the north bank of the Liffey – aided by wily developers, such as the Jervis's and Gardiner's. He instigated increased building along Dame Street, the reclamation of more land, and the building of new quays and bridges (e.g. Ormond Quay and Essex Bridge in 1678) to protect the reclaimed land and to make movement across the River Liffey easier. One of his lasting achievements was the open quays along the river; he constructed boulevards, thus reversing the trend of building houses right down to the water.[10]

This approach had huge implications for the growth and appearance of Temple Bar and Dublin. When Ormonde was promoted to viceroy for Ireland in the late 1670s, he greatly encouraged the building of what is now

Ormond Quay, persuading the local property owner Sir Humphrey Jervis that this was his price when Jervis asked for his support in the building of Essex Bridge and Capel Street. With the construction of the quay, which separated houses from the River Liffey, a blueprint emerged for future development along the river.

When the east-west-oriented Essex Street and Essex Bridge, the latter linking Temple Bar to the north city, were laid down in the 1670s, development further accelerated, to the extent that by the early eighteenth century the area could justly be considered the heart of Dublin city. Expanding on Ormonde's blueprint, much activity followed in subsequent decades. The construction of a new custom house on Wellington Quay in 1707, the building of more quay walls, and the expansion of the area to Dame Street with the building of mansions and gardens for the new colonists resulted in a busy residential and commercial area. These new landowners subdivided and leased their plots, thereby creating an evolving streetscape. Many of the north-south streets and alleys followed the lines of the former gardens of the mansions facing on to Dame Street.

All this expansion and development was accompanied by an influx of English civil servants, senior officials and administrators, up to the level of Lord Lieutenant, and entrepreneurs such as the Huguenots fleeing persecution in Europe after the 1685 Edict of Nantes. Five years later, King William of Orange landed in Dublin and consolidated the Protestant influence and control of Dublin for the next century at least. His statue graced College Green for more than 200 years.[11]

THE CONSOLIDATION OF TEMPLE BAR

Bernard de Gomme's 1673 map of Dublin shows the major reclamation and development which had taken place since the publication of Speed's map sixty years previous. It shows that the extent of the development of Temple Bar by 1673 was much as we see it today. De Gomme's is the earliest map or document specifically to refer to Temple Bar and familiar streets clearly shown in the area are Dammas (Dame) Street and Dirty (formerly Hogges, now Temple) Lane. Also shown are Fish Shamble Street, Copper Alley, Blind Key, Smock Alley, custom house Key, Poolys Ally, Wood Yard, College Green and Temple barr. Significantly, there is mention of 'Ground taken from the sea' eastwards along the River Liffey just beyond Temple Bar and north of Trinity College, essentially the Fleet Street/Westmoreland Street area.

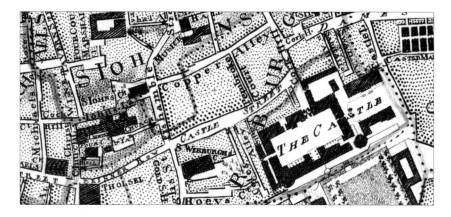

The area around Copper Alley and Cork Hill, as shown in Rocque's Map of Dublin, 1756. (Courtesy of UCD/Harvard)

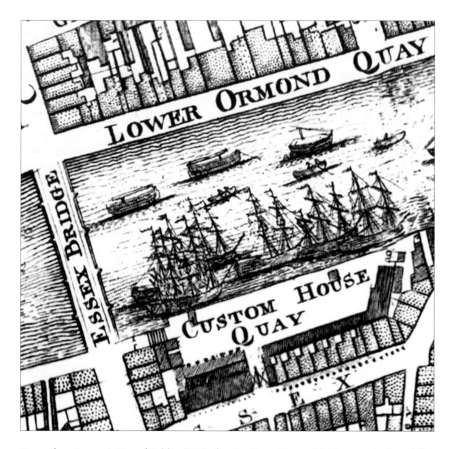

Extract from Rocque's Map of Dublin, 1756, showing Essex (Grattan) Bridge over the River Liffey and Custom House Quay parallel with Essex Street. (Courtesy of UCD/Harvard)

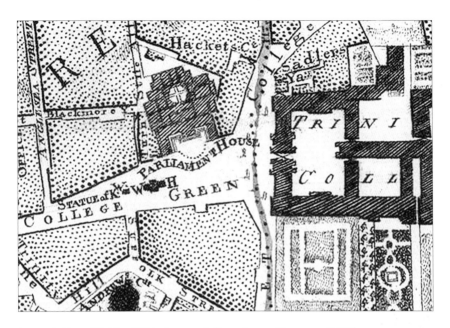

Rocque's Map of Dublin, 1756, showing College Green. (Courtesy of UCD)

Brooking's map of 1728 did not show much extra detail, but John Rocque's 1756 map of Dublin made up for that with the sheer amount of detail; it shows every house and garden in the small city. Rocque's map reveals that the intervening period saw the rapid expansion of the area, which by 1756 is densely inhabited with dwellings and buildings covering every square inch of the area.[12]

4

CUSTOM HOUSES
AND WIDE STREETS

The reclamation and development work carried out in the early eighteenth century enabled the building of a new custom house in 1707 on the site where the Clarence Hotel stands today. The location was called Custom House Quay, clearly shown on John Rocque's map of 1756, and was at the strategically important confluence of the rivers Poddle and Liffey. This was the third but most important such building in that vicinity since land reclamation from the River Liffey commenced in the early seventeenth century.[1]

The new, impressively built custom house became the commercial focus of Dublin. It was separated from the city behind with entrances via steps from Essex Bridge and an archway leading to and from Essex Street. When it opened, it brought money and a flurry of activity into the area, making Temple Bar the centre of commercial Dublin. Any goods imported or exported from Dublin were obliged by law to pass through this custom house and this port. Goods were offloaded with cranes and processed on an extensive quay front called Custom House Quay. Warehouses were built behind and adjacent to the custom house. Shops, taverns and coffee houses, printers and publishers, theatres and brothels soon sprang up in the area. Located near the custom house was a chophouse, known as the 'Old Sot's Hole', which, from the early years of the eighteenth century, had a widely celebrated reputation of having the best ale and beef steaks in Dublin. The important location of the new custom house was emphasised by the fact that the Privy Council (effectively the Cabinet for running the country) met for a few years in rooms in the building. Its importance was further emphasised when its façade was lit with 2,000 candles for the king's birthday in 1763.[2]

THE END OF AN ERA

The boom for the custom house lasted for nearly a century. In the 1770s, calls were being made for an even bigger and more impressive custom house, but in a different location. Complaints about the unsuitability of the custom house site for improving trade with England and the Continent were becoming more vociferous. It was recognised that the custom house location was in fact unsuitable for the safety and convenience of shipping due to the shallowness of the water, large vessels were unable to come up the River Liffey and had to use 'lighters' or 'gabbards' – smaller craft – to unload cargo. Moreover, some smaller vessels became stuck sailing near the place of landing on a notorious rock called 'Standfast Dick' – a large mass of hidden rock extending from Dublin Castle to Capel Street on the north side of the river.[3]

Then, in 1773, it was discovered that the upper floors of the building were structurally unsound, which would necessitate the building of additional warehouses on Essex Street East. The question was whether the old building should be refurbished or whether the custom house should be moved to a more suitable location nearer the mouth of the river. In 1774, the government eventually decided to build a new custom house farther eastwards. (It was a veritable *coup de grâce*, attributable to the exceptional influence of the Gardiner and Beresford families, who had large swathes of land on the north side of the River Liffey.) This was decided in the face of huge opposition from Temple Bar merchants, anticipating (quite correctly as it turned out) that the move would cause an eastward move of the city away from its medieval and commercial centre, leading to the fall in value of their property and the decimation of trade and business in the area. However, because of the continuous pressure from merchants, traders, brewers and manufacturers, the building of the new custom house did not commence until 1781 and it did not open until 1791.[4]

Construction was overseen the famous architect James Gandon, who was much involved in the Irish Houses of Parliament project. The new custom house was located farther downstream, nearer the mouth of the river and on the opposite side of the Liffey, on what is now (also) called Custom House Quay. It is often regarded as one of the masterpieces of Dublin's impressive eighteenth-century architecture. The Wellington Quay site became redundant. When customs officials moved into new, larger premises on the north side of the Liffey after 1791, the old custom house was converted into a military barracks.

WIDE STREETS COMMISSIONERS

Looking at Rocque's 1756 map of Dublin, we see that the street pattern of Temple Bar is virtually the same as it is today. The density of housing is indicative of the size of the population, making it a very busy area. This density, however, brought its own problems, one of which was ease of access and movement. While Rocque was drawing his map of Dublin, others were contemplating shaking up the street structure of the city. The most important statutory influence on Dublin's growth in this period was the Wide Streets Commissioners (WSC) (1757–1851). The Commission was set up by an Act of Parliament in 1757 to reduce city-centre congestion and to widen and develop the thoroughfares of Dublin city centre. The work of the WSC, which had the ability to reshape the city thanks to its powers of compulsory purchase, had a lasting impact on the fabric of Dublin city and its built heritage. Expenditure incurred was covered by a tax on imported coal. The contrast today between Crane Lane and Parliament Street, two adjacent streets, is indicative of the old and the new, with the former being part of the medieval street structure and the latter part of the work of the WSC.

Although on the one hand the WSC demolished many of the old medieval streets, houses and buildings, it also helped to create a city of fine public buildings, elegant streetscapes and residential squares. The framework of modern Dublin is largely its work. Paradoxically, this is why Temple Bar remains so important to this day – it escaped much of the demolition that took place to widen the adjacent streets and its own streetscape was left almost uniquely intact.

One of the first tasks for the WSC was to make 'a wide and convenient street from Essex Bridge to the Castle of Dublin'. This new street is today Parliament Street. Many other streets were subsequently laid out or enlarged and so we have the spacious thoroughfares of Westmoreland, D'Olier and Dame streets, as well as Carlisle (O'Connell) Bridge and onwards to Sackville (O'Connell) Street. Other Dublin streets also benefited from the work of the commissioners, including Thomas Street and adjacent streets in the Liberties. Lord Edward Street was not constructed until the late 1800s.[5]

Dublin grew even more dramatically during the eighteenth century (often described as the 'Golden Age of Dublin'), with the construction of many famous districts and buildings. Temple Bar was the epicentre of this growth and improvement, with new buildings such as the Irish Parliament House on College Green and the Royal Exchange on Cork Hill. New fashionable squares and roads were built at Rutland (now Parnell) Square, Mountjoy Square and the Gardiner Street area on the north side of the Liffey. South of the river, impressive squares were laid out: St Stephen's Green, Merrion Square and Fitzwilliam Square. St Stephen's Green was considered the largest square in Europe, the Liffey quays were admired and the new Irish Parliament House, opposite Trinity College, built between 1729 and 1739, was regarded with envy.

Dublin was also a city of magnificent balls, receptions and entertainments. There were exciting dinners, with such unusual dishes as squab pigeon, pickled penguin, badger flambé, stewed carp and venison pie. Mrs Delaney, a friend of Dean Swift, served her famous syllabub. There was the Smock Alley theatre, where David Garrick and Peg Woffington appeared and where the ladies and gentlemen in the audience were dressed in magnificent court costumes. All this prosperity and grandeur was encouraged and constructed by the increasingly confident Protestant Ascendancy and nobility that ruled Ireland at this time.[6]

5

BUCKS, BLASTERS
AND CLUBS

Eighteenth-century Dublin was notorious for the conspicuous consumption and the extravagant lifestyles of those of immense wealth, power and prestige, all connected in some way or another with Dublin Castle, the custom house (and later the Royal Exchange) and the Irish Parliament House. Visitors to Dublin were impressed by the air of gaiety in the houses of the well-to-do, which went with a peculiarly splendid way of living – a multiplicity of servants, a great profusion of dishes on the table, abundant wine. It was said that Bordeaux's best customers were to be found in Ireland. The city was famed for its hedonistic lifestyle, particularly during the winter months, when it was the social imperative for the Anglo-Irish ascendancy to flock to Dublin, to live, play and consume to excess. Even George Frederick Handel was caught up in this; during his visit to Dublin in 1741–42, he was taken ill with a paralytic stroke brought on by excessive eating.

While the Irish in the city mainly lived a life of impoverishment, inhabiting hovels, those with wealth and influence lived extravagantly off the rents paid by their tenants outside the Pale. It was a time of excessive wealth concentrated in the hands of the ruling nobility and gentry, a time of great licentiousness, drunkenness and debauchery, midnight orgies, corruption and unbridled sexual activity. Charles Manners (1754–1787), the Duke of Rutland and Lord Lieutenant of Ireland for a few years, was an example of one of the many that opted for this lifestyle. His Dublin Castle banquets were renowned. He eventually died of syphilis, although liver disease (from excessive consumption of claret) has also been cited as a possible cause of his demise.[1]

There was another outlet for those well-to-do gentry with a propensity for Bacchus, bawds and the gambling tables who were prepared to pay extra for comfort and privacy. This was the private members' clubs, which quickly became hugely controversial due to the activities associated with them. They give an interesting insight into the depraved world of the eighteenth-century young Irish gentry, where social life revolved around clubs and societies, which afforded added excuses for drinking and debauchery. Some of these clubs were the Monday Club, the No Nose Club, the Mollies Club and the Spendthrift Club, although these were relatively tame in comparison to others. Some women had their own clubs, including the Jezebel Club (for courtesans or upper-class prostitutes) and the Fair Club. There were other clubs, such as Friends of the Constitution, the Aldermen of Skinnner's Row (which was the location of the Tholsel) and Friends of the Screw (wine).[2]

BUCKS, DANDY'S AND GOLD HEADS

'Bucks' and 'clubs' were hallmarks of this era. Bucks were young male members of the wealthy classes who had little to do except enjoy themselves. The fashionable gentleman of Dublin during the period were generally styled 'Bucks', as in Buck Daly, Buck Whaley, Buck Jones, Buck Lawless or Buck English, all members of the infamous Daly's Club and some of the most legendary characters of the period. Clubs were an essential aspect of the eighteenth-century urban male lifestyle. They provided a place where the young aristocracy and 'young Bucks' could carouse. They were exclusive clubs, mainly made up of a class of rich and landed gentry who chose to pursue a certain type of enjoyment, which generally involved a mix of gambling, blaspheming, whoring, drinking, violence and even Satan worship. The young Anglo-Irish aristocracy caroused in the fashionable and not-so-fashionable parts of Dublin, from St Stephen's Green to Temple Bar. Most of them found their common ground in ceremonial drinking and dining or visiting the gambling venues, but a few allegedly focused on sex, blasphemy and deliberate ill-doing.[3]

Young bucks often spent their mornings crowding into the Smock Alley theatre to watch the rehearsals or swaggering about in Lucas's Coffee House on Cork Hill, challenging all and sundry to duels, but the evening was the time when they were at their most exuberant. On one occasion, a young buck went on to the Smock Alley theatre's stage after a performance and 'took it into his head to amuse himself by cutting to pieces a freshly painted piece of scenery'. On being asked to leave by an actor, he threateningly waved his sword and asked how a 'player' dared to talk to a 'gentleman'. On another occasion, during a performance of *King Lear* starring David Garrick and Peg Woffington, again in the Smock, a young buck jumped on stage and 'tried to make indecent liberties' with the actress. Nearby, at the brothel operated by Mrs Davis on Fishamble Street (disguised as a china shop), the premises was damaged when four bucks pushed a blind horse into it.[4]

Thomas Sheridan of the Smock Alley Theatre was so upset by the behaviour of young gentleman that he wrote a tract (pamphlet) called *An Humble Appeal to the Publick* (1758) in which he gave many instances of the misbehaviour of the bucks, including how they regularly invaded the stage and annoyed members of the cast. The wild behaviour of the bucks did not diminish over the century and the *Hibernian Magazine* of 1777 described how a group of bucks, with blackened faces, entered a coffee house in Essex Street looking for someone who had apparently offended them and broke windows, chandeliers, mirrors, chairs and other furniture. Their search continued in many of the nearby taverns, where they caused further damage. This was followed by a visit to Smock Alley Theatre, where they abused staff and actors, hit a chairman and assaulted a man who ended up with a fractured skull.[5]

A group of drunken, violent bucks also enjoyed assaulting passers-by just for the sport of it. They were known as Pinking Dindies (Pinkindindies) – a class of 'dandies' (thugs) from the ascendancy and also Trinity College Dublin students who were skilled in the art of 'pinking' or slashing their victims with the point of their swords. Another favourite weapon of the students out on a rampage was a heavy metal key attached to an innocuous handkerchief. One would not take too much notice of the handkerchief until one felt the brunt of the key on one's skull. The Pinking Dindies were also known as 'rent collectors', essentially racketeers, because they extorted money from the many prostitutes around the Temple Bar area. It was also a time when duelling peaked, particularly in the 1770s[5] and 1780s, again reflecting the confidence or arrogance of the elite. At that time, economics and politics were working together for the benefit of the ruling elite in Ireland and legislative independence was on the horizon.[6]

There was a renowned jeweller working at The Sign of the Eagle at No. 82 Dame Street in the closing decades of the eighteenth century. He was also a noted manufacturer of walking sticks of every description, especially for members (bucks) of those clubs in the vicinity to use during their nightly escapades of drinking, dissipation and destruction. These particular sticks were generally distinguished from others by the addition of a finely carved, gold-coloured metallic head with inscriptions such as 'Who's afraid?', 'Who dares sneeze?', 'The Devil a better', or 'A pill for a puppy'.[7]

FROM THE HIBERNIAN TO DALY'S

The first 'Buck Lodge' was held at Philip Glenville's house in Anglesea Street, which was called the Royal Hibernian Buck Lodge. The founder was Surgeon James Solas Dodd. He was a most unusual character with a wide variety of interests, including writing on the history of the herring and lecturing on hearts. A well-travelled individual, he had been arrested as a spy in Constantinople (Istanbul). The founder or president of the lodge was known as the 'Noble Grand' and new members to the lodge swore upon a sword the oath of the society, after which a bugle-horn was hung round their neck, and the ceremony concluded by drinking three bumpers of wine to the 'Buck' toast.[8]

A short walk from Anglesea Street and just before the Irish Houses of Parliament was a gentlemen's club called Daly's Club, situated originally at the Dame Street/College Green junction. It was typical of the exclusive clubs catering to the needs of the aristocracy and members of the Irish parliament. It was also an important centre of social and political life between its origins in about 1750 and its closure in 1823. The founder was Patrick Daly, who had originally worked in a Dublin tavern and later opened a chocolate house at Nos. 2 and 3 Dame Street. It soon became the most famous, and in later years the most infamous, establishment of its kind in Ireland.

By the late 1780s, the members decided to erect an even more impressive edifice for their meetings and plans were made to build a new club near the existing building. The new, more fashionable premises, designed by Francis Johnston, stretched from Anglesey Street to Foster Place (the building survives to this day) and was opened with a grand dinner on 16 February 1791. This new version of Daly's Club was a magnificent and sumptuous palace. According to a contemporary report of the opening in the *Hibernian Magazine* in March 1791, 'This house was decorated in a very rich style, being adorned with splendid chandeliers, inlaid tables, and marble chimney pieces. The chairs and sofas were painted white and gold, and upholstered with rich silk coverings.'[9]

Daly's reached the height of its notoriety with the opening of its new premises. It was one of the venues for meetings of the Irish Hell Fire Club, which met variously at Montpelier Lodge on Montpelier Hill, at the Eagle Tavern on Cork Hill or at Daly's. Daly's was renowned for the gambling that took place there. In 1794, a visitor to Dublin, writing in the *European Magazine and London Review* declared, 'The God of Cards and Dice has a Temple, called Daly's, dedicated to his honour in Dublin, much more magnificent than any Temple to be found in that City dedicated to the God of the Universe.'[10]

The 'itch for gaming' characterised late eighteenth-century Dublin and Daly's was not the only gambling den. Other notorious ones included Molloy's and Thornton's, both on Crow Street, Byrne's on Essex Street and another one operated by the 'Sham Squire' on Parliament Street. Stories of round-the-clock gambling, land and estates wagered or drunk away, parliamentary differences compromised and bitter quarrels settled by duels were the norm at Daly's. Strange anecdotes have been told of the happenings at Daly's. The windows of rooms were completed blacked out on some days, with the occupants inside still playing cards by candlelight. Cheaters were known to have been flung out of some of the top-floor windows and duels were frequently fought outside the premises on Foster Place. Nearly half the land of Ireland is said to have changed hands at Daly's, such were the reckless characters that frequented the club. Daly's catered very well (and discreetly) to honourable Members of Parliament and rich 'bucks' alike. To facilitate the secret entry of the former, there was an underground passage linking the building with Parliament House via Foster Place. Notable members from that body included John Philpot Curran, Henry Flood, Baron Plunkett, Henry Grattan, Sir Hercules Langrishe, 1st Baronet and George Ponsonby. They would not have engaged in the exploits of the younger members, but would not have been averse to duelling. Another member was the infamous Frederick E. 'Buck' Jones, one-time owner of the Crow Street Theatre, who was renowned for his exploits, including foiling a robbery of his own house that involved much loss of life. His name is preserved in the street name Jones's Road, which originally led to his mansion, Clonliffe House. He died in 1834.[11]

In 1787, the politically motivated expulsion of William Burton Conyngham (1st Baron Plunkett) from Daly's led to an exodus of members from Daly's, who formed the Kildare Street Club, which provided a calmer environment than the debauched Daly's and soon rivalled Daly's as a fashionable haunt.

The Act of Union of 1800 inflicted its toll on the club as many ascendancy families left Ireland. The club fell into decline and was eventually eclipsed by the Kildare Street Club. Peter Depoe, who continued in office until 1823, when the club closed down, succeeded Daly as manager. In 1841, twenty years after the club's demise, it was described in the *Edinburgh Magazine* as 'the once-celebrated, and still well-remembered, "Daly's Club"'.[12] In later

The College Buck from the *Hibernian Magazine*, September 1774.

decades, the novels of Charles Lever and the writings of Charles Dickens, a regular visitor to Dublin, enhanced its romantic, melodramatic reputation. In 1866, Dickens alluded to the fate of the Club in his *All the Year Round*:

Even now, next to the old Parliament House stands a stately building, cut up into half-a-dozen houses of business. This was once Daly's Club-house, where all the noblemen and gentlemen of both Houses would adjourn to dine and drink; where were seen Mr. Grattan, and Mr. Flood with his broken beak, and Mr. Curran, and those brilliant but guerrilla debaters, whose encounters both of wit and logic make our modern parliamentary contests sound tame and languid.[13]

The building, at Nos 3–4, still stands impressively on College Green and, in keeping with the business nature of the area over the years, has been occupied by insurance companies and stockbrokers. The former Yorkshire Fire and Life Insurance Company was located there and the old lettering of the business is still faintly visible on its upper façade. There is an unusual clock on the front elevation, possibly the only red-faced public clock in Dublin. Today the building is used as a coffee shop and as part of the expanding Trinity College complex, which also occupies the former AIB bank building around the corner in Foster Place.

BUCK LAWLESS AND PIMPING PEG

One of those most notorious young 'bucks' who frequented Daly's Club was John 'Buck' Lawless, the lover of Margaret Leeson (*née* Plunkett) for many years. Her story gives us some insight into the milieu in which he (and she) mixed in late Georgian Dublin. Margaret Leeson was one of the eighteenth century's most flamboyant characters. Lawless (although reckless and financially insecure) was for many years one of her favourites. She is sometimes regarded as Ireland's first brothel-owning madam (aka Margaret Plunkett and Pimping

Margaret Plunkett (also known as Pimping Peg), renowned courtesan and Madam. (Courtesy of Dublin Forums)

Peg) and was certainly the most famous of Dublin's eighteenth-century madams. She published her memoirs in 1797, opening the work by noting, 'I shall now commence with the most memorable epoch of my unfortunate life ...' Clever, witty and beautiful, she was a leading figure in the hedonism set of Georgian Dublin, which included members of Daly's Club, and she counted lords, lawyers and bankers among her clientele. For many years, she was the talk of the town because of her jewellery, her dresses, her carriages, her clients, her girls and, above all, her attitude.[14]

The often tragic life of Margaret Leeson began in 1727, when she was born in Killough, County Westmeath, the daughter of a wealthy Catholic landowner who was related to the Earl of Cavan. However, her idyllic rural childhood was shattered when her mother and eldest brother died and Margaret's father passed control of his estates to his cruel son Christopher, who treated the young Margaret badly. She eventually escaped to Dublin, where she met a man called Dardis, who introduced her to a life of prostitution.

FROM GAME COCK JOE TO RUFFIANS

An independent person, from the age of 15 (after she became pregnant and was abandoned by her upper-class seducer), Margaret Plunkett effectively navigated upper-class society to ensure her survival. First, she was the 'kept woman' of a succession of wealthy men and later the operator of a lucrative, high-end brothel frequented by the rich and famous of the day. She never married, but moved through various relationships. She regarded marriage as an unfair contract. She met Joseph Leeson, a wealthy English merchant from whom she took her assumed name in order to enhance her respectability. He was known as 'Game Cock Joe' and later became 1st Earl of Milltown. His name is commemorated in Dublin by Leeson Street. Leeson fell for Margaret's charms and put her up in a house in Ranelagh. When Leeson was away she would sneak in to the house of her other lover, Buck Lawless. Leeson finally found out and, upon discovering her infidelity, left her penniless. Buck Lawless went on to become her most enduring client and partner. They lived together for five years and had five children. However, tragedy struck eventually: their money ran out, the children died one by one and Lawless absconded for America, leaving Margaret heartbroken. She kept her original 'keeper's' name to ensure her social standing and so styled herself 'Margaret Leeson'. She was later to write in her memoirs that, with regard to

Joseph Leeson, she was more 'distressed by the loss of his purse that the loss of his person'.[15]

With the departure of Buck Lawless, she returned to a life of prostitution and found that many wealthy men were willing to entertain her and pay her way. She soon regained her position in high society and her first brothel in Dublin was opened on Drogheda Street (now O'Connell Street). However, this brothel was closed due to an attack by the Pinking Dindies. It was Richard Crosbie (1755–1800), the duellist and aeronaut (he famously landed a balloon in Ranelagh Gardens), who led a gang who wrecked her brothel. Not to be deterred, upon receiving compensation from Crosbie, she continued her business elsewhere (just off Grafton Street).

Her latest venture was the most luxurious brothel, fitted out with every comfort and boasting prostitutes handpicked by Margaret herself. It became a well-known establishment among well-bred men and her clients included a Lord Lieutenant – Charles Manners, 4th Duke of Rutland and Lord Lieutenant of Ireland, known for his convivial nature and ample banquets in Dublin Castle; Rutland Square, now Parnell Square, was named after him. Manners insisted on sleeping only with Margaret, swearing he would pay his fortune if only his wife was as good in bed as she was. She refused to have another Lord Lieutenant, John Fane, the Earl of Westmoreland, as a client because of his ill treatment of his wife. The famous banker and Huguenot, David La Touche, whose name still lives on in Dublin financial circles, was the governor of the Bank of Ireland and likewise a very important frequenter of her brothels. Other important clients included Walter Butler, Viscount Thurles and later the Earl of Ormond; Captain Francis Craddock, aide-de-camp to the Lord Lieutenant in 1783; the 'Curly Pated Squire' from Limerick (all he required was a night's lodgings, a girl and a bottle); and Richard Daly, variously of the Theatre Royal and Smock Alley Theatre. She also listed among her clients earls, generals, top barristers, merchants, aldermen, writers, clergymen and many at the top levels of society, one of whom was a revenue official with a wooden leg who was brought to court, successfully, to force him to pay his debts of £50 for services rendered. Most of those at that level of society had their own 'kept woman' or mistress. Many of Dublin's top-class prostitutes attended society functions. Some of them came from the environs of the Smock Alley Theatre and blended in at functions, where they were readily welcomed.[16]

MANNERS AND MASQUERADES

When Signor Carnavalli (a celebrated violinist) came to the Smock Alley Theatre to perform Italian operas, he barred certain kinds of people from attending or, as Peg put it, 'every lady of my description'. She turned up at the theatre nonetheless and took her usual seat, but, on Carnavalli's orders, she was unceremoniously thrown out by the doormen. Furious at this ill treatment, she got a warrant against them for assault and robbery (for holding the ticket she had paid for) and returned to the theatre with four of the nastiest bailiffs she could find, who then hauled Carnavalli and the doormen off to Newgate Prison.

An outspoken and shrewd woman, Margaret Leeson is perhaps best summed up by the following story. One night, Charles Manners (the Lord Lieutenant), one of her most important clients, appeared in the regal box at the theatre (Smock Alley) on the same night that Peg was attending the show with her girls. Some characters in the gallery began shouting at her, 'Oy Peg! Who slept with you last night, Peg?' Peg gave them an imperious look, threw a dramatic glance at the Lord Lieutenant and in a scolding tone, said, 'Manners, you dogs!' [17]

FROM FASHIONABLE ELEGANCE TO REVENGE

In the early 1790s, after thirty years in the business, Margaret Leeson decided to retire and cash in all the promissory notes she had accumulated. She became penniless in the process as former clients refused to pay or had disappeared. Consequently, she ended up in a debtor's prison. By this time, not only was she penniless, but had also lost her once strikingly beautiful looks. However, a few of her former admirers did help her. Francis Higgins ('The Sham Squire'), the owner of the *Freeman's Journal*, provided some assistance. Bishop Harvey of Derry, who was also the Earl of Bristol and her former client, likewise sent her money. Despite this, she attempted suicide and after the failed attempt she wrote her memoirs in a bid to raise some cash (and take revenge). She wrote *The Memoirs of Mrs Leeson, Written by Herself*, published between 1795–97, of which two volumes appeared while she was still alive, to the embarrassment of many.[18]

A casual reading of her memoirs reveals that she did not hold back her anger. For example, she describes in detail the debauched antics of the Dublin masquerade scene. The masquerade, or masked ball, was particularly popular in Dublin and people in high positions in Dublin politics and society dressed in the most amazing costumes – as sultans, Spaniards, the Devil, preachers, Peter Pan, jolly tinkers and plates. Arthur Young noted in the course of his travels in the 1770s that 'every night in the winter, there is a ball or a party'.[19]

The season, in full swing (from about Christmas time until the middle of March), coincided with the sitting of parliament and the period when the viceroy held court.

Masquerade balls were not the preserve of the aristocratic and middle-class women; prostitutes and the demimonde attended. Leeson's services as a madam were greatly in demand and, during the 1785 season, she recruited the best-looking prostitutes to portray Venus and the Graces. Of course, Leeson was maintaining the convention of 'The World Upside Down', which was partly the point of masquerades. So outrageous had the public masquerade balls become that they were eventually banned by the city authorities.[20]

In Leeson's memoirs, she complains that Dublin was home to many men who, 'however they might be deemed gentlemen at their birth, or connections, yet, by their actions, deserved no other appellation than that of RUFFIANS'.[21]

The brutal realities of life in eighteenth-century Dublin are captured in the final chapter of the life of Margaret Lesson, who died following rape and the resulting complications of venereal disease, from which she did not recover. She died at the age of 70, broken and alone. It has been said that a guard of honour at her funeral would have stretched from Parliament House to Dublin Castle.

Her obituary reported, 'She figured for a long time in the bon ton – and absolutely made the fashion. It was her practice to confine her favours to a temporary husband. In this state she lived with several gentlemen in the style of fashionable elegance.'[22]

THE DUBLIN HELLFIRE CLUB

As we have seen, in the eighteenth century, there was much debauchery and immorality among the upper classes in Dublin. However, there was also carousing of a more sinister nature. A House of Lords' Committee Report of 1737 found that there existed in Dublin a club called the 'Blasters' or 'The Hellfire Club'.[23]

The originator of this kind of club was the painter Peter Lens, who moved to England from continental Europe. He was accused of blasphemy, drinking to the health of the Devil and openly insulting God. The Hellfire Clubs of England and Ireland seemingly took their inspiration from him. In 1719/20, Sir Francis Dashood in Buckinghamshire started the first of the Hellfire Clubs in England. The club and its imitators indulged in idleness, luxury, profanity, gambling and drinking and became notorious for rumours about sexual orgies and tales of the occult. Their outrageous activities included daring blasphemies, including playing cards on Sunday, reading Lucretius (denying divine providence and emphasising instead 'chance') and eating pigeon (which they called Holy Ghost) pie.[24]

ROSSE AND THE HELLFIRE CLUB

The Dublin Hellfire Club was founded in the Eagle Tavern (Cork Hill) around 1735 by some of the elite of the Protestant ascendancy that liked to socialise in the Temple Bar area. The members were mostly young, male and moneyed, united by an enduring fascination with the forbidden fruit offered by the Devil and a desire to flirt with danger and the unknown. Richard Parsons, 1st Earl of Rosse and the humorous artist, James Worsdale, were the founders. The club motto was '*Fais ce que tu voudras*' or 'Do as thou wilt'. The club's mascot was a black cat. Besides the Eagle Tavern and Daly's Club, the many taverns, coffee houses, brothels and gambling houses in Temple Bar were their haunts.[25]

Rosse was famous for his profligacy and his wit. He was given the title 'King of Hell' in recognition of the club's location near the area known as 'Hell'. It is perhaps not surprising that he was particularly fond of the company of prostitutes, of which there were plenty in the locality of Cork Hill. However, he did not limit himself to these. He at times preferred the company of the more high-society prostitutes: 'kept women' or madams, such as Mrs Laetitia Pilkington or Margaret Leeson. Mostly though, he used Worsdale to bring the prostitutes from Copper Alley or Bagnio Slip to him. When he was dying in the early 1740s, his confessor begged him to ask for forgiveness for his 'whoring'.

He was said to have often dressed as he imagined Satan would (mainly in black with a hint of red) and he had his own special chair from which to oversee proceedings in the Eagle Tavern. The first toast was drunk to the absent Devil, who might make his appearance any time, so a chair was left vacant for him at each gathering. A satirical ballad was also recited in which the Devil was represented as summoning before him those who had the strongest claims to succeed him as King of Hell. Simon Luttrell, a member of the Hellfire Club (later Baron Irnham), was introduced in the ballad, which concluded:

> But as he spoke there issued from the crowd
> Irnham the base, the cruel, and the proud
> And eager cried, 'I boast superior claim
> To Hell's dark throne, and Irnham is my name'.[26]

Accounts of the club's meetings claim that members drank 'scaltheen', a mixture of whiskey, eggs and hot butter. It was as strong as poteen and had similar hallucinatory effects. The club was also infamous for excessive whiskey-drinking and general debauchery. In the 1740s, whiskey grew in popularity when the excise duty was lowered and it became much cheaper.

Lord Rosse gladly embraced 'all the vices which the beau monde called pleasure', according to Peter Somerville Large in his book on Dublin.[27] Another member, Lord Santry, was found guilty of murder by the House of Lords for having killed a man in a drunken fray. In 1739, at the age of 29, he stabbed a servant, Laughlin Murphy, to death with his sword for the spurious reason that the latter had spoken out of turn. This was a major scandal at the time, but he was subsequently pardoned, having been judged by his peers, which was in keeping with the usual leniency when members of the ascendancy misbehaved.[28]

Evidence of the identities of other members of the club comes from a painting by James Worsdale (one of the founders) entitled 'The Hell Fire Club, Dublin', now held by the National Gallery of Ireland, which shows five members of the club seated around a table. The five men are Henry Barry, 4th Baron of Santry; Simon Luttrell, Lord Irnham; Colonel Henry Ponsonby; Colonel Richard St George; and Colonel Clements. Years later, during excavations near the former Eagle Tavern, the skeleton of a dwarf, reputed to have been sacrificed by members of the Hellfire Club, was found.

The Hellfire Club went into decline after 1741, following the death of its main founder, Lord Rosse. He died, but not before having one last jest. As he lay on his deathbed, the rector of St Anne's church on Dawson Street, near his house on Molesworth Street, beseeched him in a letter to repent his evil ways while there was still time. Lord Rosse was amused by the letter. Noticing that it addressed him as 'My Lord', with no name, he re-sealed the letter and sent it to Lord Kildare, who was well known for his upstanding life and piety. When Kildare received it, he was furious with the rector until the truth came out. Lord Rosse would certainly have enjoyed the episode.[29]

BUCK WHALEY AND COPPER-FACED JACK

Between Rosse's death and the revival of the club in the 1770s, a number of similar clubs were established in Dublin, such as the Holy Fathers Club and the Cherokee Club (based on the name of an American Indian tribe), dedicated to their own pleasure and amusement, and involving scant respect for women, violence and duelling, copious drinking, disorderly outrages, blasphemy, general nuisance and mayhem, extravagant and startlingly colourful uniforms. Again, they comprised young members of the upper classes of Irish society.[30]

The Dublin Hell Fire Club was revived in 1771 and was active for a further thirty years. Its most notorious member was Thomas 'Buck' Whaley, born in around 1755 (d. 1800), the son of the wealthy landowner Richard Chappell 'Burn-Chapel' (he liked to burn down Catholic chapels) Whaley. A relation, Captain William Whaley, shot Counsellor Dennis Kelly dead in a duel in St Stephen's Green in July 1790. He was elected a Member of Parliament to the Irish House of Commons in 1785. On his father's death, he inherited a fortune and devoted his time to squandering his new wealth drinking, gambling and carousing. He fitted into the revived Hellfire Club well. His associates included Francis ('the Sham Squire') Higgins, notorious editor of the *Freeman's Journal*, and John Scott, who was known to his friends and foes as 'Copper-Faced Jack'. Scott bore the nickname due to his aggressiveness in legal argument and the bronzed hue of his skin, exacerbated by heavy drinking. He was the Earl of Clonmel and Chief Justice of the King's Bench. Both men were described as 'as rascally a pair as could be found anywhere' and the three together were a notorious triumvirate. Higgins and Whaley were next-door neighbours on St Stephen's Green, while Scott lived just around the corner on Harcourt Street (remembered to this day by 'Copper Face Jacks' nightclub).[31]

Some meetings took place at Daly's Club, the Eagle Tavern and Montpelier lodge (in the Dublin Mountains, far from prying eyes). Historian Constantia Maxwell noted that 'when rakish gentlemen wished for congenial society they rode up to Mr Connolly's hunting lodge, perched like Noah's Ark on the top of Mont Pelier, among the Dublin Mountains. But most of the club's meetings were actually held in the Eagle Tavern.'[32]

Whaley won great fortunes at the Temple Bar gaming tables, as well as partaking in some bizarre wagers. In one wager, he won £25,000 from the Duke of Leinster by riding to Jerusalem and back within a year. This was not a religious pilgrimage; he later boasted of playing handball against the Walls of Jerusalem and of having drunk his way there. On another occasion, for a bet of £12,000, he rode a beautiful white Arab stallion in a death-defying leap from the drawing room on the second floor of his father's house on Stephen's Green (now the impressive Newman House) over a carriage parked outside the door and on to the street, 30-odd feet below. He won his wager, surviving with a broken leg, but killed the horse. When he died in 1800, at a coaching inn in Cheshire, the Irish Hellfire Club passed away with him. As seemed to be the case with many of the young 'bucks', Whaley insisted that he had been 'born with high passions, a lively imagination, and a spirit that could brook no restraint'. His last years were spent on the Isle of Man, where he had fled his creditors. Whilst there, he built a mansion for himself, known locally as Whaley's Folly.[33]

Today, the ruins of the old hunting lodge on Montpelier Hill in the Dublin Mountains are essentially a monument to the arrogance and violence of the eighteenth-century Irish gentry.

6

BEGGARS, BAWDS AND BAGNIOS

AN AGE OF EXTREMES

The eighteenth century was Dublin's golden age. It was very similar to other cities in Europe. By the 1750s, it had a population of between 100,000 and 120,000 people, a number that was rapidly expanding because of immigration from Britain, mainland Europe (particularly Huguenots) and rural Ireland. It was regarded as the second most important city of the British Empire.[1]

The city presented vivid contrasts, however, and visitors noted the crowds of beggars, the poor quality of the inns and taverns, and the squalid wretchedness of the oldest part of the city, around Christ Church Cathedral. This was in stark contrast to the fine squares in the expanding areas of the city, the new impressive buildings, the Liffey quays and the brilliant society that lived in the newer areas. The confidence of the ascendancy was based on shaky foundations, however. Their lavish expenditure and lifestyle was only made possible by the substantial rents which came in from Irish estates and the low price of labour and provisions.[2] Dublin's impressive Georgian architecture was built largely for the enjoyment of the British-linked Protestant rulers of Ireland while the majority of Catholic Irish people lived in hovels and slums.[3]

There was a price to pay for this lavish and extravagant living. According to historian Maurice Craig, 'the dirt, the gaiety, the cruelty, the smells, the pomp, the colour and the sound so remote from anything we know – were all to be found in much the same proportion from Lisbon to St Petersburg'. However, he notes, Dublin was unique because 'it was an extreme example of tendencies generally diffused'. Craig even suggests that Dublin had more in common with Calcutta than European cities. Dublin was renowned for its squalor and the numbers of beggars on the streets. 'Ireland itself is a poor country, and Dublin a magnificent city; but the appearances of extreme poverty among the lower people are amazing', wrote Benjamin Franklin after a visit to the capital in the early 1770s. When the French political thinker Alexis de Tocqueville visited Ireland in 1835, the situation was little different. He noted scathingly in his diaries that the aristocracy was responsible for creating a deeply divided society in Ireland. For him, if one wanted to see the results of the spirit of conquest and religious hatred, combined with the abuses of aristocracy without any of its advantages, then one should visit Ireland.[4]

Dublin's oldest charity, the Sick and Indigent Roomkeepers' Society, was founded in 1790, with its premises on Palace Street, nestling up against the impressive walls of Dublin Castle and the Royal Exchange at Cork Hill. The charity is a reminder of the vivid and contrasting living conditions in Georgian Dublin. There was also an organisation called the Association for Discountenancing Vice, whose very name indicates a major problem in the area: Georgian Dublin was notorious for its pickpockets and prostitutes.

Beggars were everywhere, although to be a beggar one had to register, pay a fee and wear a special badge for six months at a time. There were around 1,000 official beggars at any one time. The situation had become compounded from the 1740s onwards by the major famine (in 1741, which was known as 'the Year of the Slaughter') and the subsequent disease that swept across Ireland, decimating the population and causing havoc, with many fleeing to the cities. If you reneged on your debts, you ended up in one of the many debtors' prisons, such as the Marshalsea on Thomas Street. Furthermore, if you were unable to pay the entrance charge, you would be dunked in sewage, naked, until the charge was paid.

There was overcrowding, filth, open sewers and cesspits off the main thoroughfares in the numerous alleys and lanes of Temple Bar, extending to the Liberties beyond Christ Church Cathedral. Farm animals, dogs, pigs and poultry roamed around and typhus, cholera, dysentery, diarrhoea, consumption and pleurisy were rife. Smog and pollution from factories, limekilns, glass factories, breweries, textile factories, slaughterhouses, brickworks and the numerous small craft businesses in the area permeated the atmosphere. Remedies for rheumatism were advertised in the *Hibernian Journal* of 1776 for those who could afford them. These included Scots Pills,

Pectoral Drops, Balsam of Life, Original Elixir of Health, Lozenges and Refined Liquorice. Worm Ointment was also available.

In the late eighteenth century, the Revd James Whitelaw, based in the heart of the Liberties, a stone's throw from Temple Bar, described the plight of the wretched he visited:

> I have frequently surprised from ten to fifteen persons in a room not fifteen feet square, stretched on a wad of filthy straw, swarming with vermin, and without covering, save the wretched rags that constitute their wearing apparel ... a degree of filth and stench inconceivable, except by such as have visited those scenes of wretchedness.[5]

Such was the shortage of space that the dead were at times buried standing up and often dug up and dumped in the River Liffey to make room for the next tenant. The area around Cook Street was known as Dublin's 'coffin colony' as there were at least seventeen undertakers vying for business, with some offering 'best second hand coffins' for those who could afford a coffin. Bully's Acre in Kilmainham was the local cemetery for the poor. Bodies would be squashed into every available space and, unlike today, the depth between the corpse and the grass above was not an issue. Shaking hands with the dead was a frequent occurrence, particularly for a wager. Body snatchers would also be hovering on the periphery at funerals, waiting for the departure of the mourners before pouncing on the newly dead and shunting them off to Trinity College for dissection.

Poverty gave rise to rampant violence. This made Dublin a very dangerous place, which was reflected to some extent in the hundreds of executions, mainly for robbery, that occurred in the closing decades of the eighteenth century. The historian W.E.H. Lecky notes that Dublin was the scene of much disorder, including savage feuds, between the Ormond Boys (butchers, slaughter works, porters, stable-boys, cattle drivers and vagabonds) and Liberty Boys (unemployed weavers), who would usually meet to fight on the quays adjacent to Temple Bar. They often used meat hooks and sharpened oak staves (tools of their trade) as weapons. Such was the savagery and loss of life involved in the faction fighting that an eminent surgeon at the time, so used to dealing with fractured skulls, eventually began referring to them as 'Ormond fractures'.

The Cornmarket open area near Christ Church Cathedral was the location for another violent pastime known as bull-baiting. This involved tying a bull to a pole with a rope of a certain length so it could move around a bit, then letting the fiercest dog possible attack (or bait) it. The poor of Dublin thought of this as a great amusement. Another source of entertainment was the Saturday hangings and the pillorying and stocks outside the Tholsel on Skinner's Row, which faced Christ Church Cathedral. The condemned, often languishing in the notorious Black Dog Gaol near Cornmarket, sometimes spent their last days playing cards on their own coffin. The grim lives of the dispossessed were sometimes lightened by black humour, as in the case of the execution ballads 'The Night Before Larry was Stretched' and 'The Kilmainham Minuet' (the dance of the hanged man), popular from the 1780s onwards.

Those at the upper levels of Irish society were preoccupied with retaining their position and possessions, so the stocks, the pillory, stretching, transportation, burnings and hangings were standard punishments meted out by the nervous upper classes to those found guilty of even the smallest crime.[6]

FROM POVERTY TO PROSTITUTION

Due to the extreme poverty experienced by the poor of Dublin and the proliferation of taverns in the area, parts of Temple Bar were particularly susceptible to prostitution. The preponderance of taverns in Temple Bar in the seventeenth and eighteenth centuries is highlighted by the name Winetavern Street, the street of taverns. At one time, there were 137 alehouses on that street alone. There were hundreds of other taverns in the wider Temple Bar area. In fact, William Petty, in the course of his work on the Down Survey in the middle of the seventeenth century, noted that there were 1,180 alehouses and 91 breweries in Dublin. These numbers did not diminish as time passed, but increased.[7]

Shebeens (places involved in the illicit sale of alcohol) were as numerous as taverns, dram shops and alehouses. Nearly a quarter of the houses in Temple Bar and the Liberties sold alcohol. It was mostly women who brewed beer and ale, cheaply, then sold it from their own taverns or from street carts. Crucially, these were times when safe drinking water was not widely available, so the drinking of beer or ale was a suitable alternative. The brewing process helped to eliminate much of the impurities of dirty water. Dublin itself had nearly 100 breweries and nearly as many distilleries. However, with the arrival of Arthur Guinness in 1759, a process of amalgamating breweries started. This was also the case with distilleries after the arrival of the Jamesons and Roes.[8]

Another reason for the proliferation of taverns was that the old docklands area around the custom house was in the very heart of Temple Bar. This is

The Quays Bar, Temple Bar.

where Dublin's original docklands area was, with ships, boats and trawlers offloading their cargos, including fish for the nearby fish shambles and copious quantities of wine and whiskey. After dark, it was not advisable to walk down the narrow, medieval alleys towards the quays in the vicinity of Smock Alley, Fishamble Street or Bagnio Slip at Lower Fownes Street unless you wished to visit the taverns or playhouses, which you did at your peril, for there lay danger and vice. The smell of horse dung and rotten fish, and the ragged individuals lurking in the shadows of badly lit streets were all indicative that, when darkness fell, this part of Dublin was not for the genteel.

Such was the demand for taverns that Christ Church Cathedral rented out part of its huge medieval crypt to accommodate them as there was a shortage of space in Temple Bar. Consequently, the area below the cathedral and in the vicinity became known as Hell. On Rocque's 1756 map of Dublin, there is an alleyway in Christ Church Yard, linking St Michael's Hill with Fishamble Street, called Hell.

Alcohol and sex went hand in hand and Temple Bar facilitated this with its taverns, theatres, numerous brothels or bawdy houses and bagnios, cockpits, gambling dens, gaming rooms and billiard rooms (the latter over the disreputable 'piazzae', behind the custom house). Several ferries plying the River Liffey from Bagnio and other ferry stations enabled customers from the north side to avail of the fare with ease.[9]

Soldiers from the barracks located in Temple Bar and at Dublin Castle, students from Trinity College and drunken sailors on shore leave were all looking for entertainment. They flocked to the disreputable taverns and bawdy houses in the back lanes and alleyways between the cockpit and the custom house. From Smock Alley, Copper Alley and Blind Quay to the Bagnio Slip area at Lower Fownes Street and on to Fleet Lane, Temple Bar was a den of debauchery, gambling and prostitution in the eighteenth and nineteenth centuries. Once darkness fell, one was likely to be accosted by streetwalkers near the bawdy houses of Smock and Copper alleys, Essex Street, Cope Street and nearby, or at the notorious Dame Street and Temple Lane junction, a favourite spot for those touting for business.[10]

Bagnio Slip (Fownes Street Lower) was where one of the Liffey Ferry stations was located. The word 'bagnio' comes from the Italian word for illicit bathing house or brothel. The term was popular in the mid-eighteenth century. In 1743, the English painter William Hogarth (whose works were very popular in Ireland) portrayed an earl catching his wife in the Turk's Head bagnio with her lover, who is endeavouring to make his escape through a window. The Turk's Head pub subsequently moved and today is located on Parliament Street. There were many bagnios in Temple Bar that masqueraded as wash houses, but were in fact were brothels. Examples include Mother Bungy's in Fishamble Street and, around the corner, the Munster Bagnio in Copper Alley. There was also the Royal Bagnio on Essex Quay and the Duke of Ormond's, for most of the eighteenth century, on Essex Street East. There was another one on Anglesea Street and still more on Blind Quay. In the vicinity of Bagnio Slip, some of the many coffee houses and taverns offered Turkish baths, which evolved into houses of prostitution. The Bagnio Slip brothels were ideally located as they were at the ferry crossing.[11]

The prostitution business was the cause of much violence, intimidation, kidnapping, rape and murder in Dublin. In 1781, a prostitute was murdered in the Copper Alley area. In the same year, the brothel of Anne McDonagh, who had a house in Little Booter Lane, was attacked by an angry mob after the murder of two more of her prostitutes. Angry mobs attacked brothels with some frequency during the closing decades of the eighteenth century due to the brutal behaviour of brothel owners towards prostitutes. McDonagh beat one of her girls so badly that she lost an eye. In 1791, four brothels had to be demolished by the authorities, such was the level of violence.

The authorities were often lax in their attitudes towards prostitution, provided bawdy houses were not too disorderly. They saw it as a necessary evil for men and a lewd or unfortunate activity for women. While prostitution was not strictly illegal, a 1565 law required that the city authorities punish brothel keepers 'according to the ancient laws of this city' and every so often the authorities would take action. In 1798, Elizabeth Crummers was tried for robbing a customer at her brothel on Sycamore Alley. In earlier decades, Margaret Flood of Copper Alley was whipped in the streets for brothel-keeping; Margaret Leary, who operated two brothels in Fleet Street, was jailed and pilloried for dealing in stolen property (presumably her customers'); Elizabeth McClean of Eustace Street was arrested and released for touting for business – she was one of the most successful and notorious; Mrs Brazen of Aston Quay was arrested for operating behind a haberdashery shop; and Mrs Maher of Essex Street was sentenced to transportation for brothel-keeping, although this severe sentence was quite unusual. Other famous madams included Alice Rice, Mrs Locker, Mrs Maher and Catherine Locker, all of whom had businesses in Essex Street, Margaret Flood of Copper Alley, Margaret Leary of Fleet Street and Margaret Molloy of Crane Lane. The latter's brothel was located above the offices of the *Freeman's Journal*, run by the notorious Francis Higgins, who was known as the 'Sham Squire'.

The *Daily Gazetteer* for October 1736 reported on a couple, the Reillys, who were tried and convicted for keeping a bawdy house. Both were sentenced to be whipped as bawdy-house keepers. The man was also sentenced to three months' imprisonment. The woman's punishment involved being paraded from Newgate Prison on Cornmarket to Trinity College and being whipped along the way. One newspaper of the time suggested that much of the crime in Dublin was associated with prostitutes and streetwalkers. A public meeting held in the Fishamble Street Music Hall in 1766 led to the establishment of a Magdalen Asylum to try to tackle the problem and provide some kind of refuge for young women caught up in prostitution.[12]

MOTHER BUNGY, MARS AND VENUS

Prostitutes and bawdy houses were much in evidence around Smock Alley, from the time of a notorious prostitute called Mother Bungy, who, in the early eighteenth century, according to historian John Gilbert, 'was in her day, a sink of sin'. Smock Alley is where one might end up murdered in 'these bottomless pits of wickedness'. Notorious taverns included the Hoop Petticoat Tavern and the Globe. However, the local residents took matters into their own hands, demolished the buildings and 'banished the unclean vermin, the place purged of infamy'. This did not last long; brothels soon reopened in the alley and gambling houses were soon busier than ever.[13]

The Smock Alley Theatre would also have attracted prostitutes to the area and confirmed the area as a place of vice. The public sometimes saw little difference between actresses and prostitutes. Thomas Sheridan, the manager of the theatre in the 1740s and 1750s, noted that 'the very fact that one part of the house was a bear-garden and the other a brothel kept respectable people away'. Sheridan also noted that at times there were up to 100 people on the stage after a performance. These people mixed with the actors so as to be nearly indistinguishable from them. Moreover, any fashionable young man could get admission behind the scenes. 'Here he would speedily be initiated into the mysteries of Mars and Venus', Sheridan noted. On one occasion, a young gentleman accosted a famous actress in the theatre, Ann Bellamy, the toast of Ireland in the mid-eighteenth century. He got up on the stage and kissed her on the neck, whereupon she slapped him in the face. Sheridan afterwards decided that henceforth no gentlemen would be allowed behind the scenes.

Despite that and despite the iron spikes Sheridan erected in front of the stage as a deterrent, the Kelly Riots of 1747 involved a drunken Galway 'gentleman' called Kelly taking liberties with an actress on stage. An actor sternly reprimanded him, but Trinity College students did not appreciate a 'gentleman' being forcibly ejected from the theatre and riots ensued two nights later when the students broke up a performance, stormed the stage and damaged the backstage area. Given this view of actresses, it is not surprising that the number of bawdy houses in the area around the theatre grew.[14]

MADDEN'S AND MENDOZA

The most notorious gambling houses on Smock Alley were Madden's, but there was also the Globe, Reilly's Tavern and a fourth at Ben Jonson's Head. Gambling was a vice that crossed social divides. When the police raided a gambling den in 1790, they found a notorious 'sharper' (a cheating gambler) called Mendoza and his gang, who operated in the area, as well as a few of the false dice used at the gambling tables. These tables were called 'stamps' or 'hazard-tables'. The police also discovered a cellar full of the skeletons of those who had fallen victim to Mendoza and his gang. It would have been easy to get away with murder as many of those who frequented the gambling houses would have been soldiers or seafaring individuals. Their families back home might have assumed they had died in battle or at sea. But there were also other cases of murder. In 1768, there were serious riots involving substantial damage to property and the loss of many lives following the murder of a butcher in Smock Alley by some of the ruffians who frequented the area. Such was the destruction and violence that the horse-mounted soldiers had to be brought in to patrol the street. The mob attacked and wrecked the houses in which they suspected the villains were hiding. The city authorities responded on numerous ways. They even changed the name of the alley – first to Orange Street, then to Essex Street West – to deter and confuse customers. However, despite these changes, it was still known as Smock Alley by residents and because of its proximity to the theatre.[15]

WENCHES AND THE ASCENDANCY

A story that survives from this unique era and area is that of Darkey Kelly, the infamous prostitute and madam of a brothel on Copper Alley (off Fishamble Street) called 'The Maiden Tower' (now home to Darkey Kelly's pub). Dorcas 'Darkey' Kelly was a beautiful woman with long, flowing black hair. A life of destitution and poverty forced her into prostitution and she became a woman of ill repute. The building, a large brick mansion where she conducted her business, survived until the late nineteenth century. It contained such a labyrinth of rooms, galleries, mirrors and doors that it was almost impossible for anyone to find their way out from the upper storeys unless they were accompanied by a guide. Access was easy, egress difficult. This was deliberate. Having paid their money, many of her unwary customers were lured into her brothel, some never to be seen again. There were many instances of customers in other brothels also being murdered, either by their enemies or by the prostitutes.

For generations, Darkey Kelly was also known in Dublin folk memory as the woman who was burned at the stake for witchcraft after she accused the Sheriff of Dublin, Simon Luttrell (1713–1787), of fathering her baby. His family had owned Luttrellstown Castle, Castleknock, County Dublin, since the early thirteenth century. He was made Baron Irnham of Luttrellstown in 1768 and became First Earl of Carhampton in 1785. In his younger days, he was one of the most active members of the notorious Hellfire Club. His rakish behaviour earned him the nickname 'King of Hell'.[16]

When Darkey Kelly demanded Luttrell's financial support, he refused to acknowledge the child and instead, in order to discredit her, he accused Kelly of witchcraft and spread rumours among the women of Dublin that she was involved in witchcraft and the murder of her baby, though no actual body was produced. Some said that having customers from the ascendancy was her downfall. It was said that men such as Simon Luttrell 'wanted the wench, but not the woman', whereas she 'wanted the money but not the man'.

Despite being accused of witchcraft, the real charge against her was much more serious. Contemporary newspapers revealed that Darkey Kelly was in fact accused of killing local shoemaker John Dowling. Investigators then found the bodies of five men hidden in the vaults of her brothel. It seemed that murder was her way of dealing with annoying or non-paying customers. She was sentenced to death and she was publicly burned in St Stephen's Green in January 1764 before a jeering rabble. Women in eighteenth-century Ireland were second-class citizens and the execution of prisoners reflected this sexism. Men found guilty of murder were hanged whereas women were strangled first, then burnt. In the wake of her execution, prostitutes rioted in Copper Alley.[17]

The Darkey Kelly case did not end there. Her sister was involved in another sensational news story in the 1780s when Simon Luttrell's son Henry, who also had the title Lord Carhampton and who was involved in the revived Hellfire Club, allegedly raped a young teenage girl in a brothel located at Blackmoor Yard, Anglesea Street. The girl, Mary Neil, aged 13, was procured for him by brothel-keeper Maria Llewellyn (Darkey's sister). Following the accusations, Henry Luttrell reportedly had the young girl and her parents falsely imprisoned. The girl's mother died in prison. Luttrell's trumped-up charges against the girl and her family were later dismissed in court. Llewellyn was described as Darkey Kelly's sister and she was condemned to be hanged in 1788 for her complicity in the affair. However, on the morning she was to be hanged, the Lord Lieutenant pardoned her as there were doubts over the testimony of witnesses. Later, one of the pimps from Llewellyn's brothel, Robert Edgeworth (known as Squire Edgeworth), was sentenced to imprisonment for perjury. As part of his punishment, he had to spend time in the stocks outside the Tholsel on Skinner's Row (Christ Church Place). The crowd threw rotten eggs and snowballs at him. In 1789, he went into the stocks again. This time he was pelted with rotten eggs, oranges, potatoes, old shoes, brickbats, dead cats, mud and filth of every kind. Today, the stocks may be seen across the road in the crypt of the cathedral.[18]

7

FROM PUE'S TO BEWLEY'S – THE COFFEE HOUSES

Besides clubs and taverns, there was another outlet for those who preferred more sober surroundings: coffee houses. Coffee was originally imported into Europe by Venetian traders, starting in 1615. In the decades that followed, the coffee house culture rapidly spread across Europe. Coffee houses made their first appearance in Dublin in the mid-seventeenth century and quickly gained a large and varied clientele, particularly among the merchant class. They became the place to meet, negotiate and find out the latest news. As Temple Bar was the centre of Dublin's thriving commercial life, many of the first coffee houses were concentrated in the area surrounding the old custom house on Essex (Custom House) Quay. Later in the century, they proliferated in the vicinity of the Royal Exchange.[1]

During their heyday, the coffee houses became hotbeds of political discussion, debates, meetings and gossip. In Jonathan Swift's words, 'Coffee makes us severe, and grave and philosophical', the exact opposite of the state of mind promoted by taverns. Besides the coffee, a large part of the appeal of coffee houses was the multitude of newspapers available to read. The selection on offer was a source of great pride to the owners, with many boasting titles from both home and abroad. Other documents were presented, such as parliamentary reports and notices from bodies such as the Wide Street Commissioners and Dublin Castle.[2]

DICK'S AND LUCAS'S

Among the more popular coffee houses in the Temple Bar area were Lucas's Coffee House in the Royal Exchange on Cork Hill; the Phoenix on Werburgh Street, where political dinners were often held; Dick's Coffee House on Skinner's Row, much patronised by literary men because it was over a bookseller's; the Eagle on Eustace Street, where meetings of the Dublin Volunteers were held; and the Old Sot's Hole, near Essex Bridge, famous for its beefsteaks and ale.[3]

Beside Fishamble Street, in Skinner's Row, on the site of what is now Jurys Inn, stood Dick's Coffee House, where auctions of books, land and property were also held. Over time, it became one of the main auction houses in Dublin and it was known especially for book auctions. The owner of the coffee house, Richard (Dick) Pue, published a newspaper called *Pue's Occurrences* from the late seventeenth century onwards. He was described by his contemporary John Dunton as 'a witty and ingenious man, who makes the best coffee in Dublin ... and has a peculiar knack at bantering, and will make rhymes to anything'. Pue was as much a printer, publisher and editor as a coffee-house proprietor. Dick's and other such establishments were central to political and journalistic discourse during this period, serving as factional centres of gravity, as they were near Dublin Castle, the Tholsel and the Royal Exchange.[4]

Of the many customers of Lucas's on Cork Hill, one of the most eccentric was Talbot Edgeworth, son of Ambrose Edgeworth and a relation of Maria Edgeworth, the author of *Castle Rackrent*, which was published in 1800. Talbot Edgeworth was renowned for his vanity, his extravagance and his fondness for fine clothing. Of women, he said, 'they may look and die'. Consequently, he was the butt of the jokes of men and the contempt of women. Another character who frequented the establishment was the notorious and battle-hardened Colonel Henry Luttrell, who was murdered in 1717, shortly after leaving Lucas's.[5]

The nearby Rose Tavern, also a coffee house, was the popular meeting place for political clubs, lawyers' clubs and benevolent clubs. The Friendly Brothers of St Patrick was one such benevolent club. Members held their annual dinner here at 4 p.m. on 17 March, having first heard a sermon in St Patrick's Cathedral. One of its members was the brewer Arthur Guinness. Dean Swift mentioned the club in 1731:

> Suppose me dead; and then suppose
> A club assembled at the Rose.

Eighteenth-century sketch of 'The Coffee House Mob'. Dublin's first Coffee House was on Essex Quay. (Courtesy of Dublin Forums)

Other popular coffee houses in Temple Bar during the first half of the eighteenth century were Dempster's, Bacon's, Norris's, The Merchant's, The Dublin, Walsh's and there was another in the custom house itself. The Anne coffee house, also called the Anne and Grecian, situated at Essex Bridge, was also used in the first two decades of the eighteenth century for book auctions. On Custom House Quay, the Cocoa Tree Coffee House was on the eastern side, near the custom house and was over the bookshop of Thomas Whitehouse. St James's Coffee House was located on the upper floor of the building. Merchants whose businesses revolved around the custom house frequented two of Dublin's busiest coffee houses: The Little Dublin and The Exchange in Crampton Court, a short walk from the custom house.[6]

THE GLOBE

Opposite the custom house on Essex Street, from the early years of the eighteenth century, was The Globe, which has been described by the historian John Gilbert as one of the most important taverns (it was also a coffee house) of the period. He notes that 'this house was the chief resort of the Dublin politicians during the reign of George II' and that it attracted 'merchants, physicians, and lawyers', among others. Gilbert quoted from a poem about the establishment, popular at the time:

> Sometimes to the 'Globe' I stray,
> To hear the trifle of the day;
> There learned politicians spy,
> With thread-bare cloaks, and wigs awry;
> Assembled round, in deep debate
> On Prussia's arms, and Britain's fate;
> Whilst one, whose penetration goes,
> At best, no farther than his nose,
> In pompous military strain,
> Fights every battle o'er again:
> Important as a new-made Lord,
> He spills his coffee on the board ...[7]

An interesting character by the name of Blind Peter, famed for his wit, recurs in many accounts of this coffee house. He liked to position himself at the entrance to the building. He was a shoeblack (polisher) who was described as 'of hideous aspect, he had but one eye, was pitted with the pox, and his face completely tattooed with the scars he received in the various battles he had fought'. Lord Townshend, when he was viceroy, stopped one day in Essex Street and after having his shoes polished by Blind Peter, asked him for change of half a guinea. 'Half a guinea, your honour,' exclaimed the shoeblack, 'change for half a guinea from me! By God sir, you may as well ask a Highlander for a knee-buckle!' Blind Peter was not just a character. He had many other talents, including pickpocketing and mugging and housebreaking. His blindness did not prove to be a disability.[8]

The popularity of the coffee houses continued throughout the eighteenth century. However, by the turn of the following century, their appeal had diminished. Dick's Coffee House was closed in 1780 and Carberry House, where it was located, was demolished. Other once-popular establishments suffered a similar fate. With the increased availability of newspapers in the mid-nineteenth century, the role of the coffee houses as the city's dominant 'third space' faded.

FROM SYCAMORE TO WESTMORELAND

There was one exception. The famous Bewley's Café on Westmoreland Street had its beginning in Temple Bar in the 1840s, when Joshua Bewley opened a small coffee and tea house at Sycamore Alley, off Dame Street. In 1896, the family opened a branch on Westmoreland Street called Bewley's Oriental Café, following the success of the South Great George's Street branch. Nearly 200 years later, the company is still trading in Dublin, notably from its landmark café on Grafton Street.

8

FROM GRATTAN'S PARLIAMENT TO THE EAGLE TAVERN

In the closing decades of the eighteenth century, the confidence of the elite in Irish society would have presupposed a different course for Irish history going into the nineteenth century. The political discussion in the coffee houses was an indication of the political turmoil and ferment in Dublin. The streets in and around Temple Bar and the individuals associated with them provided the stage and cast for some of the most important political developments from the late eighteenth century onwards, developments that were to have a resounding impact of the course of modern Irish history. At the centre of these developments were the Irish Parliament House on College Green and the Eagle Tavern on Eustace Street.

Between 1661 and 1784, the Irish parliament sat for approximately six months every two years and annually thereafter. The House of Commons was composed of Protestant English settlers. Among those early members were John Temple (author of the unquestioned and exaggerated history of the 1641 Rebellion) and William Petty, both based in Temple Bar. At the time of Grattan's Parliament in the late eighteenth century, there were 300 MPs and 100 peers, a huge number given the impotency of the parliament. The population of Ireland had reached 5 million by 1800.

Legislation imposed by the English parliament – in particular, Poynings' Law (1494) and the Sixth of George I (1719) – circumscribed the power of the Irish parliament, essentially establishing that the Irish parliament was legislatively subservient and dependent upon the English parliament and Crown. Consequently, the Irish parliament was a puppet parliament. The head of the Irish executive, the Lord Lieutenant, a nominee of the British

The Speaker entering the Irish House of Commons, from a drawing by Francis Wheatley, 1782.

government (puppetmaster), lived in Ireland only while the parliament was sitting. The day-to-day business of administration was usually shared between office holders who were English-born and Irish politicians called 'undertakers' who had agreed to manage parliament on the Lord Lieutenant's behalf.[1]

One of the most important pieces of legislation passed by this parliament on College Green was the 1666 Acts of Settlement and Explanation, which granted ownership of huge swathes of Irish land – nearly 8 million acres; more than half of the land of the country – to the Cromwellian adventurers of the 1640s and '50s. This was 'perhaps without parallel in the history of civilised nations', an English commentator noted at the time, 'its injustice could not be denied; and the only apology offered was the necessity of quieting the Cromwellian settlers and of establishing on a permanent basis the Protestant ascendancy in Ireland'.[2] It was also at College Green that the Penal Laws were enacted from 1692 onwards. These laws, following the Williamite victory at the Battle of the Boyne in 1690, were intended to break the political power of Irish Catholics.

In Jonathan Swift's famous *Drapier's Letters* of 1724, written just a few years after the enactment of the Sixth of George I (1719), he challenged this law. He was opposed to the law, along with many others. He noted that the arguments were 'invincible', as 'All government without the consent of the governed, is the very definition of slavery; but, in fact, eleven men well-armed, will certainly subdue one single man in his shirt'.[3]

He also summed up the majority opinion in Ireland in relation to the incumbents in the parliament:

> Tell us what the pile contains
> Many a head that holds no brains.[4]

Under the influence and the example of the American War of Independence (1775–83), new political ideas began to develop and calls for reform from within the Protestant ascendancy itself led to a significant constitutional change. Irish agriculture was generally inefficient and manufacturing trades suffered from restrictions imposed to protect English merchants. British policies were challenged by writers, including not only Jonathan Swift, but also Bishop George Berkeley and Charles Lucas, who was one of the founders of the *Freeman's Journal*, based in Temple Bar. Within the Irish parliament itself, a reforming group known as The Patriots eventually emerged, led by Henry Flood and the Earl of Charlemont. They believed that a more representative assembly would achieve more for Irish commerce while also preserving the Protestant interest. In 1775, Flood accepted a government post and leadership of The Patriots passed to Henry Grattan (born in Fishamble Street), a young lawyer whom Charlemont had brought into parliament.

In 1779, Grattan addressed the House on the subject of Free Trade for Ireland, which had long been a burning issue, and on 19 April 1780, he made his famous demand for Irish independence. His address, his subject and his oratorical skills were very impressive:

> I wish for nothing but to breathe in this our land, in common with my fellow-subjects, the air of liberty. I have no ambition, unless it is the ambition to break your chain and to contemplate your glory. I never will be satisfied as long as the meanest cottager in Ireland has a link of the British chain clinging to his rags; he may be naked, but he shall not be in irons. And I do see the time is at hand, the spirit is gone forth, the declaration is planted; and though great men should apostatize, yet the cause will live; and though the public speaker should die, yet the immortal fire shall outlast the organ which conveyed it; and the breath of liberty, like the word of the holy man, will not die with the prophet, but survive him.[5]

A

LETTER

To the Right Honourable the
*Lord Viscount *Molesworth.*

* * * * *

By *M.B. Drapier*, Author of the Letter
to the *Shop-keepers*, &c.

* * * * *

They compassed me about also with Words of Deceit, and
  fought against me without a Cause.
For my Love they are my Adversaries, but I give my self
  unto Prayer.
And they have rewarded me Evil for Good, and Hatred for
  my Love. *Psalm* 109. *v.* 3, 4, 5.
Seek not to be Judge, being not able to take away Iniquity,
  lest at any Time thou fear the Person of the Mighty, and
  lay a stumbling Block in the Way of thy Uprightness.
Offend not against the Multitude of a City, and then thou
  shalt not cast thy self down among the People.
Bind not one Sin upon another, for in One thou shalt not
  be Unpunished. *Ecclus.* Ch. 7. V. 6, 7, 8.

* * * * *

*Non jam prima peto Mnestheus, neque vincere certo: Quanquam O!
Sed superent, quibus Hoc, Neptune, dedisti.*

* * * * *

DUBLIN: Printed by *John Harding* in *Molesworth's Court* in
Fishamble-street.

Title page of one of the *Drapier's Letters* pamphlets, printed by John Harding, Fishamble Street.

The Patriot element demanded an end to the direct control Westminster exercised over Irish legislation. It was an opportune time as Britain was forced to withdraw troops from Ireland due to the outbreak of rebellion in the American colonies, followed by French and Spanish intervention. A Protestant militia, known as the Volunteers, was formed, ostensibly to protect against a French invasion of Ireland but essentially to protect their own power and wealth. Charlemont became their leader and the Volunteers, assuming both a military and political role, threw themselves behind the demands for reform.[6]

The Patriots now had the backing of a 40,000-strong volunteer force, which, in the 1780s and early 1790s showed its strength in many parades on College Green and Dame Street. In 1782, a fearful government gave way to their demands. In 1779, it removed most of the trade restrictions and in 1782 Westminster repealed the 1719 Act (declaring the right of the British parliament to legislate for Ireland) and the Irish parliament removed the most oppressive parts of Poyning's Law and other similar legislation. The outcome of the settlement was Grattan's parliament, the acknowledgement by the government of the right of the Irish parliament to operate as an independent legislature subject only to the Crown.

On 16 April 1782, Grattan passed through ranks of Volunteers gathered outside the Irish Parliament House on College Green, amidst unparalleled popular enthusiasm, to make a declaration of the independence of the Irish parliament.

'I found Ireland on her knees,' Grattan said, 'I watched over her with a paternal solicitude; I have traced her progress from injuries to arms, and from arms to liberty. Spirit of Swift, spirit of Molyneux, your genius has prevailed! Ireland is now a nation! She is no longer a wretched colony, returning thanks to her Governor for his rapine, and to her King for his oppression.'[7]

There was much celebration in 1782 when Ireland was granted legislative independence. The final years of the century saw great commercial activity and Dublin acquired many more of the handsome Georgian buildings for which it is known today.[8]

In recognition of Grattan's contribution, later historians established the custom of referring to the parliament of the years 1782 to 1800 as Grattan's Parliament, even though Grattan's influence after 1782 was limited and he in no sense controlled or directed parliament. Some of the important work of the parliament included the Relief Acts of 1782, 1792 and 1793, which cumulatively did away with most of the Penal Laws. Nonetheless, although parliament was now independent in theory, in practice it was still controlled by the English government, which continued to exercise its influence through the borough patrons (essentially ensuring by corrupt payments that its

Henry Grattan demanding Irish independence. (Courtesy of Dublin Forums)

The first meeting of Grattan's Parliament in Irish Parliament House in 1782. Grattan is standing to the right of image. (Courtesy of Kildare Local History Society)

preferred Members of Parliament were in the majority in the Irish House of Commons). Grattan's efforts in this supposedly free parliament met with such opposition that he retired out of frustration in 1797, returning only to oppose the Union in 1800.

1798 – FROM THE DUBLIN VOLUNTEERS TO THE UNITED IRISHMEN

Having achieved legislative independence, the Volunteer movement gradually disbanded. Despite that, some of the Dublin Volunteers coalesced with the growing movement of the United Irishmen. The Society of United Irishmen had been founded in Belfast in October 1791. Following the foundation of the United Irishmen in Belfast, Dublin quickly followed. On 9 November, in the Eagle Tavern on Eustace Street (its new home after moving from Cork Hill), the Dublin Society of United Irishmen was formed. The Eagle was not the only rendezvous as one of the society's leaders, Napper Tandy, also held meetings of the Society of Free Citizens at the Kings Arms on Smock Alley. Tandy (who lived on High Street, beside St Audoen's church) acted as secretary of the Dublin committee of the United Irishmen and was an influential man in his time. He was a popular member of Dublin Corporation who had campaigned for a boycott of English goods in Dublin and who had even led a mini-riot at the site of the new custom house in 1781 in the belief that the location of the building would have a devastating economic effect on Temple Bar and the wider city. Later in life, Napoleon is said to have demanded Tandy's release from captivity as a stipulation to his signing of the Treaty of Amiens in 1802.[9]

The society was committed to a union of all Irish people and contained within its ranks members of different Christian denominations. The founders were influenced by the ideals of the French Revolution (which began in 1789) and the American War of Independence (1775–1783). However, their vision went further than that of Grattan's Parliament. They wanted further parliamentary reform and, in particular, Catholic Emancipation. They wished for equal representation in parliament as part of a political system that included those of all religions.

During the early phase of the United Irishmen, they focused on the printed word. The works of authors such as Locke, Paine, Rousseau and Voltaire were handed out in scaled-down pamphlet form. The ideas of these men were used to highlight the political and social inequalities in Irish society.

The group was particularly successful at disseminating their message and recruiting members. Many members of the Dublin Volunteers became part of the Society of United Irishmen. In Belfast and Dublin, they had access to an established printing and publishing network, particularly in Temple Bar, which had a long history of a prolific and mostly independent printing and publishing industry. The Belfast-published *Northern Star*, the official organ of the United Irishmen, was distributed in Dublin by Dr William Drennan from his house on Dame Street, under the noses of those in Dublin Castle. Drennan was very important in the United Irishman movement and his reforming ideas reinvigorated the society, which had waned since the achievement of legislative independence. He successfully advocated the need for a secret interior circle within the movement to aggressively direct its mandate. The *Northern Star* was not the first such audacious publishing initiative. Another such newspaper, the *Volunteers Journal, or Irish Herald*, had been published from No. 7 Dame Street in the 1780s.[10]

In 1793, Britain went to war with France. The following year, the government suppressed the United Irishmen movement but in 1795 several of its leaders came together, reconstituted it as a secret, oath-bound society and argued for more revolutionary tactics. They developed a military structure and armed themselves for revolution. The war with France and the prospect of a French invasion had changed the political situation in Ireland.

Some of the leaders of the movement, such as Napper Tandy, Thomas Russell, Oliver Bond and John Keogh, lived in or near Temple Bar and it was at the Eagle Tavern that Lord Edward Fitzgerald, Wolfe Tone and other leaders met and planned the rebellion. Thomas Russell was an experienced soldier who had risen to the rank of general. He had first met Wolfe Tone in the gallery of the Irish House of Commons on College Green and, according to Tone, 'we were struck with each other, notwithstanding the difference of our opinions, and we agreed to dine the next day in order to discuss the question'. Wolfe Tone and his friends called the House of Commons' dome 'Goose-Pie' and frequently said that they were going 'to hear what the geese are saying in the pie'.[11]

The government became increasingly nervous of revolution and ensured that it was kept informed of developments by a network of spies. It reacted quickly by introducing the Insurrection Act in 1796. A tip-off by a spy who was a member of the movement led to the arrest of many of the movement's leaders in Oliver Bond's house. Martial law was declared following the arrests. The arresting police officer was Major Henry Charles Sirr, who was effectively Dublin's chief-of-police.

One of the most notorious informers in the United Irishman was Leonard McNally, a significant member of the group and a prominent barrister. When defending many of the movement's senior members, including Wolfe Tone, Napper Tandy and Robert Emmet, McNally secretly passed on the defence's arguments to the government. From 1798 until his death in 1820, he received a pension from the government and it was only after his death that it became known that he had been an informer.

LORD EDWARD AND 'THE MAN FROM GOD KNOWS WHERE'

Following the arrests of his co-conspirators in the United Irishmen, Lord Edward Fitzgerald went into hiding. The government offered a £1,000 reward for his arrest. On 19 May, he was arrested at a house in Thomas Street in the Liberties (thanks to information provided by McNally). During the struggle, he was wounded by Major Sirr. He was lodged in Newgate Prison, where he died on 4 June 1798. One of the few United Irish leaders with military experience, his capture just before the outbreak of the rebellion was a major blow to the organisation. The rebellion was put down, quickly and mercilessly, with the help of 137,000 troops.

Two locations in Temple Bar were used for the interrogation, torture and execution of rebels. The old custom house on Wellington Quay had been converted into a military barracks and used by the Dumbarton Fencibles, who were involved in suppressing the 1798 Rebellion in Dublin. They administered pitch-caps and floggings to disaffected citizens, of which there were many. Pitch-capping was a particularly torturous punishment that involved pouring boiling pitch or tar into an upturned cone, then pressing it down on the bound victim's head. The Royal Exchange at Cork Hill was used as a headquarters by Major Sirr, who was responsible for the arrest, torture and execution of many of those involved in 1798.

The chief topics of conversation among the well-to-do in Dublin were the hangings, shootings and burnings, such was the extent of the ferocity and the cruelty exacted. Several of the lamplighters were hung from their own lamp posts for neglecting to light the lamps. Every morning the dead were exhibited in Dublin Castle Yard. The reaction showed that the Protestant ascendancy were not for changing. In fact, they were extremely alarmed by developments in Ireland since the granting of legislative independence in 1782. The extension of rights to Catholics, e.g. the admission of Catholics to the Bar in 1792, and the gradual erosion of the privileges of the ascendancy was, for them, apocalyptic.

There was a reason why King William of Orange dominated the approach to College Green, across from the Irish Houses of Parliament. The Protestant ascendancy was founded on the principles of the revolution of 1688, when King William overthrew King James. This was their 'Glorious Revolution'.

Today, Edward Fitzgerald is remembered by the street bearing his name in Temple Bar – Lord Edward Street. He is buried in the family vault in St Werburgh's church nearby. Major Sirr is buried in the adjacent graveyard.[12]

Thomas Russell, a founder and leader of the United Irishmen, known as 'the man from God knows where' because of his enigmatic personality, had been arrested in Dublin in 1796 and lodged in Newgate Prison. As a result, he was unable to take part in the 1798 Rebellion. In 1796, prior to his arrest, he had written a pamphlet, in which there was a powerful analysis of the revolutionary opportunity and the importance of a united Catholic and Presbyterian front. He was also a consistent anti-slavery campaigner and once said that 'on every lump of sugar I see a drop of human blood'. He was released in 1802 and travelled to Hamburg. Later, in Paris, he met Robert Emmet, who was planning another insurrection. When Emmet was arrested in Dublin, Russell went to his rescue, but was arrested on 9 September 1803 at his temporary residence at 28 Parliament Street. The house belonged to a gunsmith named Mulvey, who was also one of the best marksmen in Ireland. Russell was executed in Downpatrick Gaol for high treason.[13]

The arrest of Lord Edward Fitzgerald, United Irishman, by Major Sirr as shown in the *Hibernian Magazine*, 1803.

Today, there is a plaque on 4/5 Eustace Street commemorating the founding of the Society of United Irishmen of Dublin, which occurred on 9 November 1791 at the Eagle Tavern 'on this site'.

CATHOLIC EMANCIPATION AND THE EMERALD ISLE

Another important leader of the movement was John Keogh (1740–1818), a Dublin silk merchant and a champion of Catholic Emancipation who had lived at 17 Dame Street from 1772 to 1788. He met Edmund Burke in London in 1792. In the same year, he formed the Catholic Convention in Tailor's Hall at Back Alley in the Liberties (the Convention was also known as 'the Back Alley Parliament'), a short distance from Temple Bar. He was much respected by Wolfe Tone and was particularly associated with the Dublin United Irishmen, whose revolutionary ideals he shared. He was arrested in 1798, but later released.

Another survivor of the failed 1798 Rebellion was the aforementioned physician, poet and political radical Dr William Drennan (1754–1820), who had a house on Dame Street. As well as being one of the chief intellectual architects of the society and the distributor in Dublin of the *Northern Star*, he is known as the first to refer to Ireland in print as the 'Emerald Isle'. He did this in his poem 'When Erin first Rose', published in 1795 in a periodical called *Erin*:

> When Erin first rose from the dark swelling flood,
> God blessed the green island, he saw it was good.
> The Emerald of Europe, it sparkled and shone,
> In the ring of this world, the most precious stone.
> Arm of Erin, prove strong, but be gentle as brave,
> And uplifted to strike, still be ready to save;
> Not one feeling of vengeance presume to defile,
> The cause, or the men, of the Emerald Isle.[14]

Interestingly, Drennan was one of the first advocates of inoculation against smallpox and of the importance of handwashing to prevent the spread of infection.

FRAUD ON THE GREEN

One of the consequences of this late eighteenth-century revolutionary fervour was that the independent Irish parliament on College Green lasted a mere

John Keogh (1740-1817), a leading member of the United Irishmen who organised the
Catholic Convention in Dublin in 1792 to petition the English king on Catholic Emancipation.
He was a silk merchant with a business on Dame Street. (Courtesy of Dublin Forums)

eighteen years. Reacting against the spreading revolutionary ideas of the French Revolution and the 1798 Rebellion of the United Irishmen, the London government induced the parliament in Dublin (through huge payments to the many corrupt members) to vote itself out of existence under the 1800 Act of Union. It was parliamentary corruption at its worst, in the view of Henry Grattan. In May 1800, in a speech in the Irish parliament against the proposed legislation, he noted that 'loyalty [to England], distinct from liberty, is corruption, not loyalty'. The *Dublin Gazette* of July 1800 announced the creation of sixteen new peerages. In December of the same year, it published a list of twenty-six more.[15]

Grattan's view was echoed by other speakers in the many debates on the legislation, including at the last meeting of the Irish parliament on 2 October 1800. The general view of Ireland's best lawyers, including John Philpott Curran (defender of the United Irishmen and father of Sarah Curran, Robert Emmet's girlfriend), was that the Act was a 'nullity' and that the whole process of passing the Act was 'radically fraudulent; that all the forms and solemnities of law were but so many badges of the fraud'.[16]

For Henry Grattan, the Act 'was a savage act, done by a set of assassins who were brought into the House to sell their country and themselves; they did not belong to Ireland: some were soldiers, all were slaves. Everything was shame, and hurry, and base triumph!' The Act of Union received royal assent on 1 August the following year.[17]

In 1803, the Bank of Ireland bought Parliament House for £40,000. From this time until independence in 1921, Irish MPs were entitled to hold seats in the House of Commons at Westminster, but, following the 1916 Rising, most abstained.

Grattan himself lived on, despite poor health, until 1820. Then, according to historian Maurice Craig, 'with brazen cynicism, the British authorities conferred on Grattan the supreme indignity by burying him in Westminster Abbey'. According to Craig, Jonah Barrington, a prominent barrister and a contemporary of Grattan's, was furious at this and who wrote at the time of Grattan being 'escorted to the grave by mock pageantry of those whose vices and corruption ravished from Ireland everything which his talent and integrity had obtained for her'.[18]

Today, a statue of Henry Grattan is located in the centre of the road outside the former Houses of Parliament, facing Trinity College.

In a way, the Act of Union marked the end of the prosperous years not only for the Temple Bar area but for Dublin and the country as a whole. Many of the ascendancy moved to London, taking their wealth, influence and prestige with them. The words of historian Mary Daly, in reference to a later period in Dublin's history, seem appropriate: the city became 'the deposed Capital'.[19]

The nineteenth-century Irish novelist Maria Edgeworth also wrote about the consequences of the Act of Union on Irish economic life in her classic work *The Absentee* (1812). Her father had been one of those who had vehemently voted against the corrupt legislation. She noted that from the time of the removal of both Houses of Parliament, 'most of the nobility, and many of the principled families among the Irish commoners, either hurried in high hopes to London, or retired disgusted and in despair to their houses in the country'. She described the effects on rural life of the displacement of the Irish elite to London and the resulting deterioration of their Irish estates.[20]

Thus began a new era. An old Dublin saying describes the situation well: 'the rich marched out and the poor marched in'.

9

THE FREEDOM BELL
AND THE FENIANS

Temple Bar played a part in the achievement of Catholic Emancipation in 1829. Following the closure of the Smock Alley Theatre, the building was used as a whiskey store until Fr Michael Blake bought it for use as a church, which was called SS Michael and John church. The construction of the church was permitted because it was not located on a main street or road; Catholics were forbidden to have any church on a main route. Dublin's Pro-Cathedral is located on Marlborough Street, behind O'Connell Street, for the same reason.

When the church bell tolled in 1811, eighteen years before Catholic Emancipation, it was the first Catholic church bell to ring out in Dublin in nearly 300 years. However, it caused great consternation because it was in direct violation of the Penal Laws. The city authorities took a legal action against Fr Blake, the parish priest of the church, but Daniel O'Connell (a lawyer) successfully defended him against the charges of defiance levelled against him. O'Connell was widely known as 'The Liberator' because of his campaign for Catholic Emancipation (i.e. the removal of Penal Law restrictions and other similar legislative impediments to Catholics). Legend has it that O'Connell rang the bell to celebrate the granting of Catholic Emancipation in 1829 and in the process created a crack, which remains visible today. The bell is regarded as Dublin's, and Ireland's, great emancipation or 'freedom bell'.

THE FENIANS AND TEMPLE BAR

The granting of Catholic Emancipation was just another stage in the struggle for freedom, a struggle that persisted throughout the nineteenth century. The printing presses of Temple Bar played a significant role in the dissemination of revolutionary ideas. This was part of a trend that began when the printers and publishers of Temple Bar first published Jonathan Swift's *Drapier's Letters*, *A Modest Proposal*, *Gulliver's Travels* and other similar political documents. This trend continued throughout the late eighteenth-century revolutionary upheavals and in subsequent centuries.

The Fenian movement was a secret revolutionary society founded in Dublin in 1858 as the Irish Republican Brotherhood and in America as the Fenian Brotherhood. It was dedicated to the goal of achieving a democratic Irish republic. ('Fenian' refers to ancient warriors in Ireland.) In the early 1860s, a Fenian newspaper, the *Irish People*, was published at No. 12 Parliament Street. Leaders of the movement were involved, including Thomas Clarke Luby, who was the editor, and Jeremiah O'Donovan Rossa, the business manager. This publication contravened the nature of the 'secret' society, but one of the movement's leaders, James Stephens, had pushed for it on financial grounds. He was supported because some members of the organisation held the view that 'the nearer you are to Dublin Castle the less you will be noticed'. The first issue was published on 28 November 1863 and the paper lasted until September 1865.

However, there was an informer in the newspaper's office called Pierce Nagle who kept the authorities up to date on the movement's activities. This, and the very existence of the radical newspaper, enabled the Castle authorities to undermine the wider movement. In September 1865, Dublin Castle moved to close down the newspaper and arrested much of the leadership, including John O'Leary, O'Donovan Rossa, Luby and James Stephens. The latter three were sentenced to penal servitude. Stephens, the leader of the movement, later escaped to America. The government strike quickly and effectively undermined the growing movement, which was significant as 1865 had appeared to be the optimum year for rebellion due to the ending of American Civil War and the consequent availability of thousands of Irish soldiers. When the rebellion did take place in 1867, informers, bad weather and a government on high alert caused it to fizzle out quickly.[1]

Also in 1867, on the heels of the unsuccessful Fenian Rising earlier in the year, two policemen were shot dead on the night of 31 October at the corner of Temple Bar (street) and Eustace Street, near the Norseman Pub.

Funeral procession of Fenian Jeremiah O'Donovan Rossa, 1 August 1915. (Courtesy of NLI Commons Collection)

A manhunt was immediately launched to track down the Fenian assailants of the two Dublin Metropolitan Policemen (DMP) Sergeant Stephen Kelly and Constable Patrick Keenan. The investigation by Dublin Castle uncovered the existence of a Fenian assassination squad that had policemen, informers and judges in its sights. Today, there is a plaque on the upper wall of the Norseman pub commemorating that event in 1867.[2]

It has been argued that the 1915 funeral of the Fenian leader Jeremiah O'Donovan Rossa in Dublin's Glasnevin Cemetery was the beginning of Ireland's Easter Rising of 1916. He was regarded as a powerful symbol of Irish republicanism and it was at his funeral that one of the Rising's leaders, Pádraig Pearse, spoke the famous words in his oration, 'Life springs from death; and from the graves of patriot men and women spring living nations. While Ireland holds these graves, Ireland unfree shall never be at peace.' Prior to the removal to the cemetery, O'Donovan Rossa lay in state in Dublin's City Hall on Cork Hill.

THE FOUNDER OF SINN FÉIN

Despite the failure of the Fenian Rising of 1867, members of the Irish Republican Brotherhood continued to work for the cause, with members working in other organisations such as the Land League and the Gaelic League, and were particularly important in the 1916 Rising. A republican political organisation called Sinn Féin ('We Ourselves') was founded in 1905, influenced by the ideals of the Fenians and the IRB. The founder of this new organisation was Arthur Griffith, a journalist by training and a member of the IRB and the Gaelic League. Sinn Féin incorporated all brands of nationalism except home rule.

Arthur Griffith published the *United Irishman* (1899–1906), a weekly radical newspaper (founded in 1899 with William Rooney) from offices at 17 Fownes Street in Temple Bar in the early years of the twentieth century. The paper played a part in the foundation of Sinn Féin itself. Griffith's editorials urged the Irish to work towards self-government. The paper folded in 1906 because of a legal action taken against it, but it was revived in the same year under the name of Sinn Féin and lasted until 1914, when the government suppressed it. However, the party survived and was to have a major role in political developments after the 1916 Rising.

What distinguished Griffith's paper was the calibre of the contributors, which included W.B. Yeats, Oliver St John Gogarty, George Russell, George Moore, Robert Lynd and Katherine Tynan. James Joyce received his first review in the paper (the review was largely positive). Other contributors included poets Padraic Colum, James Cousins, Joseph Campbell and Seamus O'Sullivan. William Bulfin was published in the paper and some of the leading activists of the 1916 Rising, including Pádraig Pearse, Maud Gonne and Roger Casement also wrote for the paper. The organisation and the paper itself had a profound influence on many of those involved in the fight for Irish independence in subsequent years, including Arthur Griffith himself, who had joined the Irish Volunteers and was involved in the Howth gun-running. Despite not actually being involved in the 1916 Rising, Griffith was imprisoned as the government considered his writings as attempts to revive the national spirit. Moreover, although the 1916 Rising was essentially a rebellion inspired and organised by the IRB, it was mistakenly regarded by the British as 'a Sinn Féin rising'. Likewise, the general public believed that Sinn Féin included all fighters for Irish freedom. This made it much easier for Sinn Féin to oust the Irish Parliamentary Party in the 1917 elections as the effective representatives of the aspirations of the Irish people.

Griffith stood down as party leader in favour of Éamon de Valera, one of the 1916 Rising leaders, but he continued to be a significant figure in the movement and was one of the delegates sent to London to negotiate the Anglo-Irish Treaty that ended the War of Independence.[3]

THE 1916 RISING, CORK HILL AND THE 'FIERCE HORSEMEN'

City Hall also played its part in the development of Irish nationalism. The funerals of the leading patriots Charles Stewart Parnell, Jeremiah O'Donovan Rossa and Michael Collins were held there. During the 1916 Rising, the building was garrisoned by the insurgents. On Easter Monday, a company of James Connolly's Irish Citizen Army marched up Dame Street and took control of City Hall at Cork Hill. The garrison was commanded by Sean Connolly and the plan was

Parliament Street, looking towards Capel Street in far distance, 1953. Tarlo's Department Store is on corner with Dame Street and the *Evening Mail* offices are on the opposite corner. Read's and Royal Exchange Hotel are also visible. (Courtesy of Fotofinish Irish Historical Images)

to use it as a base to attack Dublin Castle. The two buildings across the road on the corners of Parliament Street – the *Evening Mail* offices and Tarlo's department store – were also occupied. Besides being part of the attacking force, the occupation of these corner buildings defended the rear and covered the Christ Church Cathedral and Trinity College approaches to the garrison.

The insurgents came under intense gunfire and there were five casualties. Captain Sean Connolly was the first rebel to shoot an opposing soldier and he was also the first rebel fatality during the Rising. He was shot and killed on the roof of City Hall on Easter Monday by a sniper lodged on the Bedford Tower in Dublin Castle. Three other casualties at the City Hall garrison were Sean O'Reilly, George Geoghegan and Louis Byrne and a fourth was injured.

City Hall on Cork Hill, 1952. (Courtesy of Bureau of Military History)

Sean Connolly's death was celebrated by the poet W.B. Yeats in this verse from his poem 'Mountain to Mountain Ride the Fierce Horsemen':

Who was the first man shot that day?
The player Connolly,
Close to the City Hall he died;
Carriage and voice had he;
He lacked those years that go with skill,
But later might have been
A famous, a brilliant figure
Before the painted scene,
From mountain to mountain ride the fierce horsemen.

Lady Gregory, who had founded the Abbey Theatre with W.B. Yeats and others, also wrote a poem in memory of Connolly after 1916. Connolly had been an actor at the Abbbey as well as a member of the Irish Citizen Army.

Five of Connolly's siblings fought in the Rising. Today, there is a plaque on an external entrance pillar to City Hall commemorating the sacrifice of those men who gave their lives in the 1916 Rising.[4]

Merchant's Arch also featured in the 1916 Rising. During the Rising, a band of Volunteers had marched into Dublin from Maynooth in County Kildare. When these men arrived in the city, they went first to the General Post Office on O'Connell Street. They were later sent across the Liffey to Parliament Street, where men were urgently required to help rescue those in the City Hall garrison as well as those in the *Dublin Evening Mail* offices. One of the Volunteers, Thomas Harris, recalled that 'We were issued with two canister bombs each and instructed how to strike a match and light the fuse and then fire them. We went down Liffey Street out on the Quays and across the Halfpenny Bridge. The toll man demanded a halfpenny!' Another account of being stopped for the toll on the bridge came from J.J. Scollan, a member of a small armed group called the Hibernian Rifles that took part in the Rising. Scollan recalled that:

At 6 a.m. on Tuesday I received orders to get over to the Exchange Hotel in Parliament Street. We proceeded to the Metal or Halfpenny Bridge – eighteen of my men and nine Maynooth men. Incidentally, the toll man was still on duty on the Bridge and tried to collect the halfpenny toll from us. Needless to say, he did not get it. No attempt was ever made to collect tolls on the bridge again [during the Rising].[5]

THE WAR OF INDEPENDENCE

Another participant in the 1916 Rising, but one who survived, was Thomas Traynor (1881–1921), a shoemaker who had a shop in Merchant's Arch. He was a married man with ten children. He was captured during an ambush on Auxiliaries in Brunswick Street in March and tried in City Hall on 5 April. He was hanged in Mountjoy Jail on 25 April 1921 during the War of Independence. A song, 'The Ballad of Thomas Traynor', was written in his memory.[6]

KEVIN BARRY

A name that lives on in the story of the War of Independence is that of Kevin Barry, 'who gave his young life'. Kevin Barry (1902–1920) was born on 20 January 1902 at No. 8 Fleet Street to Thomas and Mary (*née* Dowling) Barry. The fourth of seven children, his father ran a dairy shop. He joined the IRA at the age of 15 and went on to study medicine at UCD. At the age of 18, following his capture during the War of Independence, he became the first republican to be executed since the leaders of the 1916 Rising. He was sentenced to death for being involved in an ambush on Church Street in Dublin, during which three British soldiers were killed. His execution, at the young age of 18, outraged the public not only in Ireland, but also across

A wounded soldier is carried through Temple Bar during the War of Independence. (Courtesy of Dublin Forums)

the globe. Coming just a few days after the death of hunger striker Terence MacSwiney, Lord Mayor of Cork, the two deaths precipitated a dramatic escalation of the War of Independence.

A young Kevin Barry of Fleet Street in his Belvedere College football jersey. (Courtesy of IHI)

Kevin Barry is also remembered for his refusal to inform and a ballad bearing his name is one of the most famous and sung of Irish ballads.[7]

> In Mountjoy Jail one Monday morning,
> High upon the gallows tree,
> Kevin Barry gave his young life
> For the cause of liberty.
> But a lad of eighteen summers,
> Yet no true man can deny
> As he walked to death that morning,
> He proudly held his head on high.

In Exchange Court, at the side of City Hall, high up on the end wall there is a stone plaque, which was erected in 1939 by the National Graves Association to commemorate three men who were executed in that building on 21 November 1920. The three were IRA men Peadar Clancy, Dick McKee and Conor Clune. They were tortured and executed behind the wall in what had formerly been Dublin Castle guardroom. The men had been arrested in the heart of Dublin's most notorious district, Monto, on Gloucester Street, after being betrayed to the authorities by an informer. Two of these men had served during the 1916 Rising and prior to their arrest Clancy and McKee had been involved with Michael Collins in planning the pre-emptive strike on the infamous Cairo Gang, special undercover agents of British Intelligence. This strike on 20 November 1920 resulted in the execution of fourteen British agents based in different parts of Dublin and the destruction of much British Intelligence. The execution of the three IRA men was a reprisal for the execution of the undercover agents. Moreover, as part of the reprisal, members of the Auxiliaries and the RIC opened fire on the crowd watching a Gaelic football match in Croke Park, killing fourteen spectators and wounding more than sixty. To this day, that event is referred to as Bloody Sunday.

10

FROM THE SHAMBLES TO THE EXCHANGE – THE OLD CITY

The streets of Temple Bar can be divided into two sections – the old city from Fishamble Street to Parliament Street (to coincide with the old walls and tower defences of the medieval city) and the later expanded, reclaimed and developed section that stretches from Parliament Street to Westmoreland Street. Some of the street names of the old city still reflect medieval times in Dublin, such as Fishamble Street, Copper Alley, Smock Alley, Crane Lane and Cow's Lane. The later eastward expansion of Dublin towards Trinity College, initiated and encouraged by the new English overlords of Dublin, is reflected in the names of streets, including Essex, Eustace, Fownes, Temple, Crow, Anglesea and Crampton streets.

DUBLIN'S FISH SHAMBLES

The Temple Bar district is bounded on the west by Fishamble Street, so called because it was the medieval location of the city's fish markets (a shamble was a booth or stall). Because of its closeness to the quays and the old custom house, it was also known as the 'fishmongers' quarters' in 1467, Fish Street in 1470 and Fisher Street in 1570. The Fish Shambles name is shown on Speed's 1610 map. It used to extend to Castle Street but its length was cut by a third because of the construction of Lord Edward Street in 1886. It now extends from the junction with Lord Edward Street to Essex Quay.

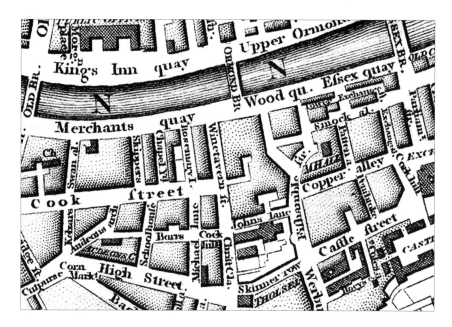

Map of 1798 showing the Fishamble Street areas.

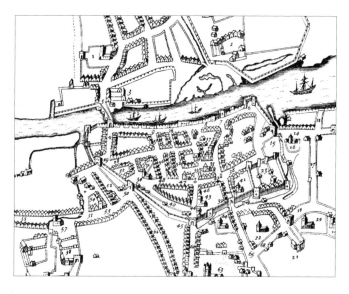

Speed's Map of Dublin, 1610.

Fishamble Street itself is one of Dublin's oldest medieval streets still in everyday use. It dates from Viking times – around the late tenth and early eleventh centuries. The vicinity was once a hive of activity, full of fishmongers, sailors, printers, publishers, lawyers, taverners, candle makers, leather workers and many other tradespeople, all jostling together in a very small area. Wicker basketmaking was also a major activity because baskets were needed to carry fish and fruit from the ships that unloaded their cargos just metres from the street. The street plunges down to the quays, which at one time would have been Dublin's docks, with the hustle, bustle and noise of trade, and fishermen offloading their catch for the fish hawkers who had their shambles nearby. The street was deliberately developed in a curving, winding fashion to make it easier for wheels, animals and people to negotiate the steep slope. As part of the port, it would also have been the location of the many vices that one finds in such areas.

Archaeological excavations in the area have revealed evidence of a row of tenth-century dwellings along the western side of the street (the street fronts of these houses correspond with the sweep of today's Fishamble Street) and evidence of a mid-ninth-century defensive ramparts of a Scandinavian enclosure. Today we are reminded of this by two pavement flagstones with sculpted images of combs, spearheads and daggers. Other findings, including Normandy pottery, revealed evidence of trade links with France and of skilled crafts such as amber working, which flourished in the late tenth century during the reign of King Amlaib Cuarán (of Hiberno-Norse extraction). All this would point to the area as a tenth-century location for regular economic activity, an important Viking trading settlement, and hence signalling early urban development, i.e. the growth of a town, rather than just a fortress. Before the construction of Dublin City Council's Wood Quay office headquarters, which borders Fishamble Street, the area was the focus for the major 'Save Wood Quay' marches of 1978. These were remarkable public demonstrations against official plans to build offices on the Viking site that extended from Winetavern Street to Fishamble Street and the adjacent streets. One of these marches involved thousands of protestors marching from the site, and along Lord Edward Street, Dame Street and Fishamble Street.

Located at the corner of Fishamble Street and what is now Lord Edward Street was, for many years, the entrance gate to the notorious district called Hell, which was marked on Rocque's 1756 map of Dublin. Hell was a laneway linking Fishamble Street through Christ Church Yard and to the corner of Winetavern Street and Skinner's Row (now Christ Church Place). The Devil's head was carved in the oak of the entrance gate. The laneway was renowned

Fishamble Street in 1967. (Wiltshire Photographic Collection, courtesy of NLI Commons Collection)

throughout Europe for its vice, taverns and debauchery. The fact that some of these taverns were directly below the cathedral, in the huge medieval crypt, further enriched the folklore about this infamous area on the edge of Temple Bar.[1]

In the 1940s, Nos 1,2,3, and 12 were listed as tenements with Nos 22-25 vacant. No. 10a was occupied by Solwaye Freres, manufacturing perfumers. Next door, No. 11 was occupied by W.G. Hickey & Co., underwear manufacturers. Kennan & Sons in No. 13 was listed as horticultural, building and steam joinery works, engineers, fence and roof manufacturers.

THEY RISE TO CONQUER

Cornelius Kelly, a renowned fencing master, lived on Fishamble Street in the mid-eighteenth century and was reputed to be the best swordsman of his day. In 1748, he easily defeated Britain's most expert professional fencer. Kelly played a practical joke on Oliver Goldsmith by persuading the writer that the home of Sir Ralph Fetherstone in Ardagh, County Longford, was actually an inn. This is supposed to have inspired the plot for *She Stoops to Conquer*.[2]

William Maple, a chemist, was one of the founders of the Dublin Society, later the Royal Dublin Society (RDS), and lived on Fishamble Street. He acted as secretary for the new organisation until his death in 1762 at the age of 104.[3]

Arthur Annesley, later Earl of Anglesea, was born on Fishamble Street in 1614. So great was his influence in the 1660s in England that it was said he was offered the position of prime minister, but he declined. The famous Trinity College Dublin scholar James Ussher (1580–1656) was also born there. He was Archbishop of Armagh and was regarded as one of the most influential intellectuals of early modern Europe. Trinity's Ussher Library was named after him.

The Grattan family resided on Fishamble Street for well over a century. James Grattan, who lived on the street until 1757, was appointed King's Counsel in 1747 and his son, the famous Henry Grattan, was baptised in St John's church nearby on 3 July 1746.[4]

William Townsend, a leading gold and silversmith in Dublin in the eighteenth century, had his business here. Another famous resident was James Clarence Mangan, composer of 'Dark Rosaleen' ('Oh, my Dark Rosaleen, do not sigh, do not weep!') and many more renowned poems. He was born at No. 3 Fishamble Street.

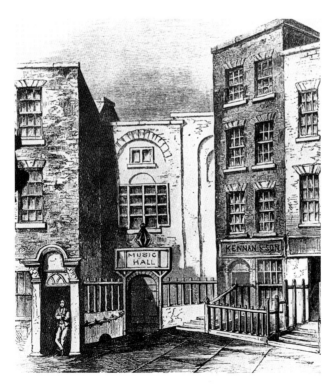

Fishamble Street in eighteenth-century showing the music hall where Handel's *The Messiah* was first performed in 1742. (Courtesy of IHI)

Fishamble Street was home to numerous interesting taverns over the centuries. The name of 'Winetavern Street', which runs parallel to this street on the opposite flank of Christ Church Cathedral, is indicative of the sheer number of taverns in the area since medieval times. Some of the early taverns on Fishamble Street included the Swan Tavern (1639); the Fleece Tavern (1666); the London Tavern (1667); the Ossory; and the Ormond's Arms. One popular venue was The Bull's Head. A musical society associated with this tavern was

The Wood Quay end of Temple Bar in the late 1960s. (Courtesy of Gemma Jackson)

central to the construction of a new music hall on the same street, which would serve as the location for the world premiere of Handel's great work, *The Messiah*. This tavern was also used for assemblies of the Grand Lodge of Irish Freemasons as well as the choirs from the nearby cathedrals. The first masquerade ball held in Ireland took place on 19 April 1776 in the Music Hall. A few years later, in 1780, the first Irish state lottery was drawn in the Music Hall, thereby adding further to the gambling frenzy in the area.[5]

On the corner of Fishamble Street and Essex Street West is a jewel of a building – the timber-framed No. 26 Fishamble Street, one of Dublin's oldest surviving houses. This listed house dates from the 1720s. It incorporates features such as oak beams from an earlier seventeenth-century structure and is built on the foundations of a late medieval or Tudor house. It has seventeen rooms. A medieval footpath may be seen in the cellar. It is believed to be the longest-inhabited family dwelling in the old city as the present family (the Casey family) have been there for almost 250 years. Following the gradual decline of the area in the twentieth century, this was the only building left standing. It almost fell down when Dublin Corporation demolished a house next door it claimed was unsafe, apparently destabilising No. 26 in the process, which had to be supported by timber beams to prevent its collapse. Commenting on the Corporation's action, Mrs Edna Casey said in 1988, 'Really and truly it is maddening what they have done to the city.' Today, No. 26 stands proudly among the recently constructed social housing and apartments. It faces, in stark contrast, the huge Wood Quay offices and so it is as if the two faces of Dublin are confronting each other. The building has Russian vines growing on its wall, which adds to its unique character.[6]

MOLLY AND APOLLO

According to Dublin folklore, one interesting resident of Fishamble Street who lived, died and had her funeral in and near the street was daughter Molly Malone, who, according to the ballad, 'wheeled her wheelbarrow through streets broad and narrow, crying "cockles and mussels, alive, alive-o!"' Her parents ran a fishmonger business at one of the fish shambles on the street and resided nearby. One day Molly dropped dead at the young age of 36, having succumbed to one of the diseases that struck the area from time to time. Her funeral was held in the church of St John, Fishamble Street, and she was buried in the adjacent graveyard. Her legend lives on and the ballad is Dublin's unofficial anthem.

Interestingly, a late eighteenth-century book containing the earliest known version of the song 'Molly Malone' hints that Molly may not have been the virtuous, tragic girl who merely sold cockles and mussels remembered in the popular ballad we hear today, but was also a 'street-walker' or a 'lady of the night'. A copy of *Apollo's Medley*, dating from around 1791, published in Doncaster in England and rediscovered in 2010, contains a song referring to 'Sweet Molly Malone' that ends with the lines:

> Och! I'll roar and I'll groan,
> My sweet Molly Malone,
> Till I'm bone of your bone,
> And asleep in your bed.
> Sweet Molly, Sweet Molly Malone,
> Sweet Molly, Sweet Molly Malone.[7]

So it seems that Molly worked part-time in the evenings and at night as a prostitute. This is not surprising considering that the area was full of brothels. Moreover, one interpretation of her name, 'Molly', is that it derived from 'moll', the slang word for prostitute. The provocative attire worn by the statue of her on St Andrew's Street today (opposite Temple Bar and commissioned by Dublin Corporation) gives some credence to this aspect of the legend.[8]

Despite this, the folklore in Dublin maintains that Molly was pretty, sweet and a fishmonger and that her ghost still haunts Dublin, crying, 'Cockles and mussels, alive, alive-o!' So when Dubliners today are singing the hearty ballad, they might well be singing to the memory of a famous prostitute – the moll Malone![9]

TENTS AND PAMPHLETS

Off Fishamble Street, there was a short alley called Molesworth Court. The name 'Molesworth' referred to a merchant based in the vicinity: one Robert Molesworth, who had been a soldier in Cromwell's army and had profited considerably for his efforts (making a thousand tents for the government). He paid only £1,500 for 2,500 acres of land in County Meath.

Molesworth Court was also where Dean Jonathan Swift's famous and notorious *Drapier's Letters* was published in 1724 by John Harding. These patriotic letters (seven pamphlets) challenged English rule in Ireland, asserting the latter's constitutional and economic independence. One pamphlet in particular covered the Wood's Halfpence controversy, which involved

Jonathan Swift.

an attempt to foist an inferior copper coinage on Ireland. Following the public outcry stoked by Swift's anonymous letters, the plan was defeated. Unfortunately, Harding was arrested, imprisoned and died in prison.

COPPER ALLEY

Also off Fishamble Street is Dublin's oldest medieval street, Copper Alley. It dates from the thirteenth century and follows the route of an earlier Viking street. In later centuries it was so narrow that carriages were unable to use it; it was only wide enough for chairs or sedans. It had an entrance where Harding's Hotel stands today and it led to Exchange Street Upper. It was built on a portion of land known as Preston's Inns and named after the copper money minted there and distributed to the poor by Lady Alice Fenton (the mother-in-law of Richard Boyle, 1st Earl of Cork). Today, the once infamous alley runs through the reception area of Harding Hotel, parallel to Essex Street and Lord Edward Street.[10]

The *Copper Alley Gazette*, published in 1766 in the *Freeman's Journal*, contained a satirical account of the actions of politicians of the day. Other prominent publishers had their printing presses along this street, including Andrew Cook, the King's Printer General for Ireland (1673–1727), and Edward Waters, who printed one of Jonathan Swift's famous pamphlets, which denounced England for interfering in Ireland's export trade of linen and woollens and rejected anything wearable coming from England.

An interesting advertisement in an eighteenth-century newspaper under the heading 'Mendicity', advised that 'The Public are requested to refer BEGGARS, in future, to the New Mendicity Office, in Copper Alley, from nine till three each day.' Copper Alley is also where the family home of Catherine McAuley, foundress of the Sisters of Mercy, was located.

The street was renowned for its taverns and eating houses, including a famous one called the Unicorn Tavern. Like the nearby Smock Alley, the area was full of brothels, the most notorious being the Maiden Tower. In fact, Copper Alley was the centre of a hectic, and at times rowdy, social life in the area.[11]

Artist Tom Cullen (1934–2001) made a painting of the alley called 'Copper Alley off Lord Edward Street'. The artist depicts two buildings on either side of the entrance to the alley being held apart by two timber beams to prevent them from collapsing. Alexander Williams RHA also made a painting of Copper Alley.[12]

FROM SMOCK ALLEY TO ESSEX GATE

Around the corner from No. 26 Fishamble Street is Essex Street West. Arthur Capel, Earl of Essex and Lord Lieutenant for Ireland from 1672 to 1677, gave his name to Essex Street East, Essex Street West and Essex Bridge (now Grattan's Bridge), which links Capel Street to the City Hall and Dublin Castle via Parliament Street. Essex Gate was another of the gates guarding the perimeter walls of the old city. The old walls extended from the quays of the Liffey and curved around near Exchange Street and Essex Street West, close to present-day Parliament Street, and on to Dames Gate on Dame Street and farther again towards Dublin Castle. Before Parliament Street was built, Essex

Arthur Capel, 1st Earl of Essex (1631-1683). This portrait was painted in 1672 to commemorate his appointment as Lord Lieutenant of Ireland. (Courtesy of Dublin Forums)

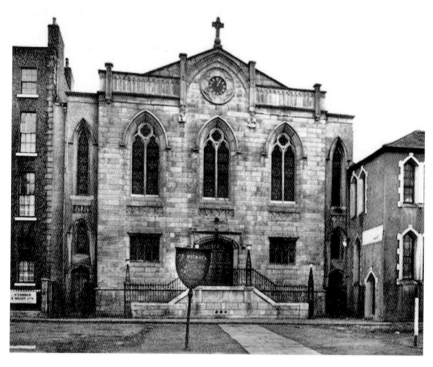

SS Michael and John's church in the 1950s. It is now the Smock Alley Theatre. (Courtesy of IHI)

Gate was the link between Essex Street West (in the old city) and Essex Street East in the developing Temple Bar. It was built on the site of the former Buttevant's Tower, another of the towers protecting the medieval city. Finn's Tower was located a few metres in front of the Smock Alley Theatre along what is now Lower Exchange Street.[13]

Essex Street West, dating from the early 1600s, was formerly named Smock Alley and gave its name to the famous Smock Alley Theatre. The thriving theatre is located in what was formerly SS Michael and John's church, on the same site as the original seventeenth-century theatre. Contrary to popular belief, the church was not originally a theatre – it was just built on the site of the former theatre. The church, an important example of the Regency Gothic style, was the first purpose-built church in Dublin in the early nineteenth century and one of the finest buildings of its type. The name derived from two old, nearly forgotten nearby churches – St John's on Fishamble Street and St Michael's on St Michael's Hill/Winetavern Street. Richly ornamented, it had elaborate Gothic plasterwork, a large gallery, a decorated timber organ loft and an ornate marble altar. The church opened in 1811 and it was deconsecrated in 1988. For a few years afterwards, it housed Dublin's Viking Adventure. The *Independent* newspaper (England) noted that 'the curious project involves the destruction of authentic history to make way for a world of conjecture and make believe'.[14]

The building was subsequently purchased as a site for a theatre. Prior to construction, much archaeological excavation was undertaken by Linzi Simpson in 2009. More than 200 artefacts were discovered, including wine bottles, clay pipe fragments and an actor's wig curler. Unfortunately, much of the interior, including the gallery, was destroyed when the building was being converted to a theatre. The finely decorated ceiling survived, as did the exterior church bell and crosses, front and back. The clocks on both north and south granite elevations also survived; they have copper faces and gold numbers. Why the magnificent interior was removed is not clear.[15]

The street had various names over the years, partly because of its terrible reputation as the location of brothels and gambling houses. It witnessed serious riots in 1768 with the destruction of much property and loss of life. It has variously been called Stable Lane, Cadogan's Alley and Orange Street. Since 1839, the alley has been called Essex Street West, but for generations residents still called it Smock Alley.

Located next to the famous theatre is the Gaiety School of Acting, founded by Joe Dowling in 1986, which occupies a nineteenth-century former primary school that had been beside the church. The building was a clothing

Shops on Essex Street in the 1960s. (Courtesy of Irish Historical Images (IHI))

warehouse in the 1970s – Trend Fashions – and subsequently part of the short-lived Viking museum. Between the theatre and the School of Acting a wall sculpture depicts a Viking ship sailing up the River Liffey. Grace Weir's wall relief, for the former Dublin Viking Adventure, gives a visualisation of the site's history with the emphasis on the coming of the Vikings. Nearby, there is the old firm of locksmiths, J.A. Powell's, which is still thriving and deals in all manners of locks. Rathborne's Candle Makers was located on Essex Street for a few years. Seemingly, each generation of the family liked to move premises and the business was located on different streets of Temple Bar over the centuries. Today, the company makes church candles in the same way as they were centuries ago – using beeswax.

The back of the theatre faces the stepped, newly built Cow's Lane, which leads to Lord Edward Street. There appears to be no historical basis for the name 'Cow's Lane', except for the fact that there are a few lanes in the surrounding area with names such as Lamb's Alley and Bull Alley Street. Today, Cow's Lane has a substantial residential component, with shops, cafés and restaurants at ground level and a farmer's market at weekends. When the whole development of nearly 200 apartments and shops was granted planning permission in the late 1990s, it was part of one of the most important urban renewal schemes in Dublin for decades. There are no pubs in the immediate area, which has resulted in a pleasantly quiet, residential atmosphere. Looking down Cow's Lane from Lord Edward Street, towards Smock Alley Theatre, the view is attractive, if somewhat off-axis. The reason for this is that the city's planners would only allow a wider street to facilitate weekend market stalls.[16]

BLIND QUAY AND ISOLDE'S TOWER

A lane extending from one of the old walled city's towers (Isolde's Tower) to Cork Hill was known as Scarlett Lane in medieval times and was later changed to Blind Quay (because it was behind buildings overlooking the River Liffey quays). Lower and Upper Blind Quay were renamed Lower and Upper Exchange Street towards the end of the eighteenth century due their proximity to the Royal Exchange (built between 1769 and 1779), now the City Hall. For generations, this was an important street linking the quays to Dublin Castle (before the construction of Parliament Street) and running along the inside wall of medieval Dublin. It is one of a few remaining narrow, sloping and winding medieval streets in Dublin. The name Blind Quay lives on today in the name of a block of apartments located opposite the remains of Isolde's Tower.[17]

The old defensive wall of the medieval city extended eastward by the bank of the Liffey, near the present-day Smock Alley Theatre and Wood Quay offices. A purpose-built path leading to the Wood Quay venue follows the old wall and then turns southwards along by present-day Parliament Street to Dame's Gate (near City Hall) and onwards to Dublin Castle. Four of the guarding towers of Dublin once stood along this curving line from the River Liffey to Dublin Castle – Case's Tower, Buttevant Tower, Finn's Tower and Isolde's Tower.[18]

In the late 1990s, when digging the foundations for the new apartment block mentioned above, archaeologists found a substantial part of the original Isolde's Tower near the junction of Lower Exchange Street and Essex Gate. There was also evidence of the foundations of the old city wall, which extended from two sides of the surviving lower part of the original tower. It was estimated that the tower stood at nearly 40ft, with walls 13ft thick, before it was demolished in 1675. The tower was built in the mid-thirteenth century to protect the north-eastern part of the city wall from attacks via the River Liffey. The tower was named after Isolde, an Irish princess who was supposed to marry a Cornish nobleman, Prince Mark, but, after taking a love potion, instead fell in love with the knight, Tristan, who was bringing her to England across the Irish Sea. Their tragic love story ended with both drinking a poisonous concoction. The legend gave its name to Isolde's Tower. The story also inspired Wagner's opera, *Tristan and Isolde*.

When the tower was demolished, it was replaced with dwellings called Essex Gate (near the corner of Parliament Street). Its ruins are still to be seen, preserved and surrounded by a modern apartment block, at Lower Exchange Street. At the back of this block there was once a number of Georgian houses on Essex Quay, which were demolished in the face of a major public outcry in 1993 and replaced by a new office-apartment complex.[19]

The Irish name on one of the street signs for Lower Exchange Street is Sráid Iosóilde (Isolde's Street). This is not the correct translation but is rather a former name for the street. Opposite Isolde's Tower is a site that has been vacant for more than twenty years. Previously, it had been occupied by many businesses, including Blazes Restaurant, which, true to its name, was destroyed by fire in the late 1980s.

Several pubs in and around Temple Bar spent time in Huguenot hands in the late seventeenth and early eighteenth centuries, such as the Three Tuns on Blind Quay purchased by Jean Chaigneau for £200 in the 1720s. Members of that community also owned Ruben's Head and the Two Friends Tavern, just off Crow Street.

Lower Exchange Street (or Blind Quay at the time) was the first location of Sir Patrick Dun's Hospital in 1792. Dun (1642–1717) was a physician and head of the Royal College of Physicians. His hospital later moved to Lower Grand Canal Street. It was under the patronage of the College of Physicians and provided clinical instruction for medical students. It originally occupied part of what subsequently became the presbytery for SS Michael and John's church. Many booksellers and publishers were also located on this street.[20]

In the twentieth century, O'Reilly's Fine Art Auction Rooms was located on Upper Exchange Street for many years, occupying some of the former despatch offices of the famous Dublin newspaper the *Evening Mail*, which was located on the adjacent corner of Parliament Street. The O'Reillys have been in the area for generations; they were originally located on Winetavern Street and latterly on Francis Street, Dublin's Antique Quarter, in the Liberties.

THE WOODEN BUILDING

It has been said that one of the successes of Temple Bar Properties (TBP), charged in 1991 with renewing and revitalising the area, is the strength of its residential developments in the area. Examples of this are the ten-apartments-over-shops complex built around a courtyard at the Printworks (Essex Street East and Temple Lane), designed by Derek Tynan Architects, and the new apartment developments in the Upper Exchange Street/Cow's Lane area, including the Wooden Building. This square, tower-like structure by architects de Blacam & Meagher is a wonderfully clad building with brick and timber predominating. The building comprises a five-storey south block and a nine-storey north block. An interior courtyard presents a different aspect of the building, with a central portion being more like a tower, with brickwork taking central stage. Dating from 1995 to 2000, it forms part of the residential development of the west end of Temple Bar.

The building's location on land that slopes towards Lord Edward Street helps make it appear higher than it actually is. On a narrow street, the head has to be lifted to see the top levels of the building. The inspiration came from medieval timber-framed buildings originally in the vicinity and the building ascends in stages, each appearing to project out more than the one below. It is constructed of wood, stone and glass, thus linking the past with the present, a constant theme in the renewal of Temple Bar in recent years.

11

LORDS OF THE HILL – CORK HOUSE TO THE CATHEDRAL

There is a beautiful view of Dublin Castle and the Rates Office building from Upper Exchange Street. The street brings us to the junction of Lord Edward Street and Cork Hill. The fine building facing the side of City Hall, now the Dublin City Council's Rates Office, was once Newcomen Bank, designed by the renowned architect Thomas Ivory and first Master of the School of Drawing in Architecture in Dublin. It was later the Hibernian Bank. It is also where Éamonn Ceannt, one of the leaders of the 1916 Rising, worked.

The building itself dates from different centuries, despite appearing to be one complete structure. The original building, constructed in Portland stone, was just half the size of the present structure. The later construction mirrored Ivory's original design and a new portico was added to link the two sides together. The left side was built around 1781, whereas the right side dates from 1866. The distinguishing feature of the different eras is that the older part has its decorations and swags worked in stone, whereas the same features on the later part are in plaster. This building also has a very impressive staircase. There is an interesting drinking fountain shaped like a large seashell set into the side of the building.

The bank closed in 1825, following a number of bank failures in Dublin in the 1820s. Following the bank's collapse and the consequent ruination of his family (some members of which had been given peerages to persuade them to vote for the Act of Union in 1800), Thomas Viscount Newcomen shot himself in his office at the age of 48.[1]

One side of the Rates Office overlooks Cork Hill, which is today a very short street (more of a terrace) stretching from the corner of Parliament Street to Lord Edward Street. However, as architectural historian Maurice Craig once said, 'it was very much at the centre of things' and originally covered a much wider area. Cork Hill took its name from Richard Boyle, First Earl of Cork. In the early seventeenth century, Boyle had a forty-year lease on the land from the treasurer of St Patrick's Cathedral and he owned Cork House. He built his house on the site of the former medieval church, St Mary del Dam. Its location, adjacent to Dublin Castle, was very important.

The street has a chequered history, both socially and architecturally. It was originally lined with the mansions of the well-heeled of Dublin society, including Boyle's. The street suffered when many of the buildings were demolished to make way for the Royal Exchange, the development of Parliament Street and the opening of Lord Edward Street.

However, before that demolition took place, Cork Hill stretched to Essex Quay, Smock Alley and Blind Alley and included, behind the mansions, a veritable warren of alleys, lanes and winding passages that could lead anywhere. There was no public lighting at night and it had no night watch. Pedestrians at night were liable to be attacked passing the entrances to Lucas's Coffee House and the Eagle Tavern and it was said that the waiters at these establishments often amused themselves by pouring chamber pots upon passers-by.[2]

FROM THE ROYAL EXCHANGE TO CITY HALL

Shortly after Boyle died in 1643, Cork House appears to have been used for government offices, including the Committee of Transplantation (1649–1680), which oversaw the implementation of Oliver Cromwell's 'To Hell or Connaught' policy. During the reign of Charles II, Cork House began to be used for the management of financial transactions. In 1670, the 'Farmers of the King's Revenue in Ireland' occupied the building. Subsequently, the Commissioners of Customs used an 'exchange place' in the garden (formerly the graveyard of the St Mary del Dam church). Here, 'merchants and others met every day at the ringing of the bell to treat of their business'. Soon, the house was called the Cork 'Change' as it had become the meeting place for merchants and traders. In the late eighteenth century, the name evolved into the Royal Exchange when the prospering merchants decided they needed a more appropriate meeting place for their transactions.[3]

The new meeting place, now Dublin's City Hall, is an important building whose story begins in 1761, when the merchants of Dublin formed themselves into a society, the objects of which were 'the defence of trade against any illegal imposition and the solicitation of such laws as might seem beneficial to it'. Seven years later, in 1768, the society advertised an architectural competition for the design of a new exchange building to be erected on a site at Cork Hill, previously occupied by the church and Cork House. The international competition attracted a total of sixty-one entries and was won by the architect Thomas Cooley, whose design was preferred to the entry submitted by his more illustrious contemporary, James Gandon. Gandon was later to design the new Four Courts building and the new custom house, as well as making improvements to the Irish Parliament House on College Green. Cork House was demolished in 1768 and construction on the new edifice began the following year. The new exchange was completed ten

View of the Royal Exchange from Essex (now Grattan) Bridge at end of eighteenth century. (Courtesy of IHI)

years later, in 1779, for the 'encouragement of trade and the advance of his Majesty's revenue'.[4]

The Royal Exchange, as the new building was named, is without doubt one of Dublin's finest and most sophisticated eighteenth-century buildings. It marks the introduction to Ireland of the European neo-classical style of architecture fashionable on the Continent. The sheer size and sumptuous fittings of the Royal Exchange reflect the prestige of Dublin in the late eighteenth century. The building forms a square, one side of which is hidden by Dublin Castle. The ground plan of the interior consists of a circle within a square. The circular entrance hall, or rotunda, with its spacious dome supported by twelve columns, is surrounded by an ambulatory, where the merchants strolled and discussed business. John Gilbert, in his *History of the City of Dublin* (1854), records a contemporary description of the new building:

> The inside of this edifice possesses beauties that cannot be clearly expressed by words, being a great curiosity to those who have a taste for architecture. The dome is spacious, lofty and noble, and is supported by twelve composite columns, which, rising from the floor, form a circular walk in the centre of the ambulatory; the entablature over the columns is enriched in the most splendid manner, and above that are twelve elegant circular windows. The ceiling of the dome is decorated with stucco ornaments in the Mosaic taste, divided into small hexagonal compartments and in the centre is a large window that lights most of the building ... in the space between the columns, are elegant festoons of drapery and other ornamental decorations.[5]

Interestingly, Gilbert also noted that the Exchange 'does not appear to have been over extensively used for the objects for which it was originally designed'. In fact, at times the outside of the Exchange was used more often than the inside. It was a favourite meeting place for public and political meetings. On many occasions in the years prior to the 1798 Rising, the Volunteers of Ireland gathered there for reviews or campaigns. The chamber was chosen in 1783 as the meeting place of the delegates of the National Convention for Parliamentary Reform. In 1798, the Exchange was converted into a military barracks for court martials and punishments, including torture, for those involved in the insurrection. Major Sirr was located here during the 1798 Rebellion and used it as a place of interrogation and torture. In addition, it was here that the Catholics of Dublin went to protest against the Act of

Union on 13 January 1800. At this meeting, Daniel O'Connell made his first speech in public criticising the proposed legislation.[6]

In September 1852, Dublin Corporation acquired the Royal Exchange as its new headquarters and initiated a series of alterations designed to create much-needed office space. Today, there are four statues between the twelve columns: Daniel O'Connell (who replaced a statue of George III); Thomas Davis, the Young Irelander and founder of *The Nation* newspaper; Charles Lucas, the eighteenth-century patriot politician and one of the founders of the *Freeman's Journal*; and Thomas Drummond, Under-Secretary for Ireland in the 1830 who coined the aphorism, 'Property has its duties as well as its rights'. There is also a statue of Henry Grattan in the vicinity.

The room at the front of the building, once used by the merchants of Dublin as a coffee house (Lucas's), is now used as the Council Chamber.

JACOB'S LADDER AND CRAZY CROW

The early meetings of the Dublin Philosophical Society (later the Dublin Society) took place at Cork Hill from the 1680s onwards. One of the attendees at the meetings of that society in the early eighteenth century was George Berkeley, the philosopher who became renowned for his views on spirit, ideas, language and perception. He was then attending Trinity College Dublin.

It was also the location for coffee houses and taverns, including Lucas's Coffee House, Jacob's Ladder, Solyman's Coffee House, St Laurence's Coffee House and the Union Coffee House. Famous taverns included the Globe, the Hoop, and the Cock and Punch Bowl. The Eagle Tavern was the best known; however, when it was located at Cork Hill (later Eustace Street), it was also one of the most dangerous and the yard behind it was the scene of numerous duels and brawls. Customers gambled on the possible outcome of the duels. It was frequently referred to as 'the surgeon's hall', such was the frequency of bodies that came from the tavern, either dead or requiring urgent medical care. It was here that the notorious Hellfire Club was founded and had its meetings.

Beside the Royal Exchange, there was a short alley called Swan Alley, which was the location of a notorious tavern in the eighteenth century – the Swan Tavern. Beside it were several gambling houses, frequented by sharpers (pickpockets and hustlers) and gamblers, including one of Dublin's most eccentric and notorious low-life characters of his day, the ferocious-looking Crazy Crow, who was a musician. He dropped dead in the tavern in 1762. He had been fined and imprisoned twenty years previously for stealing corpses from St Andrew's churchyard, off Dame Street. It was said that his voice was 'as frightful as Etna's roar and equally hideous was his well-known face'.[7]

Cork Hill was also the location of many booksellers and newspaper publishers in the seventeenth and eighteenth centuries. The *Flying Post* was published here in the early 1700s. James Esdall, who was the printer of the works of the patriot Charles Lucas in 1749, was in business on Cork Hill, at the corner of Copper Alley.

In addition, Cork Hill was home to some of Dublin's best engravers, including John Brooks and Michael Ford. Brooks was the inventor of transfer printing on pottery.[8]

COCKPIT FIGHTING

One of Ireland's most popular sports in the eighteenth century had its headquarters at Cork Hill. The location of Dublin's largest cockpit, the Cock Pit Royal, was near where the City Hall is now. The sport of cockfighting had its heyday in the mid-eighteenth century with cocks (roosters) being specially bred and trained for fighting the length and breadth of Ireland. Cocks were particularly suited to this blood sport as the males feel a congenital aggression towards other males. The sport originated in ancient Greece.

The Cock Pit Royal was a large area with tiered seating around it for paying customers who placed bets on the outcome of the fighting between two cocks, often called 'game cocks'. Sometimes up to twenty or even thirty cocks fought at the same time, with gamblers placing bets on each of the cocks, but with only one winner – the only survivor. Cockfighting tournaments or festivals often lasted for at least a week and were a regular event in the eighteenth century when the sport was at its most popular. The sport attracted gamblers from all parts of the country and there was much drinking, carousing and, of course, visiting the local brothels.[9]

LORD EDWARD STREET AND WHISKEY DISTILLING

Cork Hill connects with Lord Edward Street and both offer a splendid view of the eastern side of Christ Church Cathedral. Lord Edward Street is directly aligned with the tower of the cathedral. The street is named in honour of the 1798 patriot and son of the Duke of Leinster, Lord Edward Fitzgerald (1763–1798), who is buried nearby at St Werburgh's church. The street was part of the plans of the Wide Street Commissioners for street improvement in Dublin, but it was not laid down until the late 1880s. The land was formerly occupied by houses, courts, yards and alleyways. The street's construction involved major demolition of property (including the church of St John). Hitherto, only Castle Street linked Dame Street and Cork Hill with Skinner's Row (now Christ Church Place, opposite the cathedral). Fishamble Street extended to Werburgh Street. The new, wide and convenient Lord Edward Street was parallel to Castle Street, which quickly became a little-used lane.

The new street was officially opened in 1886 by Timothy Daniel (TD) Sullivan MP, Lord Mayor of Dublin and a strong Nationalist. It was he who wrote the rebel song, 'God Save Ireland', that was so popular in the closing decades of the nineteenth century. Local residents quickly gave the street the nickname 'Roe's Row' after George Roe, who owned one of Ireland's largest

Lord Edward Fitzgerald,
Hamilton. 1796.

Lord Edward Fitzgerald (1763-1798). Lord Edward Street in Temple Bar is named after him. (Courtesy of Kildare Local History Society)

whiskey distilleries, located on Thomas Street (where the old windmill with the image of St Patrick is still located), opposite Guinness's brewery. Roe had helped financially in the refurbishment of Christ Church Cathedral towards the end of the nineteenth century. The Guinness family helped to refurbish St Patrick's Cathedral around the same time. There was much competition between the brewery and the distillery. The Guinnesses regarded their stout or porter as the 'nurse of the people' and Roe's whiskey as 'the curse of the people'.

Two large late nineteenth-century redbrick buildings on the new street replaced older dwellings. These are distinctive and are at either side of a long, grey-bricked building (former Excise and Revenue offices) occupying the right-hand side of the street if one is looking towards the cathedral. These fine buildings are the Parliament (previously Arlington) Hotel and the former Harding Boys Home (now a hostel). The latter was a school and home for poor teenagers founded in 1876. The old name plaque still adorns this building. It was also Ireland's first technical school. It was originally established to provide 'comfortable and healthy lodgings at cheap rates for boys who were earning their bread'. It retains the fine decorative work around the windows, on the top gables and over the entrance, where one can observe finely carved technical-drawing instruments. Today, it is named Kinlay House after a former president of the Union of Students of Ireland (USIT), Howard Kinlay. USIT provided student accommodation here in the late twentieth century.

The grey-bricked building is a little-known example of civic architecture of the early twentieth century, built by the Office of Public Works in 1915. It is very much in the style of the then-being-completed Royal College of Science on Merrion Street and was designed by Harold Leask (later to become Inspector of National Monuments) and Martin Joseph Burke (later to become Assistant Principal Architect for the OPW during the war). Today, it houses the Irish Film Board, Heneghan Peng Architects and other notable bodies.[10]

Across the road, the ornamental drinking fountain on the wall of the Rates Office and below the 1886 Lord Edward Street plaque is one of the last of this type of street furniture still in existence. It was put there when the street was opened in 1886.[11]

Farther along the street on the same side is the 1927 building of the Carnegie Trust for Child Welfare. This is another impressive building with a grey centrepiece adorned with pillars and red-bricked walls on each side. Above the entrance, there is a sculpted image of a child watched over by angels. The Coolmine Building, further along Lord Edward Street, dates from 1887.

12

SWORD MAKERS AND ROPE DANCERS – PARLIAMENT STREET TO FOWNES STREET

Parliament Row, at the Westmoreland Street end of Temple Bar, commemorates Parliament House (Bank of Ireland) on College Green, but Parliament Street's name commemorates a 1757 Statute of Parliament, which granted the money for the compulsory purchase of all the properties near a proposed street to be built between Essex Bridge and Dublin Castle. It was the first project of the Wide Streets Commissioners (WSC).

Once the new custom house had been built on Essex Quay, there was increased traffic both on the river and the adjoining streets. In late 1759 a parliamentary committee looked into the traffic congestion at Essex Bridge, caused by traffic moving in the direction of the Irish Parliament House, Cork House (later the Royal Exchange) and Dublin Castle, and they decided that a new street should be built to solve the problem. The Dublin alderman Philip Crampton, who owned much of the land involved in the plan, proposed that it be called Parliament Street and in 1762 the new street opened. It is also thanks to the support of the Wide Streets Commissioners that the original proposal was successful. The building of Parliament Street may be regarded as the first step in their grand vision for the city.[1]

Although Parliament Street was a great success in many ways, it was a less welcome project for those residents in the area who woke one morning to find the slates from the roofs of their properties had been stripped off overnight at

Capel Street with Temple Bar, Essex Quay, the old Custom House, Essex Bridge and the Royal Exchange in the distance. From James Malton's *Picturesque and Descriptive View of the City of Dublin*, 1792-99.

the instigation of the WSC, in order to speed up their removal. Compensation was paid to some businesses, including one Francis Booker, a respected maker of carved and gilded mirrors. He was forced to relocate from Essex Street to a nearby corner on the quays. Adjacent to him was a goldsmith's business, owned by Isaac D'Olier of the Huguenot family whose name is remembered by D'Olier Street.[2]

The new street was occupied by five-storey buildings – four floors over the ground-floor shop or business. It must be noted also that Parliament Street is not an axial street; the view towards City Hall is off centre.[3]

Over the years, there have been many different businesses on Parliament Street. Booksellers and newspaper publishers were based here, including the Fenian newspaper the *Irish People* at No. 12 and George Faulkner's early eighteenth-century, influential *Dublin Journal* at No. 27. Silk mercers and lace-men opened for business in the early years. The opening of the Hibernian Silk Warehouse in early 1765 was attended by the ladies of the principal rank and fortune in Dublin. The vestment warehouse at No. 9 was owned and run for many years (1860–1920s) by Miss Catherine Cahill and was one of the leading houses in Dublin for clerics and nuns looking for the appropriate attire for personal and ceremonial use. Today, a reminder of this is carved over a first-floor bay window – 'Vestment Ware Rooms'.[4]

There was also a medical hall, a hat manufacturer, a fringe and lace coach manufacturer, and the Association for the Propagation of the Faith. There was a famous shoeblack, Thady O'Shaughnessy, one of the wittiest shoeblacks in Dublin, who 'will throw out more flowers of rhetoric in the true vein of laconic abuse, in one hour, than Counsellor Plausible will to in a twelvemonth at the Four Courts'.[5]

The tall and distinctive building on the corner of Parliament Street and Essex Gate has the monogram 'LF & Co.' and the date 1780 carved into it. These refer to the business of Lundy Foot and Company, whose name is still on display on the apex of its upper level. They were manufacturers of snuff, and tobacco such as Bristol Roll, Common Roll, Pigtail and Irish Rapees and 'Superfine Pigtail for Ladies', another specialist tobacco brand. This business started originally as a tobacconist's in 1758 and accidentally became famous over the years for its snuff. Apparently, a particular brand of snuff became burnt and the customers, unaware of the fact, happened to like it very much, so, business being business, Mr Foot continued to sell the improved product.

Foot amassed a small fortune from his business and had a fine house in the Dublin Mountains (now St Columba's College) beyond Rathfarnham. He was also a magistrate and over the course of this career was responsible for helping to hunt down three brothers accused and subsequently executed for conspiracy to murder in 1816. He survived a murder attempt a few years later, but in 1835 he was attacked, stoned and almost hacked to pieces.[6] For many years, the business had its warehouse behind the present building, which is now called the Czech Inn. The warehouse was later used by Rockwell Textiles.

In 1996 the Porter House independent craft brewery and pub courageously opened its doors at No. 18 at a time when taking on the bigger Irish breweries was a huge and at times very difficult and daunting challenge. Oliver Hughes, a craft brewer and publican, founded it. The success of this endeavour has since been emulated across the country; many craft breweries have sprung up and the public's taste for craft beer has become more refined. A new lexicon devoted to craft beer has evolved. Porterhouse Red is an example of the type of beer described by Hughes as 'a nice, well-brewed, sessionable craft beer, 4.2 per cent, caramel malt, a bit of crystal malt, chocolate malt, wheat malt'. The layout of the pub is unusual, described as being 'a cross between a Wild West bar and a Hieronymous Bosch painting'.[7]

There has been a pub operating on this site since 1864. Before the Porter House, there was a famous pub called Rumpole's and before that T. McLoughlin ran a pub there. A distinctive and fine James Anderson black triangular clock dating from that time hangs forlornly on the wall, all but abandoned.[8]

Across the road is the Turk's Head Chop House (a term from old Dublin that refers in a roundabout way to a cross between a bagnio and a steakhouse), which was established in 1760, although the modern incarnation is much different to the tavern of the mid-eighteenth century, which was located a few streets away (still in Temple Bar). It is decorated in two completely different styles, one modern, the other 1930s. It is a stylish bar, famous for its extravagant design, with mosaics and Spanish-style internal architecture, and is for that reason different to many of the more traditional pubs in Temple Bar.

The Royal Exchange Hotel, Read's, Tarlo's and shops along Parliament Street, 1952. (Courtesy of Bureau of Military History)

Farther along, on the opposite side as one moves towards City Hall, the name of the famous Royal Exchange Hotel is still visible on the façade of what is now a block of apartments. The name of the hotel came from the former name of City Hall – the Royal Exchange. This hotel had an unusual rule – it was a temperance hotel and did not serve alcohol to residents or visitors. This is perhaps not surprising given its location across from Miss Cahill's, a religious bookshop and the Association for the Propagation of the Faith. The customers of these establishments, particularly those from outside Dublin, would have journeyed to Dublin, stayed in the hotel (or in the Clarence) and made their purchases nearby. In this way, it is similar to the twentieth-century tradition of Wynn's Hotel, across the road from the Veritas bookshop (formerly the Catholic Truth Society of Ireland) on Lower Abbey Street.

DUBLIN'S OLDEST SHOP –
CUTLERS AND INSTRUMENT MAKERS

For many years, Temple Bar was renowned for some of the country's finest craftsmen, jewellers, silversmiths, goldsmiths, engravers, mirror makers, embroiders, lacemakers, those with other clothing skills and those involved in printing, publishing and bookbinding. In 1670, long before the building of Parliament Street, James Read & Co. opened a knife- and sword-making shop and a forge on Blind Quay (Lower Exchange Street). James Read died in 1744 and his nephew John Read succeeded him. In 1750, he acquired a property on Crane Lane, then a busy Dublin street. Crane Lane was a direct route from Dame Street to the docks and the

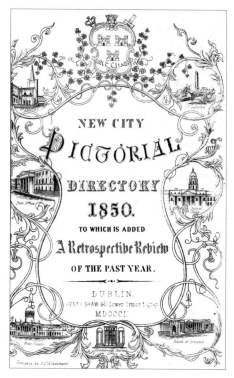

Cover of the *Dublin Directory* of 1850.
(Courtesy of IHI)

Custom House Quay. A couple of decades later, when Parliament Street was being laid out, Read purchased a plot of land at the rear of the Crane Lane premises. From the 1760s, he used the Parliament Street side for his shop entrance at No. 4 and Crane Lane for his workshop and forge.

This shop fulfilled the needs of all classes of Dublin people: for some, it was the purchase of an expensive sword and for others, simple items of table cutlery. Or perhaps one needed the world's smallest pair of working scissors – scissors small enough to trim a fly's whiskers? This Lilliputian scissors measured a quarter of an inch. If one needed the world's largest penknife, with 576 blades, Read's had it. Furthermore, Read's used to make and design surgical instruments for the surgeons at the college on St Stephen's Green. This demanding and skilful work was undertaken using the surgeon's rough sketches.[9]

PASSION FOR DUELLING

Later in the eighteenth century, Read's catered for the needs of the gentry and army by making magnificent crafted swords. The 1780s and 1790s were decades when Read's swords were highly regarded and sought after. One of the reasons for this was that it was the era when duelling was at its most feverish, reflecting the confidence of the ruling landed elite. These were Irish-made swords. Imports were not required for years.

In the eighteenth century, duelling experience was considered an indispensable part of a young man's education. The two questions a man would be asked by the family of a prospective wife were, 'Who are your family?' and 'Do you ever blaze [duel]?' The duel proved the young man's bravery, as well as cementing relationships with one's opponent, if he survived. But duelling was also about personal honour and public reputation. There were a number of duelling clubs where young men could train.

People took out their swords (or pistols) for all sorts of provocations. Richard Daly, manager of the Theatre Royal on Crow Street, fought nineteen duels in two years – three with swords and sixteen with pistols. Even prominent people fought duels, e.g. John Fitzgibbon, Lord Chancellor of Ireland and Earl of Clare fought John Philpott Curran, Master of the Rolls and a famous orator, politician and lawyer. Daniel O'Connell also had no hesitation when it came to a duel. His last was in 1815, with both parties using pistols (each with a notch indicating previous kills). In this particular duel, O'Connell met John D'Esterre, a member of Dublin Corporation who claimed O'Connell had insulted him in the course of Corporation business. D'Esterre was known to be a crack shot, but O'Connell shot him in the groin and he died two days later. Likewise, Henry Grattan was prepared to support his arguments with a pistol. He fought Lord Earlsfort and the Chancellor of the Exchequer, Isaac Corry. The duel with Corry was because of Corry's support for the proposed Act of Union legislation. Grattan managed to wound Corry in the arm. Duels were often fought in the fields near Merrion Square or in the courtyard

A young Henry Grattan (1746-1820), wearing the uniform of the Irish Volunteers by Francis Wheatley, 1782.

of Lucas's Coffee House on Cork Hill. Patrons of the coffee house used to observe the laws of honour and the proceedings from the windows above the courtyard and often laid wagers on the possible outcome. Most duels here did not end with fatalities, but at least two did. Newspapers at the time often complained of stray bullets, a particular danger for passers-by. Visitors to Dublin were advised to avoid any disagreeable encounters. The Phoenix Park became a popular location for duels.[10]

John Read died in 1776 and his son Thomas inherited the business. The business bore this name up until recently. In 1988, Jack Read Cowle, the last descendant of the Read family, retired and, for the first time the firm came under the ownership of a different family, the Butlers. The business ceased trading in 1997 and so one of Dublin's oldest shops entered the annals of Dublin folklore and history after nearly 300 years in business. The shop is still there and Dublin City Council, recognising the urgent need to save the shopfront and the unique signage and interior for future generations, is currently drawing up plans for its restoration and preservation. It is clearly an important part of the social history of Dublin and it has been suggested that it is one of the oldest retail brands in Europe.

Reads is a perfect example of a building that has survived since the 1760s. It is a unique example of an eighteenth-century merchant townhouse and shop and is one of the few Wide Streets premises to survive with much of its interior intact. It is the only one of the 1760s Parliament Street houses to retain significant decorative features and unique fittings, including display cases, drawers and counters. Moreover, the shop still retains its old-world charm. Thomas Chippendale supplied the shop's beautiful display cabinets, which are still in situ today. Fine examples of swords bearing Read's name still exist and may be viewed at the Arms and Armour collection of the National Museum of Ireland at Collins Barracks.[11]

Interestingly, the original founder of the firm, James Read, had a sister named Elizabeth, who was born in 1698 and died in 1742. Elizabeth married Richard Guinness and gave birth to the great Arthur Guinness, who went on to found the world-famous brewery firm (the Reads and the Guinnesses were both originally from County Kildare). Arthur Guinness's younger brother Samuel took a different route and became a goldsmith. His business was around the corner from Thomas Read's on Crane Lane.

It is believed that the property developer Hugh O'Regan and his public house holdings owned the building and the Thomas Read Pub (now The Ivy) on the corner, but his business went into liquidation in 2009. The location of the pub on the corner of Dame Street was known in the mid-twentieth century as Tarlo's Corner because there was a famous department store of that name located here. Before that, the building was occupied by Henry & James, Clothiers. The opposite corner, at Nos 38-40, were the offices of the *Dublin Evening Mail* and the *Irish Weekly Mail*. Another famous store, Alex Sloan & Co. (Sloan's), was located next door to the *Evening Mail*. On Parliament Street, there was also a well-known twentieth-century business, Garnett & Keegan's, an old-style gun shop. Hackett's Seeds were in business at No. 15 Parliament Street for many years. No. 30 is occupied by a firm of solicitors and has an attractive first-floor bay window. No. 34, now occupied by the Front Lounge pub, is a wide and elegant red-brick building that is part of a terrace of early and fine residential properties, built in a style appropriate to their location near Dublin Castle.

In the 1940s, Nos 1 to 3 were occupied by Tarlo's, gentlemen's outfitters. The offices of the Corporation of Dublin Dangerous Buildings Department and the City Architect were also located here. No. 10 was Mitchell & Co., a business that specialised in the manufacture of upholsterer's trimmings, fringe, web and coach lace. No. 9, Oate & Co., specialised in stationery and fancy goods. In No. 15 was the City of Dublin School Attendance Committee. No. 19 was occupied by a famous name in the history of gambling in Ireland, J. Kilmartin, Turf Accountant. No. 21, the beautiful, ornate and colourful Sunlight Chambers, was listed as Lever Bros (Ireland) Ltd, toilet and household soap and glycerine manufacturers. No. 37 was Rea's Gramophone Stores.

ESSEX STREET EAST

Continuing eastwards from Parliament Street, we have Essex Street East (named after Arthur Capel, Earl of Essex and former viceroy). Today, near the south-facing corner of Parliament and Essex streets, there is a modern building with a small number of loading bay doors all the way up its front and a hoist at the top gable. This is a reminder of the cranes and warehouses behind the old custom house on Essex Quay and the frenetic activity that characterised the area for centuries. A painting by Hugh Douglas Hamilton called *A Shoe Boy at Custom House Gate, 1760* captures some of the activities that took place around the old custom house, including ships unloading at the quays, drays carrying barrels, cranes, a shoe shop and a shoe boy working, as well as the architecture and the clothes of the era. It reveals that Essex Street, and the wider Temple Bar, was an important location of commerce.[12]

The street dates from the time of the building of the old custom house in the early seventeenth century, so it is of newer vintage than Essex Street West in the old city. Its construction was facilitated at the time by land reclamation along the shoreline of the River Liffey, which resulted in the building of the quays and the creation of the Temple Bar thoroughfare, on to Fleet Street. Many of the new dwellings along the quays had types of viewing rooms (conservatories) overlooking the river so that in the summer the new residents could enjoy the view. The building of the custom house greatly stimulated the construction of houses and businesses along the quays and on the new streets. Furthermore, the custom house itself was the regular meeting place for the Irish Privy Council (the advisory council to the Crown, but it was, in reality, the Cabinet for the administration of the country), which would meet in the Council Chamber of the building. In general, the building enhanced the area's importance in political life.

As well as warehouses, merchants, shops and residences, there were many taverns, brothels and gambling houses to cater to those visiting the custom house. There were also many publishers and printing houses, and shoe and hosiery shops. A well-known shirt shop on the street was called the Golden Peruke.

THE ELEPHANT AND THE THREE NAGS' HEADS

There were many taverns on Essex Street, including the Crown and the Three Nags' Heads. The Elephant tavern took its name from a bizarre incident in the history of the city. On 17 June 1681, an elephant, which had been brought to Dublin to be displayed at an exhibition, was to meet a tragic end when its Essex Street stable caught fire. This spectacle brought huge crowds on to the street. When the fire was quenched, there was a mad rush to take parts of the elephant as souvenirs. The remains of the elephant were dissected by Allan Mullen, from Trinity College Dublin, who published his findings, including several illustrations, in a pamphlet called *An Anatomical Account of the Elephant Accidentally Burnt in Dublin*.

It also appears that the Elephant tavern served as a meeting place for the first Catholic Committee in the 1760s, a forerunner of the influential Catholic Association of Daniel O'Connell in the nineteenth century.

On each side of the rear of the custom house stood a line of piazzas (not in the modern sense, but a colonnaded footpath for people to stroll up and down) and there were many taverns and alehouses located here. At night, this part of Essex Street attracted the worst types of both sexes. There were billiard tables in some of the taverns, which also brought many young men to the area and frequently led to fighting and general mayhem.[13]

THE WOODEN MAN AND THE DOLPHIN

Towards the end of the seventeenth century, an oaken figure celebrated in Dublin as the Wooden Man stood on Essex Street, near Eustace Street. In 1705, the official government publication, the *Dublin Gazette*, was published from Essex Street, giving details of expenditure and official matters. It is still going strong in the twenty-first century, now called *Iris Oifigiúil*, but it is no longer printed on paper and is instead available online. George Faulkner (1699–1775), founder of the *Dublin Journal* newspaper (*c*. 1725), had his printing works on this street too (and a shop around the corner on Parliament Street at what is now the Turk's Head pub). Such was the esteem in which he was held that he was one of the main printers of the works of his friend Jonathan Swift, who was the Dean of St Patrick's Cathedral.

On the corner of this street and Crane Lane, there is a fine Ruskin-influenced Victorian building called Dolphin House, built in the closing years of the nineteenth century as the Dolphin Hotel. There had been an hotel there from the early nineteenth century known as the Dolphin Hotel and Tavern. The Nugent family later bought it. It was designed by J.J. O'Callaghan and was owned by Michael Nugent, a wine and spirit merchant. The building has an impressive redbrick exterior and an elaborate interior (including a fine staircase). The Gothic entrance is crowned with a gilded dolphin and two maritime mythological figures. Over the first-floor windows, the name of the hotel and restaurant are finely sculpted. The metal flags over the dormer windows in the roof are pierced with the initials DH. The main entrance was on Essex Street East, not on the corner with Crane Lane as is the case at present.[14]

It was a highly regarded hotel. While not on a par with hotels such as the Metropole and the Shelbourne, which, in 1913, boasted passenger lifts, electric lighting and even fire escapes, the Dolphin was a very popular hotel. The restaurant was considered to be one of the best in the city well into the middle of the twentieth century, particularly among the well-to-do of Dublin society. Other popular restaurants in 1913 included Mitchell's, Bewley's and Jammets. Farther along the street was Michael Nugent's 'Whiskey Bonders' (now Bad Bobs mega pub) – 1879 and the initials MN are still to be seen ornately carved over the entrance to the pub. The same family owned both this property and the hotel. The hotel ceased trading in the late 1970s, but the striking exterior is still intact and the building is now part of the Courts Service.[15]

In the 1860s, John Rathborne & Co., was listed in *Thom's Directory* at No. 44 as a wax and spermaceti candle manufacturer, spermaceti oil refiner, and general oil merchant. Rathborne Candles was Dublin's oldest firm of candle makers, dating from 1488. The business started making candles on Winetavern Street.

They later had premises at 49 Essex Street and at the corner of Crampton Court in the middle of the nineteenth century. They had an unusual habit of frequently moving premises and returned to Crampton Court in the early twentieth century for a few years. For many years, they were located across the River Liffey at St Mary's Abbey and today are based in East Wall. Before the advent of gaslight for streets, Rathborne's supplied the city with candles for streetlights. They were also the suppliers for lighthouses and churches. In the 1940s a company called Fox's Brass and Nickel Plating Works and Foundry operated from Nos 13-14. At No. 19 was Berkell & Parnell's Slicing Machine Manufacturing Company. No. 21 was occupied by Pasley & Co., memorial and brass plate engravers, stencil cutters and rubber stamp makers.

MOB RULE ON ESSEX STREET

Across the road from the hotel is the rear of the famous Dollard House on Wellington Quay, home to Dollard House and the Dollard Printing Works since 1856 (the date is still on the rear of the building on Essex Street). Next door is the back entrance to the Clarence Hotel, which faces the Projects Arts Centre and the controversial Connolly Books (now housing the New Theatre upstairs), located here since the 1930s. The bookshop takes its name from James Connolly, a long-time trade union organiser, a socialist, a founder of the Irish Citizens Army and one of the executed leaders of the 1916 Rising.

The building occupied by the bookshop (and the New Theatre) is one of the oldest in Temple Bar, having been a former Huguenot 'Dutch Billy'-style house built in 1691. Sir John Rogerson (1648–1724) had owned it in the early years. He was a former Lord Mayor of Dublin who owned a number of houses in the area.

Connolly Books has been selling Communist and left-wing literature for many years. It has also been the cause and scene of many a riot and blaze as Catholic Actionists took umbrage against any hint of Communist literature (or any kind of literature regarded as 'indecent or obscene') or activity from the 1930s onwards in the newly independent, conservative Ireland. The original bookshop on Winetavern Street was forced to close in the early 1930s due to the disapproval of the influential and powerful in Irish society.

A Lenten sermon delivered in the Pro-Cathedral on 27 March 1933 against the 'dangers' of socialism led to a mob marching to the bookshop. They ransacked the building and then set it on fire. Three people in the building were lucky to escape with their lives. Other shops selling republican, radical or indecent literature were also attacked. The bookshop was again attacked and burnt to the ground in Pearse Street in 1956 (following the Russian invasion of

Hungary). The shop was effectively chased all over Dublin. It found a home at 14 Parliament Street in the late 1950s, before finally moving to 43 Essex Street East in 1977. If one wished to read Marx, Engels or even James Connolly in the middle decades of the twentieth century, then Connolly Books would have been the only place one could find such writings.[16]

CRANE LANE

This long and narrow street connecting Essex Street East with Dame Street is historic in its own right. The narrow thoroughfare, now known as the location of the Boilerhouse Gay Sauna Club at No. 12, was once one of two of the primary routes to Dublin Castle (the second was Blind Quay/Exchange Street) before Parliament Street was built. Its width was typical of many of the streets in the area, in contrast to the nearby Parliament Street. It takes its name from a public crane used to unload ships that was erected in 1571 near one of the earliest custom houses along the quays. A previous crane had been put in place here by the Normans in the thirteenth century. Today, a reminder of its importance is the hoist and the loading bays on the relatively new apartment building opposite the entrance to the lane at the corner of Essex Street East.

Ireland's first synagogue was founded at Crane Lane by Portuguese Jews. It was in existence from at least 1700. Businesses on Crane Lane included wig, paper, watch and stay makers. The *Dublin Gazette* (another one) was printed in Crane Lane at the Custom House Printing Office from 1705 to 1764 by Edward Sandys. It was 'Published by Authority', meaning it was an official organ. The *Dublin Evening Post* was first published from Crane Lane in 1732 (another one was founded in 1778 by John Magee). Since English copyright laws did not apply to Ireland, there were no rights attached to ownership of a title. An early issue reported that burying corpses in wool was no longer permitted. This was because they wanted to stimulate the use of wool in Ireland by the living rather than the dead. The famous and controversial paper, the *Freeman's Journal* (1763–1924), which later became the *Irish Independent*, was printed here in the late eighteenth century.[17]

On the opposite side of the street from the Boilerhouse, most of the buildings are original four-storey brick-built buildings. Fogarty's locksmiths, now around the corner in Dame Street, was located on this street from 1834. For many years, a large doorkey protruded from the entrance and acted as the sign for the shop.[18]

The Bear Tavern on Crane Lane was kept by a man named David Corbet until his death in 1787. He is described by John Gilbert as a Freemason, as well as 'an excellent musician, and leader of the band of the Dublin Independent Volunteers'. There was a host of other local taverns, including the Raven and Punch Bowl, which Gilbert dates to 1729, and the Dog and Duck, which was said to be 'noted for good ale'. The Turk's Head Chop House, which he dates to the 1760s, was originally located here. In more recent years, the name has been applied to premises on Parliament Street.[19]

CRAMPTON COURT AND 'TOMMY THE SHOE MAN'

Another old street running parallel to Crane Lane is Crampton Court. The only reminder of the age of the narrow lane is the line of original

The doors of Crampton Court, between Essex Street East and Dame Street. The doors date from c. 1750. (Courtesy of IHI)

flagstones running from the Essex Street entrance to the internal square, halfway to the Dame Street exit. In 2015, the square was re-surfaced in bright colours by Dublin City Council. Now a narrow zigzagging lane, this was formerly called Horse Guard Yard because it was used by Dublin Castle as a barracks. Its present size bears no relation to how big it used to be; it once occupied part of what is now the Olympia Theatre. It was later sold to Philip Crampton and subsequently named after him. He was a wealthy bookseller and Lord Mayor of Dublin in 1758. The Cramptons were also major landowners in the Temple Bar area of Dublin. Crampton Lane, Crampton Quay and Crampton Court were named in his honour. In 1755, his brethren in the Corporation of Stationers presented Alderman Crampton with a large silver cup as an acknowledgment of his vigilance as sheriff. He was instrumental in suppressing gambling houses and ball-yards in the city. He was also sheriff when, because of the riots in Dublin, it was found necessary for the protection of the citizens to post guards on horses and on foot in various parts of the city, including Temple Bar. Crampton died at his Grafton Street residence in 1792, aged 96, having long been known as the 'Father of the City'.[20]

Crampton Court was the site of two of Dublin's most famous eighteenth-century coffee houses – the Little Dublin Coffee House and the Royal Exchange

Dame Street, 1973. (Photographer Michael S. Walker, courtesy of NLI Commons Collection)

Coffee House. Flora Mitchell, in her excellent *Vanishing Dublin* (1966), describes these as the unofficial 'exchange' for Dublin before the Commercial Buildings on Dame Street opened at the end of the eighteenth century. Due to its proximity to the old custom house, the merchants frequented Crampton Court and commercial auctions were held there. Several notaries and insurance companies kept their offices in the court. With the opening of the Royal Exchange in 1779 and the Commercial Buildings in Dame Street in 1799, the merchants transferred their dealings to the new buildings and Crampton Court became known for jewellers, watchmakers and shoemakers.

For a long time, the main entrance to the Olympia Theatre was in Crampton Court. Today it is still possible to see this entrance, but it is now blocked up. The result of this change was that the stage area is nearer the new entrance, which is the opposite to most other theatres.

An important bookseller and printer, Luke White, opened his first bookshop in Crampton Court in 1775. He went on to have more premises on Dame Street and Dawson Street. At the time, many of the bookshops sold lottery tickets. White amassed enough of a fortune from the sale of books and lottery tickets to buy Luttrelstown Castle in Castleknock, County Dublin. Luke White's was regarded as *the* trendiest bookshop in town, full of the latest imported books from Paris and Switzerland. Another bookseller, John Archer, also started in Crampton Court and had a shop there from 1782 to 1787. Other businesses included a gunsmith, engravers, watch and glass makers, a bakehouse, and boot and shoemakers, including one called Jordan's which operated there until 1995.[21]

In the middle of the twentieth century, there was a renowned shoemaker at No. 5 Crampton Court called Tom Malone, who was a master of his craft. He specialised in handmade shoes and riding boots. 'Tommy the shoe man', as he was known, was the last of such skilled traders and was still working until the 1980s. There was also a famous china repair antique shop run by a Stephen Jackson. Besides repairing and selling china, the business used to lend props to the Olympia Theatre next door. Fogarty's locksmiths had been in Crane Lane since 1834 before moving to the present location, around the corner on Dame Street, in the latter half of the twentieth century.[22]

Today it is difficult to believe that this narrow alleyway was a bustling street in the eighteenth century. Amongst the many businesses and residences, there was an attractive pair of four-storey buildings (Nos 17 and 18) side by side, with matching doors that survived until the middle of the twentieth century. A letter to *The Irish Times* in the early 1930s described the location as 'a part of Dublin which still seems to suggest its ancient history'.[23]

In the 1940s, Nos 9 and 10 were occupied by Ada Yeates & Sister, stationers. J. Byrne, in No. 16, ran a billiards room while in No. 17 J. Jackson specialised in china repairs and J. Carson at No. 18 was a harness maker.

Crampton Lane, now Court, was celebrated by the artist Tom Cullen (1934–2001) in a 1984 painting, *Crampton Lane* (Old Dublin Series). In it, he captures the atmosphere of old Dublin, the winding narrow lane, the crowded buildings and the varied rooftops.

Part of Crampton Court in the 1960s. (Courtesy of IHI)

SYCAMORE STREET – WINE AND COFFEE

Sycamore Street (formerly Sycamore Alley) links Essex Street East to Dame Street. It also has a pedestrian link to Meeting House Square. Part of one side of the street is occupied by one of the exterior walls of the Olympia Theatre and provides access to its Upper Circle. It is a mid-seventeenth-century street and evolved in a similar fashion to the wider area, with bookshops and publishers, warehouses, residences and taverns. The Quakers had a meeting house here from the 1690s, before extending into the adjacent Eustace Street. The General Post Office was located here from about 1709 to 1755, when it moved to Fownes Court. Isaac Manley, the Postmaster General, was a friend of Dean Swift and Esther Johnson (Stella) and they often socialised together. Swift used his influence to ensure the unpopular Manley retained his position. It was to everyone's advantage that Manley kept his job as he frequently sent Stella a dozen bottles of wine at a time.[24]

Friends Meeting House on Eustace Street in the 1960s. (Courtesy of Dublin Quakers)

Nos 17–19 Sycamore Street was originally a substantial, purpose-built commercial warehouse and office built for Joshua Bewley (whose family were Quakers) in 1846. He also opened a tea/coffee house below the offices and at No. 6 Dame Street. The Bewleys were Quakers who moved to Ireland from France in the eighteenth century. They were involved in the tea trade and in 1835 another family member, Charles Bewley, landed an unprecedented cargo of 2,000 chests of tea shipped directly from China to Dublin, thereby breaking the East India Tea Company's monopoly. The Bewley family subsequently expanded into the coffee trade and in the late nineteenth century opened cafés in South Great George's Street (1894) and Westmoreland Street (1896). In the early twentieth century, the family bought Danone in Rathgar, where they had a dairy herd which they used to supply cream to their cafés. It is now the high school. The Grafton Street branch of Bewley's opened in 1926.[25]

MEETING HOUSE SQUARE AND IDLER'S CORNER

The Designyard is an eighteenth-century re-furbished building on Essex Street East, facing an entrance to Meeting House Square, and which has had many tenants over the years, including a china warehouse and a jewellery gallery. In recent years it was occupied by the Temple Bar Cultural Trust (its functions were transferred to Dublin City Council in 2016). At ground level are four wrought-iron narrow gates, reflecting the four bay windows on each of the upper levels, with carving showing the cities of Dublin, Manhattan, Vienna and Madrid. The gates were forged in Dublin by Harry Page, working to a design by Kathy Prendergast. There is also a serpentine mosaic inlay (designed by Sarah Daly) from the entrance to the yard behind the building and it is a reminder of the River Poddle that flows beneath the building.

Continuing along Essex Street East, one sees an image of a guitar hanging on a wall that leads into Meeting House Square, Temple Bar's architectural set piece. This is in honour of the renowned Irish blues guitarist Rory Gallagher of the famous late 1960s' rock group Taste. The guitar is a detailed replica of his trademark battered 1961 Fender Stratocaster and is sculpted in bronze. It was unveiled by U2's The Edge on 16 June 2006. The name of the square itself derives the nearby Friends' Meeting House and the Presbyterian Meeting House (now The Ark) on Eustace Street. In the seventeenth century, the horse stables for Dublin Castle were located here. In the latter part of the twentieth century, it served as a car park.

Entrance to Meeting House Square. (Courtesy of DubhEire, Wikimedia Commons)

In the late twentieth century, this derelict space was transformed into a new public space. The transformation was completed in 1996 and orchestrated by various architects of the Group '91 collection of architectural practices (including Paul Keogh, Shane O'Toole and Michael Kelly, O'Donnell and Tuomey), which also undertook significant work in the wider Temple Bar area. Meeting House Square contains award-winning buildings. The original brief for the architects and planners was for a purpose-built, open public square. The nearby, eclectic buildings house the Irish Photography Centre, which has three main elements: the Dublin Institute of Photography, the National Photographic Archives and the Gallery of Photography (est. 1978), the national centre for contemporary photography.

One also notices a giant metal theatre curtain, enclosing a stage (at the rear of The Ark on Eustace Street, facing onto the square). This is a cast-aluminium 'stage curtain' for the square, adapted from a design by the renowned Santiago Calatrava. During the winter, plays for young people take place inside, with the actors performing for the audience in the theatre inside. However, during the summer they open the door and the actors can turn around on the same stage and perform for the audience sitting in the open-air square.

Classic films are also shown on the square using one of the purposely designed walls that rolls down from above a huge window. There is a little metal box set into the red brick, behind which there it is the projection booth for the screen on the opposite side of the square. At weekends, there is a food market. In case of rain, there are four huge upturned umbrellas which open to provide shelter. The rain that gathers in these umbrellas is fed down through the supporting pipes.

A fine addition to the square is the exit to Eustace Street, described as 'the exquisitely detailed flight of steps' carved through the ground floor hall of a Georgian house (No. 11 Eustace Street), with decorative wall art overhead. The corner wall beside the bottom step is Diceman's Corner. The Diceman was a popular street mime artist (Thom McGinty) on Grafton Street during the 1980s and early 1990s. A colourful, bilingual plaque commemorates him. Embedded into the wall below the plaque is a shiny black granite sculpture. This was added in homage to the architect Michael Scott, who designed the iconic Bus Áras bus station in Dublin. The corner is also known as 'Idler's Corner' due to its long tradition of 'corner boys', who use the black granite sculpture as a back support.[26] The pedestrian archway, with cascading steps, is of Carlow granite with walls of white limestone.

EUSTACE STREET AND DAMASK HOUSE

Meeting House Square and Essex Street East lead to Eustace Street. This beautiful street offers a wonderful vista and a link from Dame Street, through Eustace Street and over the pedestrian Millennium Bridge (opened in December 1999). In the opposite direction, there is a view of the impressive former Burton's Store on Dame Street.

Eustace Street was laid down in the later decades of the seventeenth century. It developed around Maurice Eustace's Damask House and garden, which fell into disrepair over time and was eventually demolished, leaving much room for building. This street is one of Temple Bar's oldest and finest and it is now host to an eclectic collection of architectural styles, ranging from the Eustace Buildings, The Ark, the Focus Ireland building and its immediate neighbours, the Huguenot 'Dutch Billy' residences, and the Shamrock Chambers on the corner with Dame Street.[27]

On the corner of Eustace Street and Essex Street East, there is a plaque on the wall of the Norseman pub above the ruins of an ancient well on the widened footpath. The plaque states:

This well was probably constructed when Eustace Street was laid out between 1680 and 1720. Before that this area was a salty tidal shore of the right bank of the River Poddle where it joined the River Liffey just outside the walls of medieval Dublin.

The well (St Winifred's), 6 metres deep, was discovered in 1991 when builders were laying down cobblestones on the street. It seems to be of medieval origin, considering its proximity to the former St Augustine's Monastery nearby on what is now Cecilia Street. The monastery was closed and confiscated during the sixteenth-century Reformation. Following the development of the street, the well would have been used by the early residents of the new street, who would have been delighted to have access to underground freshwater coming from the River Poddle.

The residential development and naming of Eustace Street took place over three generations of the Eustace family, starting with Sir Maurice Eustace, Speaker of the House of Commons and Lord Chancellor (1644), who died in 1665 and whose house and gardens stood on the site of this street on what was part of the reclaimed land where the River Liffey and River Poddle met. No trace of Damask House survives today, but it is known to have been one of the largest houses in Dublin (with at least seventeen rooms) and both the house and the gardens were much admired by Jonathan Swift. Eustace, together with the Duke of Ormond, was responsible for the creation of the Phoenix Park.[28]

In 1708, the name Eustace Street appears in official correspondence relating to property in the area. It was mainly a residential street. Some of the buildings survive today thanks to organisations such as the Irish Landmark Trust and the Irish Georgian Society. Nos 17, 18, 25 and others have been carefully restored in recent decades.

FROM THE QUAKERS TO THE ARK

Eustace Buildings is occupied by the Religious Society of Friends and the Irish Film Institute, as well as a music store, Paul Ryan's, which specialises in woodwind and brass instruments. In 1692, the Religious Society of Friends, also known as the Quakers, opened their meeting house in Sycamore Alley in Temple Bar. The Quakers then extended their property to No. 6 Eustace Street in the early years of the eighteenth century. The Quakers have been in Ireland since the middle of the seventeenth century. Some of the best-known businesses in Dublin today were founded by Quakers, including Jacob's Biscuits (located on Bishop Street for many years and

The entrance to the Irish Film Institute, Eustace Street, formerly part of the Friends Meeting House.

employing 3,000 at one time); Bewley's (which started on Sycamore Alley); Pym's Department Store (South Great George's Street, across the road from Temple Bar); and Webb's (of the famous Crampton Quay bookseller's fame). The Quakers also provided major Famine relief during the mid-nineteenth century. This was organised by the Dublin Committee, operating from Eustace Street, which established soup kitchens as well as aid for farmers and fishermen.

Towards the end of the twentieth century, part of the Quaker property was converted into the Irish Film Centre (1992) (now the Irish Film Institute/IFI). This space was imaginatively restored and renovated. The principal meeting room was converted into a cinema in the mid-1980s. The interior square is covered and it is surrounded and overlooked by the backs of former, restored Georgian houses. The centre of the square's floor is designed to remind one of a reel of film. Underfloor lighting and special glass tiling highlight individual pieces in the reel of film and lead in and out of the complex.[29]

The Irish Film Institute has a long history. It was founded as the National Film Institute (NFI) in 1943 under the patronage of the controversial Archbishop of Dublin, John Charles McQuaid, enthusiastically assisted by Fr Richard Devane, who had been instrumental (with the help of the Catholic Truth Society of Ireland/CTSI) in the introduction of the draconian Censorship of Publications Act, 1929. Unsurprisingly, it later took its mandate from the 1936 Papal Encyclical, *Vigilanti Cura*, with 'vigilance' the operative word. This was vital in the face of what was seen by Catholic Church authorities as the 'celluloid menace' and the 'school of corruption' in the film industry in Hollywood. Consequently, the NFI saw itself as the teacher and moral guardian of the cinema-going public. With this in mind, it distributed films to schools, colleges and associations and became involved in the production of safety, health and educational films from the 1940s to the 1960s. With the decline in Church influence from the 1980s onwards the board of the NFI deleted the encyclical references from its articles of association. It also changed the organisation's name to the Irish Film Institute. This heralded an era of reinvention and reinvigoration, including the decision to acquire part of the eighteenth-century Quaker Meeting House on Eustace Street to hold a new Irish Film Centre and similar cultural organisations. The new centre was officially opened on 23 September 1992 by Taoiseach Albert Reynolds. In the decades since it moved to Eustace Street, the IFI has become one of the busiest and most dynamic arts organisations, not only in Temple Bar, but in the country.

The first film ever shown at the IFI was *Waterland*, which was introduced by its stars Jeremy Irons and Sinéad Cusack. In 2012, the IFI celebrated 20 years at 6 Eustace Street. During that time, it has shown 5,900 different films. The most popular of those films was *The Diving Bell and the Butterfly*, which attracted 11,000 attendees in 2008, narrowly beating the previous IFI favourite, *Crouching Tiger, Hidden Dragon*. The building also houses the Irish Film Archive, many film organisations, and educational and conference facilities. The Irish Film Archive staff are custodians of Ireland's unique and precious film heritage, with 611 different collections and over 26,000 cans of film, the oldest of which is a Lumière brothers' film of Dublin and Belfast that dates from 1897.[30]

THE ARK AND THE COVENANT

In 1728, the Presbyterian congregation on New Street moved to Eustace Street. The congregation was described as the richest Presbyterian congregation in Ireland and one of the most charitable. The old Presbyterian school (where the Presbyterian community met from 1725 and later housed a printing works) was refurbished in recent years and is now The Ark, a children's cultural centre (at No. 11a Eustace Street). The impressive façade was repaired and restored and it still has its original slanting windows at the upper level. It is unique as it is Europe's first and only dedicated cultural centre for children. They can explore theatre, music, literature, art, film, dance and more as the centre houses galleries, studios, theatres and a workshop.

The completed design included a performance space with a stage that opens out on to Meeting House Square at the rear of the building, as mentioned above. With the redevelopment of Temple Bar from the 1990s onwards, the conversion of the former Presbyterian school was one of the key cultural projects promoted by Temple Bar Properties Ltd in order to ensure the urban renewal of Temple Bar as Dublin's cultural quarter. There is no doubt that The Ark contributes to Temple Bar's status as a cultural centre.[31]

STAGS, KNAVES AND SHAMROCKS

In the eighteenth century there were several notable taverns in Eustace Street, including the Punch Bowl, the Sign of the Three Stags' Heads and the famous Eagle Tavern, where Freemasons, Masonic Templars, the Irish Volunteers and the Society of United Irishmen held their meetings.

SOCIETY OF
UNITED IRISHMEN
OF DUBLIN
Founded
9th November 1791
at
THE EAGLE TAVERN
on this site

One of the most famous of Temple Bar's eighteenth-century taverns was the Eagle Tavern, which is commemorated today with a historical plaque on Eustace Street. The Eagle was the location for the first meeting of the Dublin Society of the United Irishmen in 1791. The Eagle also has a historical connection to Dublin's infamous Hellfire Club.

Some of the earliest businesses and residents from the early eighteenth century onwards included merchants, stonecutters, furriers, a card maker (a business called The Knave of Clubs), a cider importer, a water bailiff, a gunmaker, silversmiths and James Swift & Co. Bankers. Later residents included Sir Thomas Blackhall, merchant and city sheriff, and the Fetherstonhaugh family, who occupied 17 Eustace Street from around 1780 until 1950. No. 5 housed the Stamp Office of Ireland, a tax-collecting centre operating from 1773. James Vallance, the most important book auctioneer of late-eighteenth-century Dublin, occupied the building next door for some time. The Dublin Library Society also used rooms in his building.[32]

'DUTCH BILLY' AND THE CELTIC REVIVAL

Many of the houses on Eustace Street today date from the early eighteenth century. The Ark dates from 1725 and other buildings on Eustace Street, including Nos 11, 17 and 25, date from approximately 1730. No. 17 contains a rare, early timber-panelled stair hall and staircase. The almost-intact early eighteenth-century panelling is the single most important feature of No. 17. Today it houses the Irish Theatre Institute. No. 18 dates from around 1780-1810, while No. 25 Eustace Street, another fine Georgian property, is under the auspices of the Irish Landmark Trust and gives some indication of the splendid residential properties that were a feature of the fashionable Eustace Street and some other Temple Bar streets in the eighteenth and nineteenth centuries. This house, dating from around 1720, is a much-restored example of an early 'Dutch Billy'-style residential house built by the Huguenots who flocked to Dublin from the late seventeenth century onwards. These were Calvinist Protestants fleeing persecution, particularly in France. The word 'refugee' was first used to refer to Huguenots, who were noted for their industriousness and hard work. The popularity and refinement of the style flourished with the Dutch influence of the Huguenot immigrants who settled in Dublin, as well as supporters of King William III,

Statue of King William of Orange on College Green in the early twentieth century. St Andrew's church can be seen in the background. (Courtesy of IHI)

who brought the same style from England after 1690, hence the popular title 'Dutch Billy'. Some 10,000 Huguenots, from twenty-one communities, came to Ireland and were very important in businesses such as weaving, banking, wine and brandy, farming, property, horticulture and crafts, such as silversmiths and goldsmiths. Names such as Le Fanu, D'Olier and La Touche are reminders of their influence. Their word was their bond and an expression in Dublin – 'as honest as a Huguenot' – testified to this.[33]

This terraced townhouse style remained fashionable right up until the 1750s, at which point the flat Georgian parapet became standard. Most gables were built up or demolished during the following century to conform to this fashion. Many of these houses, including the example on Eustace Street, survive, cloaked behind a modified Georgian façade. It also contains a rare surviving example of a panelled staircase and a restored panelled drawing room with an original fireplace. In this room, one of the panels has a small knob on it, which opens the panel to reveal the original brickwork behind it. The dining room is also panelled. The casement windows are nearly flush with the building's façade and there is a fine Gibbsian cut-stone doorcase (a style pioneered by architect James Gibbs in the 1720s). The timber flooring gives some idea of the age of the building because it is inclined to slope in places. In the basement, excavators discovered an old tunnel leading to the River Liffey, which was either used by an early woollen merchant to bring his bales to the river or as an escape tunnel. The preservation of this house is hugely important as it is part of an extraordinary phase in Ireland's (and Temple Bar's) architectural history.[34]

A number of interesting people occupied No. 25 over the years, not all of whom used it primarily as a residence. In 1830, it was the respectable home of J.D. Williams, a woollen merchant. More than ten years later, it was the counting house of W.T. Meyler & Co. Merchants. Five years later, Patrick Costello, a merchant tailor, shared the building with William Bloomfield, a solicitor, who continued to operate his business there until 1890. During his tenure, Bloomfield shared the house with an average of eight solicitors at any one time. One of these solicitors, from 1876 to 1879, was Standish O'Grady (1846–1928), a man who was very proud of his Gaelic heritage. W.B. Yeats called him 'the Father of the Celtic Revival'. O'Grady began his monumental work on legends and tales of ancient Ireland, *O'Grady's History of Ireland* (1878–80), while working in Eustace Street.[35]

Towards the Dame Street end of Eustace Street, Lipton's grocery establishment, a more recent business, occupied the notable Shamrock Chambers building, which curves around the corner onto Dame Street.

The side of the building on Eustace Street has sculpted bowls of fruit positioned over some of the ground-floor windows. Lipton's Tea and Provision Merchants was a household name in Dublin until well into the 1960s and had offices and a shop in the building. Across the road from the former grocery, there are four carved heads on the exterior wall of a fine building with distinctive windows, now occupied by a hostel.[36]

In the 1860s, some of the businesses located here included, for example, in Nos 12 and 13 the United Kingdom Alliance for Suppressing the Traffic of Intoxicating Liquors, the Draper's Early Closing Association, and warehouse of a brush, carpet-bag and case business. In the 1940s, Hayes and Finch, church furnishers and altar-candle manufacturers were at No. 3. The Easter Week Men's Association was located at No.7, as was the Irish Tailor and Tailoress Trade Union Hall. In Nos 12 and 13, Alexandra Buildings, was an organisation known as the Strangers' Friends' Society. Bovril (Eire), food specialists were at No. 14, Pye (Ireland), radio manufacturers, was at No. 19 and William King, a law stationer and printer, was at No. 18. In this building also were many offices of solicitors.

CURVED STREET

Just off Eustace Street, almost opposite The Ark, connecting Eustace Street with Temple Lane South, is a recent addition to Temple Bar – Curved Street – which derives its name from its shape. It was constructed in the 1990s. It serves as a street and an open space for various markets. The street was described as 'one of the most adventurous architectural innovations in Temple Bar' and it affords an excellent view of the impressive historic buildings at each entrance.

Some award-winning buildings, including Filmbase (originally Art for Media), were specially commissioned in the planned construction of this street. The Filmbase building has a curved façade with possibly nautical lines and large windows designed to facilitate ease of access for works of art. The Debbie Paul Gallery is an example of a gallery that displays concept-driven objects with a view of opening one's consciousness to the thought and practice involved in their creation.

The Irish Rock and Roll Music Experience Museum opposite Filmbase is one of the main businesses on the street. The Button Factory, at No. 2 Curved Street, is a popular venue in Dublin's live music and clubbing scene.[37]

TEMPLE LANE SOUTH

Temple Lane South is a quiet, picturesque street during the day, but it is a stone's throw from bustling Dame Street. In medieval times, it was used as a path leading to the Augustinian monastery. As a result of excavations undertaken by archaeologist Linzi Simpson in the closing years of the twentieth century, Temple Lane South has been shown to be one of the earliest lanes in Dublin and probably of Viking origin. Before the name change to Temple Lane South, this old street, pre-dating Temple Bar, was called Hogges Lane, after the nearby Hoggen (now College) Green, until the late seventeenth century and then Dirty Lane in the early eighteenth century. Later it changed to Temple Lane, when it was occupied by warehouses and stables. Access to the 'pit' of the old Theatre Royal on Crow Street was from this lane and nearby, in the shadow of the theatre, was the Shakespeare Tavern. One of the ferry stations for crossing the River Liffey was located at the end of the lane – Temple Lane Ferry. As with many of the streets of the area, the main businesses on Temple Lane South included wigmakers, wine merchants, printers and bookbinders, as well as goldsmiths, tailors and engravers.

THE GREEN AND THE GRANARY

There is a bizarre and beautiful building hidden on Temple Lane South. It is the Green Building (1994), one of the most important buildings in the area. The Green Building is an environmentally friendly building with solar panels on the roof that give surplus energy to the National Grid. Murray O'Laoire Architects designed the building, in collaboration with Tim Cooper's Conservation Engineering. Facing east and west, with a door on Crow Street, it is a building very much ahead of its time. The building is heated by a borehole more than 160 metres deep, using a system that exploits the heat generated below the Earth's crust. The solar cells atop the building provide plenty of electrical power. In the summer, the roof opens to allow excess heat to escape.

It has a striking, ornamented copper door, which is a work of art in itself (designed by Maud Cotter and Remco de Fouw). At first glance, part of the artwork looks like the debris from a building site. From a Belfast sink on the door, a tree-like structure grows. Copper pipes and taps were used in the construction of the tree. The upper balconies are constructed from recycled bicycles. The work of artists and artisans on the external façades adds a richness of detail that is an additional treasure on the street. The Crow Street door is similarly ornamented, where copper pipes, have been imaginatively converted into a most unusual piece of art, with submarine-like portholes. The doors have names – 'The Tree of Life' and 'Absolute Jellies Making Singing Sounds'. The building was described by art critic Aidan Dunne as 'blurring the edges between art and architecture'.[38]

A few doors down from the Green Building, the huge Wall of Fame for the Irish Rock and Roll Museum Experience looms colourfully, extending around the corner into Curved Street. The museum itself is dedicated to some of the most famous icons of Irish music over the years.

Near the junction of Temple Lane South and Essex Street is a white-painted building – the Printworks – with its entrance gates and staircase on Essex Street. This is a small residential development dating from the mid-1990s, designed by

The entrance to the Green Building on Temple Lane South. (Courtesy of Fotofinish)

Derek Tynan Architects and developed around a first-floor courtyard. It is an award-winning development, described as 'an oasis in the midst of street level urban activity ... a singular example of how highly crafted design can contribute to the quality of renewal and regeneration for the future of urban living'.[39]

Other important buildings with well-preserved nineteenth-century frontage are two former warehouses, one facing Curved Street at No. 20 (now called the Granary, it dates from around 1850), the other farther down on the opposite side. Both have unusual façades and are a reminder of early manufacturing and commercial activity in the area. The Granary is particularly striking as it is in a prominent location, overlooking Curved Street, with four loading-bay doors, one on each floor, to facilitate the movement of stock to ground level. The size of the doors would allow for bales of material, whether it was textiles or tea chests, to be moved with relative ease. At one time, the stock in the warehouse, according to *Thom's Directory*, consisted of tea, coffee, spices and fruit for Adam Woods & Co.

In 1994, the building was converted by architect Peter Twamley into an apartment complex with 'loft apartments'. The former *Irish Times* environmental correspondent Frank McDonald remembers when one of the early tenants of the ground floor of the refurbished building was the renowned Fat Freddy's Pizzeria, the first of its kind in Dublin using a wood-burning oven. The building won the Royal Institute of Architects Award in 1996.[40]

Farther along Temple Lane South, on the opposite side of the road, is another distinctive former warehouse, this time with three storeys and with different yet matching circular windows on each floor. At street level, a door at each side guards the coach entrance to the warehouse.[41]

In the 1860s some of the businesses here included wine and spirit merchants, tea and coffee merchants, spice and fruit dealers, bookbinders, tailors, and Forster & Co., engravers to Her Majesty, embossers, and chromo-lithographers. In the 1940s No. 1 was occupied by Hynes & Co., who ran a Red Bank oyster stores. No. 4 was Newsom's Ltd, sugar importers, and No. 8 was occupied by a company specialising in spice products. Other buildings were occupied by silversmiths, engravers, signwriters, printers, stationers, stables, and millinery agents. No. 17 was the Dublin Feather Company.

CECILIA STREET – SAINT OR SINNER

Crow Street intersects Cecilia Street, which is reputed to have been named after St Cecilia, the patron saint of music. However, there have been suggestions that it was in fact named after a member of the Fownes family, Cecilia Fownes. In medieval times, the site was occupied by an Augustinian monastery. The site was then bounded by the southern shore of the River Liffey. The new owners (Fownes) extended their holding by reclaiming much land from the river. The Friary apartment complex on Cecilia Street is a reminder of the former inhabitants of the area.

Cecilia House, the main and most distinctive building on the street, is of historic significance as it is located on the site of the famous Crow Street Theatre. Part of the theatre was rebuilt in 1836 by the Company of Apothecaries and was later taken over by the Medical School of the Catholic University of Ireland. Two of its famous students were James Joyce and Oliver St John Gogarty. Some of the other buildings on this street were warehouses

THE MEDICAL SCHOOL
OF
THE CATHOLIC UNIVERSITY OF IRELAND
FIRST RECTOR JOHN HENRY NEWMAN
AND OF ITS SUCCESSOR
UNIVERSITY COLLEGE DUBLIN
WAS SITUATED IN THIS BUILDING
1855 – 1931
ERECTED BY THE U.C.D. MEDICAL GRADUATES ASSOCIATION

For many years, Cecilia Street was the location for the Catholic University of Ireland Medical School. This plaque is located at the side entrance to Urban Outfitters on Cecilia Street, Temple Bar.

for woollen merchants and wine and spirit merchants. A famous publication, the *Dublin Penny Journal*, was published in the area in the 1830s.[42]

THE CLADDAGH AND THE CHIEFTAINS

Claddagh Records at No. 2 Cecilia Street is a haven for Irish traditional music lovers. The name 'Claddagh' derives from a quayside area in Galway city, which was one of the oldest fishing villages in Ireland. The name also refers to a traditional Irish ring. In the shop, there is everything from early traditional recordings to rare folk albums to the most recent releases. This is where one will find collections by the famous Tulla Céilí Band, the Kilfenora Céilí Band or Willie Clancy. Most importantly, Claddagh is a renowned recording label. Garech Browne founded Claddagh Records in Dublin in 1959. The first album it produced was the classic *Rí na bPíobairí* (King of the Pipers) by Leo Rowsome, one of the most renowned Irish pipers. The second Claddagh album was *The Chieftains*, the very first recording of the now world-famous traditional group. Claddagh went on to make many more fine albums with The Chieftains.

Over the years, Claddagh Records has released music by many of the best traditional Irish artists. It was a revolutionary label, in the sense that it set out to showcase the leading literary figures in Ireland. Poets such as Patrick Kavanagh, Austin Clarke, Michael Hartnett, John Montague, Thomas Kinsella and Seamus Heaney have made records for Claddagh and the label has also recorded major Scottish poets, such as Hugh Mac Diarmid, Sorley MacLean and George MacKay Browne.[43]

The great Uileann piper Seamus Ennis (1919-82) used to play in the Mechanics' Institute which had a venue on Essex Street East. His other connection with Temple Bar was that he worked in the Three Candles Press, at Aston Place, off Fleet Street, when he was in his early twenties.

CROW STREET AND SPRANGER'S YARD

Cecilia Street brings us to Crow Street, which was named after William Crow, owner of part of the land of the suppressed monastery of St Augustine. The street was laid down in the early seventeenth century and was where Crow built his house, the 'Crow's Nest'. The Dublin Philosophical Society was subsequently based in his house and William Petty, William Molyneux and other illustrious figures met there from 1684 onwards. The house was also used as government offices (including for the Down Survey). The famous Theatre Royal/Crow Street Theatre was also located on Crow Street, on the site of the Crow's Nest.[44]

A famous resident of this street was Hugh Douglas Hamilton, the eminent eighteenth-century portrait painter, many of whose paintings grace the National Gallery of Ireland.

In the middle of the nineteenth century, approximately seventeen tailors and dressmakers had their businesses here, probably because of a tradition stemming from the proximity to the former Crow Street Theatre. There was also an engraver and copperplate printer here. Every Tuesday and Thursday, the *Dublin Gazette* was printed and published at Nos 8 and 9 Crow Street 'by the King's Authority'. This paper was started by King James II in 1689 but after his defeat the paper stopped being printed. There were a number of other papers that used the name subsequently.

The west front of the Green Building is located at No. 3. Nearby, No. 5 is an ornate, old residential-style building with the date 1856 carved on the wall near the roof. However, at the level of the second floor there is another date attractively sculpted, with the number '18' over '81' (1881). Two doors down, No. 7 is also of the original residential stock and its Gibbs-style doorcase is noteworthy.

On the junction of Cecilia, Fownes and Crow streets, there is a large apartment block called Spranger's Yard, that derives its name from the famous eighteenth-century actor Spranger Barry, who was also the owner and manager of the famous Theatre Royal on Crow Street. The building has an eye-catching roof: sculpted, tentacle-like structures appear to be clawing at the air. The apartments and shops at Spranger's Yard were designed in the mid-1990s as part of the attempt to revitalise Temple Bar. The building contains both refurbished and new elements, which successfully co-exist – a recurring sight in Temple Bar.

In the 1940s No. 1 was occupied by Alex Thom who were printers, publishers, bookbinders, stationers and cartonbox makers, printers of the famous and very bulky Dublin street directory since 1844 (*Thom's Directory*). They were originally based in Abbey Street, but moved to Crow Street following the 1916 Rising which destroyed much of central Dublin.[45] Thom's also occupied part of No. 2 and another tenant in this building was John Falconer, a government, law and general printing, publishing and bookbinding establishment. From here was published the *Irish Law Times & Solicitors Journal*, and the *A.B.C. Railway Guide & Hotel Directory*. The *Garda Review Office*, the official organ of the Garda Síochána, was also published here. Foyle's Libraries Ltd had its lending depot in No. 7. In No. 9 was Irish Leathermac Co., who specialised in the manufacture of leather coats. British Insulated Cables occupied No. 17.

FOWNES STREET, LUNATICS AND ROPE DANCERS

Fownes Street Upper and Lower take their names from Sir William Fownes, a prosperous merchant, Lord Mayor of Dublin in 1708 and a member of the Irish House of Commons for Wicklow. The street dates from the time when Fownes lived in his mansion there. His property adjoined that of the Temple's. The Fownes family established a network of streets adjacent to their mansion named after family members: Cecilia Street, Cope Street and Fownes Street itself. Fownes also had other occupations over the course of his life, including Ranger of the Phoenix Park and Master of the Game for all the woodlands of Ireland. Fownes suggested to Jonathan Swift that a 'Bedlam' for lunatics should be established. Swift managed to do this by leaving an endowment in his will. This 'Bedlam' became St Patrick's Hospital, James's Street, Dublin.

Lower Fownes Street nearer the quays was formerly known as Bagnio Slip, which was the slope or slipway for the ferry station. The ferry station was removed at the time of the building of Wellington Quay and the Ha'penny Bridge in the early nineteenth century. Before the building of O'Connell Bridge,

'On yer bike!' Fownes Street from Lower to Upper in the early 1970s. (Courtesy of Tangos)

there were at least two ferry crossings of the River Liffey from Temple Bar – one at the bottom of Temple Lane and the other at Lower Fownes Street.

In 1727, Fownes's house was taken by Madame Violante, a French rope-dancer and pantomime artiste. It was subsequently a chocolate house and then an educational establishment run by, among others, the famous educationalist Revd Thomas Benson, who had his school there from 1749 until nearly the end of the century. Another part of Fownes's mansion was used by the General Post Office of Dublin, which remained there until 1783. Towards the end of the century, a group of Dublin merchants bought the property, refurbished it and in 1799 the Commercial Buildings opened and operated in a similar way to a Chamber of Commerce for the merchants.[46]

Fortunately, some of early fashionable Georgian houses on Fownes Street have survived, notably Nos 3, 4 and 5, by the Foggy Dew pub; they are some of the oldest properties in Temple Bar. These are mainly four-storey, brick-built houses packed with period details, with two windows on each floor and two or three steps leading up to the panelled front door with a handsome, cut-stone surround – the typical Gibbs-style stone doorcase. The dwellings also have some attractive panelled rooms illustrative of a different era. Some also have dormer windows, which add to their pleasing appearance.[47]

In later years, as the nearby areas of Dame Street and College Green became centres for Dublin's insurance and banking sectors, Fownes Street was occupied by related businesses. There is a striking redbrick building on the corner of Fownes Street and Temple Bar. For years, this was home to the Alan McShane office equipment business and, before that, it was the warehouse for Hoggs wine importers.

The founder of Sinn Féin, Arthur Griffith, had offices at No. 17 Fownes Street and this was where the *United Irishman* newspaper was published.

Significant architecture on corner of College Green. (Courtesy of Psyberartist, Wikimedia Commons)

THE FOGGY DEW

Old taverns located on Fownes Street included the King's Arms and the Shakespeare. Today the Foggy Dew pub at No. 1 has both an impressive old-world exterior and interior dating from 1901. The pub overlooks Central Bank Plaza. It is named after an Irish ballad, 'The Foggy Dew', sometimes known as 'Down the Glen', written by Canon Charles O'Neill in 1919. There was another ballad of the same name in the 1840s, written by an Edward Bunting. O'Neill's song chronicles the Easter Rising of 1916 and encourages Irishmen to fight, not in the world war, as many did, but for the cause of Ireland:

> As down the glen one Easter morn to a city fair rode I,
> There armed lines of marching men in squadrons passed me by,
> No pipe did hum nor battle drum did sound its loud tattoo,
> But the Angelus Bell o'er the Liffey's swell rang out through the foggy dew.

The Halfpenny Bridge Inn at the opposite end of the street, on the corner where the street meets the quays, is a long-established traditional music pub. It takes its name from the nearby bridge over the River Liffey. A few doors away, a restaurant called Caverna has a 300-year-old, barrel-vaulted ceiling in its basement.

The Foggy Dew pub, No. 1 Upper Fownes Street, with Commercial Buildings reflected in window. (Courtesy of Christopher Brown, Flickr)

No. 14 Fownes Street Upper has been the home of the famous business of John J. Cooke & Co. for nearly seventy years. The jeweller and silversmiths shop, with its distinctive blue-timbered exterior and its impressive interior, has been in business in Temple Bar since 1951. The shop is responsible for the maintenance and care of the silverware for soccer league cups and GAA club trophies.

On 28 June 1980, the former Minister for Health Dr Noël Browne unveiled a brass plaque at No. 10 Fownes Street Lower. This was the location for the new Hirschfeld Centre, the first full-time lesbian and gay venue in Ireland. 'Gay group opens new headquarters in Dublin' ran the headline in *The Irish Times*. The new venue contained, among other things, a social centre, a cinema and a meeting place for Dublin's LGBT community.[48]

Dr Browne himself, a courageous doctor famous for his involvement in the eradication of TB in Ireland, was known for going against the tide. As Minister for Health, he had been involved in promoting the famous Mother and Child Scheme (to enhance the welfare of the family by providing free, State-funded healthcare to mothers and their children) in the late 1940s, but he encountered opposition from Catholic Church authorities, the medical profession and political opponents, which resulted in political turmoil, his resignation and a change of government. Despite this, Browne continued to be involved in politics and activism for many decades afterwards and his unveiling of the new Hirschfield Centre was a testament of his courage and commitment. It was also a landmark event for the gay community.

Dr Noel Browne unveiling a brass plaque and dedication at 10 Fownes Street, The Hirschfeld Centre, on 28 June 1980. (Courtesy of Derek Speirs and NLGF Collection, IQA/NLI/ Credit- FB.com/IQAadvisorygroup)

13

THE HEART OF TEMPLE BAR –
THE SQUARE, THE CROWN
AND THE FLEET

Part of Fownes Street overlooks Temple Bar Square. The name Temple Bar originally only applied to the street between Essex Street East and Fleet Street. The street took its name from Sir William Temple, but the name has since become a generic term for the area stretching from Fishamble Street to Westmoreland Street and from Dame Street to the River Liffey. Temple Bar Square is between Fownes Street and Crown Alley, overlooked by the Central Bank.

Sir William Temple (1555-1627).
(Courtesy of Dublin Forums)

The Temple Bar thoroughfare leading to the square was the site of the mansion and gardens of the family of William Temple (1555–1627). Temple was a renowned teacher and philosopher who had entered the service of the Lord Deputy in Dublin in 1599, serving as secretary to Robert, Earl of Essex. Ten years later, in 1609, he was offered the position of provost of Trinity College. He built his house and gardens on newly reclaimed land on what is now the corner of Temple Bar and Temple Lane South. In 1656, his son, Sir John Temple, further extended the holding as the land reclamation and the building of sea walls continued apace.[1]

The heart of Temple Bar.
(Courtesy of Thorsten
Pohl, Wikimedia
Commons)

BARS AND BLACK EYES

Along the street, there were many publishers, booksellers and taverns. The Turk's Head Chop House was located here for a while in the late eighteenth century (the name was applied to different taverns in Temple Bar over the years). The Horseshoe and Magpie was the regular tavern for performers in the Crow Street Theatre and others. This tavern was managed by Mrs Mullins, wife of the landscape painter George Mullins, and not by her husband. He concentrated more on painting than pouring pints. Such was the esteem in which he was held that he also became a teacher of his craft. One of his students was Thomas Roberts (1748–1778), who became the most renowned Irish landscape painter of the eighteenth century. He died in Lisbon at the young age of 30. Roberts made extra money by painting the black eyes of the customers in Mrs Mullins' bar who had been fighting on the premises the previous night.[2]

Today, another modern tavern, the Temple Bar pub, is an atmospheric attraction along the thoroughfare. In 2006, a newspaper reported that there has been a pub on the premises since 1728, although the pub itself puts the date at 1694. Yet another source claims the correct date is 1840. During all that time, the property has been subject to many different names (including Farrington's), auctions and buy-outs. The interior has been renovated three or four times at least. It is a highly popular establishment with tourists visiting the area, as is the case with many of the pubs in Temple Bar. The pub is now ten times its original size.[3]

Across from the pub, at No. 4 Temple Bar, is the Library Project, which specialises in art books, and the Black Church Print Studio. Both are situated above Photo Ireland, an artists' collective established in 1982. It is one of the leading contemporary fine art print studios in Ireland. The studio, spread over three floors, is a purpose-built print studio that aims to give people an insight into fine art printmaking processes, some of which date back to the 1500s. Photo Ireland is an organisation dedicated to stimulating a critical dialogue about photography in Ireland. It also promotes the work of Irish artists internationally.

The entrance to the Turk's Head on Parliament Street.

In the 1860s there were many building here listed as tenements. There were also many small businesses such as grocers, dairy and provision dealers, hairdressers, cabinet makers, chandlers, hat makers, and nailers and slaters. There was also a grocer, tea, wine and spirit dealer. In the 1940s Moss & Gray, in Nos 1 and 2, were wholesale tea and sugar merchants and Nos 3, 4, & 5 were tenements. Other businesses included wholesale jewellers and cutlers, painting contractors, woollen merchants, tailors, locksmiths, the City Typewriting Company and the National Time Recording Company.

THE SQUARE – UNION ONLY IN TRUTH

Temple Bar Square was a critical part of the regeneration of the Temple Bar area. In the early 1990s, the brief for the architects from Temple Bar Properties, which was managing the rejuvenation of the area on behalf of the Irish government, was to create a modern space that was also sympathetic to the historic surroundings. It was to be a place where one could pause and enjoy the energy and colour of Temple Bar. The new public space was created on a derelict site that had been used as a surface car park for many years. Critically, the square provided a readily identifiable centre within the warren of streets that make up Temple Bar. All streets seem to lead to this square, with its variety of new and old buildings. During its construction, two fine redbrick-and-stone buildings were revealed.[4] These two building, on the east and west sides, now partially frame the square. The larger of the two faces Merchant's Arch, Crown Alley and the square itself, adding further to the attractiveness of the stepped square. This impressive building was Dublin's first purpose-built Telephone Exchange, which opened in 1900. It was taken over by the Post Office in 1912. One of the problems experience by the telephone operators in the early years was the noise outside: not boisterous party-goers but the clip-clop of horses' iron shoes and the rattle of wheels on the cobblestones.[5]

Facing the side of the Exchange is Rory's Fishing Tackle shop. It is not the kind of business one might expect in Temple Bar, but it has been thriving since the early 1960s and is one of the area's oldest shops. Its founder used to work with the ESB in Fleet Street. He was 'mad about fishing' and always had a dream of owning his own fishing tackle shop. The dream came true when the shop became vacant and the family still run it to this day. On the other side of Merchant's Arch, on the Fownes Street corner, beside the Quays Bar, is the Regent's Barber, which has been trading since 1953. A few doors down is an original, old-style, musty Dublin pub – the Halfpenny Bridge Inn. All types of music are on offer here, from jazz to traditional, and its comedy clubs (including The Battle of the Axes) are famous. On the opposite corner is the Temple Bar Gallery and Studios, founded in 1983 by Jenny Haughton, who rented a disused shirt factory from CIE and invited artists to take over the space. There is an eye-catching semi-circular metallic sign perched on the roof. It reads 'OUR UNION ONLY IN TRUTH' and faces the square. This is an artwork by Garret Phelan, crafted in mild steel, that serves as a landmark for the building while also sharing a message both subjective and positive. The building houses the studios of thirty artists, who work in a variety of media, including painting, sculpture and photography. This is an iconic building. According to the Temple Bar Gallery and Studios:

The Regent Barber Shop, Temple Bar, 1967. (Courtesy of IHI)

Sun and shadows at Merchant's Arch, 13 January 1965. (Courtesy of *The Irish Times*)

The early 20th-century industrial building, which extended through a block from Temple Bar to the Liffey quays, provided the framework of spaces for artists to work in, although the conditions were problematic and at times hazardous. The activities of the artists – studios, exhibition space, cafe, sculptor's annex – influenced the atmosphere of Temple Bar in the 1980s, establishing the area's reputation as a cultural hub and contributing to its regeneration as Dublin's Cultural Quarter.[6]

The establishment of Temple Bar Properties in August 1991 spurred the rejuvenation of the area. The Group '91 architects won the competition for the architectural framework plan. Temple Bar Gallery & Studios (TBG&S) was recognised as a flagship project and it was one of the first cultural organisations rehoused by the Temple Bar Cultural Quarter regeneration scheme. The old shirt factory was extensively refurbished and custom-designed by Irish architects McCullough Mulvin. The artists returned to their studios in the building in November 1994.[7]

THE ARCH AND THE OVAL

Merchant's Arch is a most striking and attractive entrance to the Temple Bar area and is named after the adjacent former Merchants' Guild Hall. This building is currently the refurbished Merchant's Arch pub and restaurant and has an interesting oval room at the rear, which extends from the ground floor to the roof. It is illuminated from above by an eye-like roof window. Access to the top-floor restaurant is via the oval room and an impressive original, refurbished winding stone staircase – another hidden treasure.

CROWN ALLEY – OMAN AND THE BAD ASS

Lying on a north-south axis, linking the Ha'penny Bridge to Dame Street via Merchant's Arch, is Crown Alley. This is home to some of the most colourful and eclectic shops, restaurants and pubs adorning the area. It is possible that Crown Alley derived its name from a tavern with the sign of the crown. It was originally a right of way across a field seen on Brookings 1728 map of Dublin.

An eye-catching building here is the former warehouse of Oman's Furniture Removal business (later Eamon Doran's music pub and now the Old Storehouse bar and restaurant). The name and nature of the old furniture business is

Merchant's Arch in the 1960s. (Courtesy of IHI)

still attractively displayed near roof level. The style of the sign is unusual and appears to be printed in a hand-written font. Some of the words hark back to a different era of colonies and steamships. The sign reads, 'A. Oman & Sons. Household removal contractors and warehousemen. Domestic, colonial and foreign removals throughout the entire system of Railway and Steamship Lines.'

Across the road, in another converted warehouse, is the famous Bad Ass Café, operating since 1983. It has one of the oldest cash payment systems in Ireland. Its mascot is a donkey and there is a hoof-print sculpted into the pavement outside. The café has a colourful history, including an incident when it was nearly burnt to the ground. It also claims that the famous singer Sinéad O'Connor worked there during her early career. Among some of the other legendary Crown Alley shops in the 1970s and 1980s were Rumours, a popular second-hand clothes shop, and the Cheesecake HQ, where 'cakes made in heaven' were to be savoured.[8]

COPE STREET AND CHAMBER POTS

Running along the south-facing flank of the Central Bank Plaza is Cope Street, named after Robert Cope, a Huguenot, who married Elizabeth, the daughter of Sir William Fownes. The remains of some merchants' warehouses may still be seen here. No. 7 Cope Street was the location for the manufacture of chamber pots and water closets, the first to be made in Ireland, according to an advertisement in the *Hibernian Journal*.[9]

The Graphic Studio Gallery located in a former warehouse on Cope Street is the oldest gallery in Dublin. It deals exclusively in original, contemporary fine art prints. Established in 1960, under the name Graphic Studio Dublin, to teach traditional printmaking skills, it also provides studios and technical assistance to artists making fine art prints. The gallery itself is an offshoot of the studio, having been opened in 1988. It holds many exhibitions every year and has a visiting artists programme. It is a significant cultural centre in Temple Bar, which has a tradition of printmaking-related activities.[10]

ASDILL'S PLACE – CRAMPTON BUILDINGS

On the opposite side of Temple Bar Square, proceeding towards Fleet Street, is Asdill's Row. It derives its name from a wealthy merchant, John Asdill.

Asdill's Row manages to be nearly invisible in Temple Bar, yet it stretches from Crampton Quay to Temple Bar (at the corner of the Elephant & Castle restaurant, whose motto is 'Copied by many, excelled by none'). The east side is dominated by Crampton Buildings, one of Dublin's oldest and more unusual flat complexes. The community has been here long before the late twentieth-century changes in the wider area. The green Victorian courtyard, whose plants and mature trees make it almost park-like, is surrounded and framed by fifty-four flats, twenty-seven on each of the two floors. It was built in 1891 by the Dublin Artisans' Dwelling Company and it was privately owned by Sir Robert and Lady Goff for more than 100 years. The ground floor had shops, including the famous George Webb's booksellers at one time. An unusual feature of the complex is that the chimneys are flush with the façade of the exterior walls of the flats and nearly above the upper-floor windows. Another of the many features of this old development is the unadorned metal stairs, which gives access to the flats on the higher levels of this red-brick Victorian building.

The Dublin City Council bought the flats in 1998 (when the Goffs decided to sell) after residents became concerned about eviction. Treasury Holdings had shown an interest in owning the complex, having purchased the ground-floor shops and restaurants, including the Elephant and Castle underneath the flats. Work is currently being undertaken to reconfigure and refurbish the flats and to reduce the existing number.[11]

Nearby is Bedford Row, which takes its name from the fourth Duke of Bedford, the Lord Lieutenant of Ireland from 1757 to 1761.

ANGLESEA STREET AND THE BATTLE OF RATHMINES

Leaving Crampton Buildings and walking towards Fleet Street, we are immediately arrested by the brightly decorated Oliver St John Gogarty and the Auld Dubliner pubs, which introduce us to Anglesea (originally Anglesey Street). The name commemorates another prominent resident of the area, Arthur Annesley (d. 1686). His house was on the eastern side of the street and was known as 'the great house on Anglesey Street'. This earl was great-grandfather of James Annesley (1715–1760), the principal figure in the famous and strange Anglesey peerage kidnapping case (heard in Dublin's old Four Courts). The story is said to have inspired Sir Walter Scott's *Guy Mannering*.

The street dates from the late 1650s and was laid out on the Anglesea Estate. It is shown on Dublin maps of 1685 and 1728 (Brooking's). Like Crowe, Temple, Crampton and Eustace, Annesley had acquired leases in 1657, 1658, and 1662 from Dublin Corporation on plots of land in the vicinity (up to the watermark, i.e. the Liffey shoreline before land was reclaimed and the quays built) and developed them over the years. It was an opportune time as this was when the eastward reclamation and expansion of Temple Bar was underway.[12]

Arthur Annesley was also involved in the famous Battle of Rathmines of 1649, accepting the surrender of the Royalist forces under the Duke of Ormond. This defeat facilitated the landing of Oliver Cromwell in Dublin. Annesley was created Earl of Anglesey in 1661.

FROM MONTO TO BUCK MULLIGAN

Perched on the footpath outside the Oliver St John Gogarty pub are statues of Gogarty and James Joyce, one seated, the other standing, apparently in

Arthur Annesley, 1st Early of Anglesey. He was born in Fishamble Street. Anglesea Street in Temple Bar is named after him. (Courtesy of Dublin Forums)

animated conversation. They were friends from their Trinity College Dublin days at the turn of the nineteenth century and Gogarty was the inspiration for Buck Mulligan in *Ulysses*. Joyce and Gogarty would also have been regular visitors to the most notorious red-light district in Europe, Monto, in north inner-city Dublin, so it may be more appropriate to have their statues outside a pub in that area. (In fact, it has been suggested that the mega pubs of Temple Bar would be more appropriately located in a restored Monto than in Temple Bar and the remaining pubs should concentrate more on supporting cultural activities. The annual and growing Temple Bar Tradfest is an opportunity for further development in this respect.) Both Joyce and Gogarty attended UCD's Medical School in nearby Cecilia Street before the former moved to Paris and the latter to Trinity. Gogarty lived a colourful life and was variously a doctor, an author and a senator in the new Irish Free State.[13]

On the building's wall, above the heads of the statues, the date 1941 is shown, with 'Éire' wedged in between the nine and the four.

Notable residents of Anglesea Street included the architect of the Royal Exchange (City Hall) and the Four Courts, Thomas Cooley, who died at his house there in 1784 (James Gandon completed the Four Courts after Cooley's death). Richard Edward Mercier, publisher of *Anthologia Hibernica* (which included some of the work of Thomas Moore) and other works, also lived on this street. Other residents included a famous line engraver called Patrick Halpin, whose works included Rocque's map of Dublin. Dean Swift's doctor, Thomas Kingsbury, also resided on the street, as did the famous actor, Isaac Sparks. For many years, No. 6 was the home of late eighteenth-century master violin maker Thomas Perry. His violins are often compared to the Stradivarius and are much sought after to this day.[14]

A QUEEN ANNE REVIVAL

No. 10 Anglesea Street is one of the most striking properties on this street. An ornate building with carved decorative brackets at each end of the shopfront, it is occupied by a firm of solicitors. Its elaborate exterior makes it a good example of the Queen Anne revival. Dating from late 1898, it has

The Oliver St John Gogarty pub in Temple Bar captures the colourful atmosphere of the area. (Courtesy of australiaphotos.co.uk)

been described by Pat Liddy as 'perhaps one of Dublin's finest examples of a wooden shop-front'.[15] It has been occupied at various times by firms of solicitors and stockbrokers, appropriately, given its proximity to the Irish Stock Exchange. The Latin words 'SPECTEMUR AGENDO', meaning 'Judge us by our actions', are carved into the building's façade.

The fine building that is the Irish Stock Exchange (ISE) has been located at 28 Anglesea Street since 1878. Before that, it was located at the Commercial Buildings on Dame Street and prior to that, it was at the Royal Exchange (City Hall) building as it had been founded in that building's coffee house in 1793. The interior of the building on Anglesea Street has an impressive old Victorian atmosphere to it. At the outbreak of the First World War in 1914, the offices closed for six months, but the brokers continued to trade on the steps outside the building and in the immediate vicinity. The Exchange itself made history in 1925 by admitting Oonagh Keogh, as a member. She was the first woman admitted to any stock exchange in the world.

The ornate No. 29, next door to the ISE and opposite Blooms Hotel, is a four-storey, brick, Georgian-style premises with an attractive shopfront on the ground floor. It has 'rebuilt in 1895' carved in wood over the ground-floor bay window.

Blooms Hotel was originally built (in 1979) on the site of the old Hogg's warehouse as an extension to the old Jurys Hotel, which fronted on to

Ornate shop front and entrance steps at 13 Anglesea Street.
(Courtesy of Psyberartist, Wikimedia Commons)

The Irish Stock Exchange on Anglesea Street. (Courtesy of Psyberartist, Wikimedia Commons)

Dame Street. Jurys moved to Ballsbridge in the 1970s and the part fronting Dame Street was then demolished. The new extension continued to operate as a separate hotel and incorporated the neighbouring late-nineteenth-century Vat House pub. Because Jurys featured in James Joyce's *Ulysses*, the new hotel was called after Leopold Bloom, one of the main characters. In recent years, the whole exterior has been painted by the designer James Earley in a striking and novel way, featuring the main characters from *Ulysses*. This kaleidoscope of vibrant colour is a most unusual, yet attractive, addition to Temple Bar. The Vat House pub, on the ground floor, with its decorative exterior (and interior), also adds to the bohemian atmosphere.

Stockbrokers and solicitors had offices on this street in the 1860s. There were also other occupations, including jewellers, bootmakers, tailors, gilders and pictureframe makers, printers, robe makers, booksellers, and printers. In No. 3, Salmon, Rice & Co. were plaster of Paris and Roman cement manufacturers, and in No. 30, Julius Sandheim, Chief Rabbi of the Hebrew Congregation, had his residence. The Irish Bloodstock Agency operated from No. 7 in the 1940s. No. 17 was a down quilt manufacturer called Pownall & Hamson and a hairdresser, Edward Finn in No. 22.

Window of a shopfront
on Anglesea Street.
(Courtesy of Psyberartist,
Wikimedia Commons)

FLEET STREET AND THE DIFFERENT POWERS

Fleet Street (along with the street called Temple Bar and Essex Street East) once formed the southern boundary of the River Liffey before the new residents started reclaiming the land in the early seventeenth century and developing the area. The name probably derives from the old English word '*fleot*', meaning creek or inlet. Another possible interpretation of the name is that it refers to fleets of ships coming up the river to moor here. It was called Fleet Street towards the end of the seventeenth century and, like its English counterpart, in later years became a favourite meeting spot for media and literary types.[16]

The Irish Times was published on the corner of D'Olier Street and the eastern end of Fleet Street until 2006. Westmoreland Street, laid out in 1799, separated the D'Olier end of Fleet Street from the main part in Temple Bar. In the nineteenth century, it was the location for many Dublin-based foreign officials who had their offices there.

One of the main buildings on Fleet Street from the late nineteenth and for most of the twentieth century was the redbrick building that housed the Electric Light Company of Dublin Corporation, which had been a power station in the late nineteenth century. The famous Dublin ironworks company, Hammond Lane Foundry, was involved in its construction and it opened in 1892. Electric street lighting followed and seventy-eight lamp posts were installed from Grafton Street to O'Connell Street. The famous Shelbourne and Metropole hotels were among the first businesses in Dublin to be connected to the huge dynamos in Fleet Street. Business boomed and eventually the power station moved to Ringsend and the Pigeon House Fort. Fleet Street continued to be used as a central distribution network. Further developments followed the establishment of the Electricity Supply Board (ESB) in 1927, including the construction of a control centre across the road on Bedford Row. This corner building is an architectural gem as it is one of the few examples in Ireland of Egyptian art deco.

The ESB remained in Fleet Street until the late twentieth century, operating a bill payments office and a showroom for electrical goods from the late 1950s until the end of the twentieth century.

One famous resident of Fleet Street was Isaac Weld (1774–1856), an Irish topographical writer, explorer and artist. He was a member of the Royal Dublin Society. His name stems from his great-grandfather's close friendship with Sir Isaac Newton; both his grandfather and father were also named Isaac.[17]

DELIA, THE DOLPHIN AND THE LAUNDRY STRIKE

The Dublin Lockout of 1913 was perhaps the first significant event in Ireland in workers' struggle for the right to join a trade union, union recognition, and improved working conditions and pay. The Irish Women Workers' Union was on the front lines in the battle over all these issues, and many more, and courageously fought despite adverse circumstances, with many union members being sacked because of their activities on behalf of their fellow workers.

The headquarters of the Irish Women Workers' Union (IWWU) was located at 48 Fleet Street for many years and this union achieved some notable successes for Irish workers in the first half of the twentieth century. The union was established at a public meeting held on 5 September 1911 in the old Antient Concert Hall on Great Brunswick (later the Academy Cinema on what is now called Pearse Street). For many years from the time of its foundation, it had its headquarters at Fleet Street. Jim Larkin became the union's first president and his sister, Delia, was its first secretary. Among those to address the first meeting was Constance Markievicz, who said that the union would not only give women a greater voice in the workplace but would also help to win them the vote and improve their status in society. Within weeks, the new organisation, which had effectively started out as a semi-autonomous branch of the Irish Transport and General Workers Union, was involved in a successful dispute over pay with Jacob's, then the largest employer of women in Dublin, employing over 3,000 at its site on Bishop Street (now DIT). Rosie Hackett was one of the leaders in that dispute.[18]

THE DOLPHIN AND THE SWASTIKA

In 1945, the IWWU's members won the historic 'Laundry Strike' and earned a second week's annual holidays for all Irish workers. The strike began with many of Dublin's most famous hotels – the Hibernian, the Shelbourne and the Dolphin in Temple Bar – among those most affected. Hospital laundries were exempted from the action. Affluent areas served by the Dartry Laundry, the Kelso Laundry in Rathmines and the Swastika Laundry in Harold's Cross (which had the swastika as its logo on laundry vans) were particularly affected. One disgruntled resident was overheard bemoaning 'those obstreperous lassies'. Copies of a song, to be sung to the tune of the popular wartime song 'Lilli Marlene' were printed and sold by members and supporters to bring in much-needed cash to support the strike.[19]

Today, another radical organisation, also fighting for human rights, is located in the former premises of the trade union. Amnesty International Ireland has its Dublin headquarters in the building, now called Seán MacBride House after one of the organisation's founders (it was founded in 1961). Seán MacBride (1904–1988) was also the organisation's International Chairman. He was the son of Major John MacBride and Maud Gonne. His father was executed after the 1916 Rising. An Irish government minister, a prominent international politician and a former chief of staff of the IRA, Seán MacBride received the Nobel Peace Prize in 1974 for his tireless fight for human rights.

THE PALACE BAR – AMBIENCE AND TRADITION

Of the many pubs in the Temple Bar area, there is one establishment that is one of best-preserved pubs in Dublin. There is disagreement about the exact date on which the Palace Bar on Fleet Street was established: some say 1823 and others 1848. However, before it assumed the Palace name, it was Murray's Grocers, Wine, Tea and Spirit Merchants. It was also owned by a James Hall and, before that, a John Sandford. The consensus is that there has been a pub on this site for nearly 200 years. The Palace Bar is universally acclaimed as one of the few original Victorian pubs in Dublin. It is a priceless

Delia Larkin, of the Irish Women's Workers Union, had a long-time base at 48 Fleet Street. Jim Larkin became the union's first president with his sister, Delia, its first secretary. (Courtesy of IWWU)

jewel of the nineteenth century as it affords one an idea of what pub design was like in Dublin at the time. The original interior has rich mahogany fittings, carvings and counter divides, ornate stained glass, bevelled mirrors, brass fixtures and high ceilings (with a vaulted, stained glass skylight). There is also the Palace Snug, close to the entrance, as was typical.[20] The pub has not been tainted or spoiled by the passage of time.

THE ICON WALK – ASTON PLACE AND PRICE'S LANE

Linking Fleet Street to Aston Quay, Aston Place was originally called Lee's Lane. It was laid down around the same time as Aston Quay and it was renamed Aston Place in 1885 after the eighteenth-century Dublin merchant Henry Aston. John Ward, the famous violin maker of the mid-eighteenth century, lived here. As was the case in much of the Temple Bar area, it was a centre for bookshops and the well-known printers of the twentieth century, Three Candles Print, was located on the narrow street. Another narrow street leading to the quays is Price's Lane.

Today, there is what is called 'The Icon Walk' linking these back lanes and streets between Fleet Street and the quays (Aston Place, Bedford Lane and Price's Lane). A challenging and energising concept, this 'Love the Lanes' project has

The Palace Bar in Fleet Street, est. 1823. (Courtesy Mark Megs, Flickr)

done much not only to change the character of the lanes by brightening and decorating the walls of these forgotten cobbled alleyways, but in so doing it also tells the story of Ireland through icons of Irish history and culture. It was created by the Icon Factory, an artists' co-operative based at Aston Place.[21]

PARLIAMENT ROW AND THE TURNSTILE

Across from the Palace Bar is Parliament Row, named because of its proximity to the former Parliament House. The street was originally called Turnstile Alley and connected Foster Place to Fleet Street. It was laid down in the mid-seventeenth century and the name was changed in 1775 to reflect that it was adjacent to the new Irish parliament building on College Green. It was widened considerably and renamed Foster Place after John Foster (1740–1828), the last Speaker of the Irish House of Commons. For hundreds of years, it was possible for Dubliners

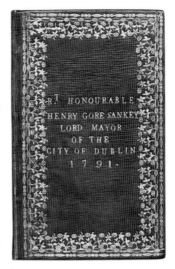

1791 book cover for the Lord Mayor of Dublin. This would have been typical of the standard of book covers produced in Temple Bar in the eighteenth century. McKenzie's at the College Arms on Dame Street was renowned, as was John Archer on Crampton Court. (Courtesy of Dublin Forums)

to cross from College Green to Fleet Street via Turnstile Lane and Alley and come out on Fleet Street near Lee's Lane (near Aston Place). When the Bank of Ireland, which had bought Parliament House in 1803, built its bank armoury, it restricted proper use of the link. A narrow alleyway still linked the two but this was finally closed off in 1928. The 'Irishman's Diary' column in *The Irish Times* in 1928 noted that 'the closing of the passage at the "back of the bank" ... is causing much inconvenience to the many busy people who found it a short cut'.[22]

This part of our sojourn through Temple Bar brings us to the eastern boundary of the district, which is marked by Westmoreland Street, called after the tenth Earl of Westmoreland, Lord Lieutenant for Ireland from 1790 to 1794.

14

FROM THE ROYAL MILE TO THE BOOKEND – PERIMETER PLACES

We will now circle Temple Bar, looking at the perimeter streets of this unique area as we move from Dame Street to Westmoreland Street, around to the quays, finishing at the Bookend Building near Fishamble Street.

The interesting and undulating Dame Street, with its variety of buildings and house types, is one of the boundaries of Temple Bar. The street takes its name from the medieval church of St Mary del Dam, built in around 1385. The church was demolished in the seventeenth century. The location was at a crossing point of the River Poddle, where there was a dam (hence the name of the church). Today, the Poddle still winds its way to the Liffey, but now it does so under the Olympia Theatre.

Sir Maurice Eustace, Lord Chancellor of Ireland from 1606 to 1665, built his townhouse, Damask, on part of the site that stretched to Eustace Street. Richard Boyle, Earl of Cork built on another part of the site. The street was originally a path linking the various monastic settlements in the area. The opening of Trinity College in 1592 spurred developers to build on the link, which commenced at one of the defensive gates of the old city, Dame's Gate, near the present-day City Hall. Further improvements were carried out by the Wide Streets Commission. The WSC regarded the street as the most important route in the city, linking as it did Dublin Castle and the Irish Parliament House, as well as being at the heart of commercial Dublin. Over a period of three decades from the mid-1760s, the old buildings were demolished and replaced with a classical streetscape. Dame Street eventually became a street filled with some of Dublin's most impressive residential dwellings – a Royal Mile. In the following century, building on its long-standing reputation as the heart of commercial Dublin, even more splendid Victorian mercantile architecture became (and remains) a feature of the street.[1]

A FULL CAST WITH KITTY CLIVE

James Malton's prints of Dublin in the late eighteenth century show Dame Street lined with impressive houses and even more impressive public and commercial buildings. Such was the importance of Dame Street that the Earl of Kildare had a mansion there in the early part of the eighteenth century. It is clear from Malton's images that the vista from the Royal Exchange to Trinity College was astounding: it was lined with fine houses, businesses and buildings all the way to the wide-open green area that fronted the college. It is still possible to appreciate a version of this vista by standing outside City Hall. The street was soon filled with mansions and their gardens stretching to the River Liffey, particularly after the building of Chichester House on College Green to house the Irish Parliament which was used it from 1673 onwards. The outlines of the gardens of these mansions, running north-south, would greatly influence subsequent development in the seventeenth and eighteenth centuries and even up to the present day.

John Keogh, a champion of the United Irishmen movement and Catholic Emancipation, lived at No. 17 Dame Street from 1772 to 1788. Other prominent residents included Dr Bartholomew Mosse, founder of the Coombe Lying-in Hospital in the Liberties. John Rocque, the eminent cartographer, lived on the street from the time of his arrival in Dublin because of the number of booksellers, printers and publishers in the area. He lodged for a time at the Golden Hart opposite Crane Lane. George Faulkner's *Dublin Gazette* announced his arrival in the city. Rocque went on to draw up some extraordinarily detailed maps of Dublin in the ensuing years, maps that are still referred to today. James Petrie, artist and father of the historian George Petrie, lived on the street. The eminent Dr William Drennan, physician, poet and political radical with the Society of the United Irishmen, also lived on Dame Street.

Kitty Clive, the famous English actress and soprano, lived on the street for a while around 1763. Her father was Irish and had moved to London after a stint in the French army. It was there, at the age of 17, that she was discovered by the theatre community when she was overheard singing while cleaning the front steps of a home near a tavern that actors and playwrights regularly patronised.[2]

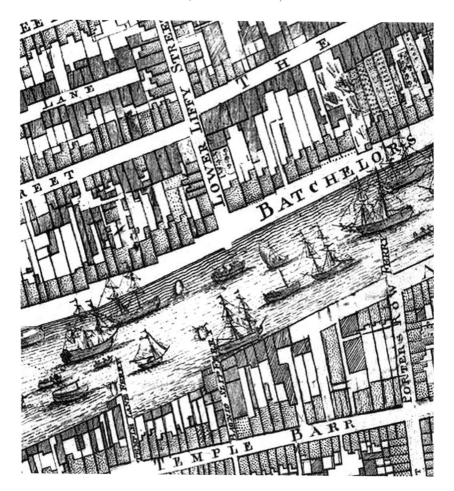

Rocque's Map of River Liffey and Temple Barr showing Bagnio Slip, 1756. (Courtesy of UCD/Harvard)

THE DUBLIN SOCIETY

The Dublin Society, later the Royal Dublin Society (RDS), has its origins in Dame Street, at Shaw's Court (occupied now by the Central Bank Plaza). Its forbear, also called the Dublin Society, had originally met in the 1680s in a coffee house on Cork Hill before moving to the Crow's Nest on Crow Street.

The society reincarnated in 1731 in the Philosophical Rooms in Trinity College nearby, before moving to Dame Street. The premises of the society consisted of a coach house, a stable, a large warehouse and a garden acquired in 1756 by Samuel Moyneux Madden and Thomas Prior (Thomas Prior House in Ballsbridge is named after him). The aim of the society's founders was to improve Ireland's economic conditions by promoting the development of agriculture, arts, industry and science. It was the society's first secretary, William Maple, an apothecary from Fishamble Street, who found the premises for the society. One of its most prominent members was the subsequently renowned philosopher George Berkeley. The Dublin Society remained at Shaw's Court for ten years before moving to Grafton Street.[3]

The society did much to promote Irish industry in the face of English-imposed restrictions, particularly in the woollen, silk and linen industries. It did this by giving grants and successfully pressuring the government to relax restrictions on the exports of woollens from Ireland. The society opened a woollen warehouse in Castle Street. It also encouraged the silk industry, in part by opening the silk warehouse on Parliament Street in 1765. Both these initiatives proved very successful and did much to stimulate the industry. Likewise with linen and cotton, the society was instrumental in promoting these industries. The society's influence was crucial in these industries' ability to employ some 15,000 weavers towards the end of the century.[4]

After the society left the building, it became auction rooms and then a small private theatre in 1786. The first play was deferred, however, as the Irish Parliament was sitting a short stroll away in Parliament House, College Green. It was deferred because many of the performers were members of the House of Commons and they were required at this time. Shaw's Court itself was subsequently demolished to make way for the construction of the Commercial Buildings.

BOULEVARD OF FINE SHOPS AND BUSINESSES

Coinciding with the widening of Dame Street, a building boom in Dublin in the latter decades of the eighteenth century resulted in streets and squares with fine Georgian houses in the city as a whole. Interior design flourished as houses were embellished with ornate plasterwork ceilings, painted wallpaper, beautiful furniture of polished wood and gilt, paintings and sculptures, print collections, and libraries filled with books in exquisite bindings. The burgeoning of the wealthy classes in eighteenth-century Dublin created a market for luxury goods such as watches, fine china, gold jewellery and more. The new, prosperous, Anglo-Irish residents needed shops, so Dublin in the late eighteenth century became a shopper's paradise. Dame Street was *the* place to shop. If one were to stroll along the fine boulevard in the 1780s and 1790s, one would pass beautiful shops full of the finest clothes and silk, linen and wool, lace, hats, perfumes, fine wines, music, prints, jewellers, bookshops, lottery offices, coffee houses, taverns and private clubs. In the streets and alleys off Dame Street, some of Ireland's best craftsmen, including silversmiths and goldsmiths, provided the best materials to meet the demands of the ascendancy. One of the most prestigious silversmiths of nineteenth-century Dublin, Waterhouse & Co., was based at No. 25 Dame Street. Today, the old Seiko watch sign over a building by the Olympia Theatre is a reminder of the prominence of jewellery shops on what was a major shopping street in the eighteenth century.[5]

THE LOTTERY AND LIPTON'S

During the lottery mania at the end of the eighteenth century, there were nearly as many 'Lottery Office' shops as there were booksellers, with names such as Royal Exchange Lottery Office, Old Lottery Office, Dublin Lottery Office and the Government State Lottery Office. A popular stationer was called the King's Arms and Two Bibles.

Another prominent business on Dame Street until the early twentieth century was Lipton's grocery establishment, a household name in Dublin until the 1970s (one of last branches was in Rathmines). This business occupied premises on the corner of Dame Street and Eustace Street, now

The Irish State Lottery in Fishamble Street from the *Hibernian Magazine*, June 1783.

known as Shamrock Chambers. Sir Thomas Lipton (1848–1931) was the owner of the business and was also the owner of some of the largest private yachts in the world. Lipton's tea was famous throughout the country and there was a sign on Dame Street over the shop (really an emporium) stating: 'Liptons, the largest tea and provision dealers in the world'. Lipton grew up in Glasgow, Scotland, but he had roots in County Fermanagh (his parents were forced to emigrate during the Famine). He believed in the power of advertising. He often boasted that one of the secrets of his successful empire of 300 grocery stores in Ireland and England and elsewhere was selling the best goods at the cheapest prices. There are reminders of this business beside the original entrance on Eustace Street, where decorative stucco panels, depicting bowls of fruit, are carved at each side of the doorway and windows.

FROM LUCKY COADYS TO A SHOOTING GALLERY

Other prominent businesses (and buildings) on the south side of Dame Street included the Pen Corner (1901), an elaborate curved shop front topped with an impressive ornate structure which also houses a clock, and Lucky Coady's, whose fine Victorian façade also has attractive curved window. This shop, built in 1869 at No. 39, originally housed an insurance company. It acquired its name in later years, after it was converted into a shop, because it sold many winning tickets for the hugely popular Irish Sweepstake.

Other prominent businesses that continued until the last quarter of the twentieth century included Burton's, Hely's (toys, printers and stationery; mentioned in James Joyce's *Ulysses*) and Callaghan's (horse-riding equipment) near the junction with South Great George's Street. Burton's Tailors was located on the street from 1929. The building has a most unusual sandstone façade and colouring and its blue-tiled roof is particularly remarkable. The word 'The Tailor of Taste' is still carved on the upper level. Callaghan's were in business from 1869. The only reminder of the business on the redbrick building with its limestone dressings is a Chancellor clock high up on a gable. There was a gun and rifle maker, Kavanagh's, operating from No. 12 Dame Street for most of the nineteenth century. There was a shooting gallery on the premises where customers could ensure they were satisfied with their purchase.[6]

VENETIAN PALACES

Very few of the early residential and older houses survived the widening of the street. It is possible that the buildings from the Olympia Theatre to Crow Street junction have an eighteenth-century background. The short terrace betwcen Temple Lane South and Crow Street survives from the late eighteenth century. Besides the many and varied businesses, Dame Street and College Green are dotted with the architecturally notable buildings of present and former banks and insurance companies. In the nineteenth and well into the twentieth century, Dame Street was filled with banking and insurance companies. Some of the oldest insurance companies, including the Sun (1710) and the Commercial Union (1696), were located here. The insurance companies were responsible for the city's fire brigade service and they only quenched fires in buildings that were insured. Today's Dublin Fire Brigade is a direct descendant of this service.[7]

There are a few impressive bank buildings that have survived, e.g. the 1824 Hibernian Bank (now occupied by H&M, with the French Renaissance carved detailing and wording of the bank's name still intact both inside and outside the building). The former National Bank's head office on College Green (No. 34), now occupied by Abercrombie & Fitch, dates from 1842. The style is reminiscent of the Renaissance palazzos preferred by Italian merchant banking families. To emphasise its patriotic leanings, the figure of Erin, sculpted by James Pearse (father of 1916 Rising leader, Pádraig Pearse) and Edmund Sharp in 1889, adorns the crest of the front elevation of the building. This is a typical Celtic Revival image. The inscription 'Eire go bragh' (anglicisation of an Irish phrase meaning 'Ireland forever') is below the figure representing Ireland, beside a harp, an Irish crown and a wolfhound. Another impressive former bank building is the brownstone on the same side, now occupied by a restaurant named The Bank. The exterior of the Ulster Bank is also noteworthy, though the architecture of the interior is mostly hidden by modern furnishings.

The AIB bank opposite the Olympia Theatre on the corner with Palace Street, built in the early 1870s, was modelled on the architecture of Venetian palaces. This theatre has the letters 'MB' and '1873' carved on its exterior limestone elevation, signifying the Munster Bank, which formerly occupied the premises. This is a splendid bank, with a high ceiling and much ornamentation in the interior of the building itself (called the Great Hall). Thomas Newenham Deane's design for the building was influenced by the Venetian Gothic style. Inside, there is an unusual and beautiful clock with Arabic numbers on an interior wall. The corner entrance to the bank is striking, all the more so when one sees the two-storey bank chamber inside, with its elaborately decorated plasterwork. The floors are laid with Connemara and Italian marble inlaid with designs. According to historian Peter Pearson, Dame Street 'has some of the best Victorian carving to be found anywhere in the city' and the bank buildings are proof of this.[8]

The striking building at Nos 46 and 47, on the corner of Dame Street and Fownes Street Upper, is the former Crown Life Insurance building. It later housed the Hibernian Insurance Company and subsequently a hotel. It is one of Dublin's finest Victorian buildings and a landmark in Temple Bar. It was built in an Italianate/Venetian palace style in 1869, with the interior as richly decorated as the exterior. A stone building, it has much carved detail, including balconies, cornices, windows, chimneys and roof. The lower arched windows on the Fownes Street side are stepped to complement the parallel staircase on the inside.[9]

IN THE SHADOW OF A BANK

In direct contrast in style to this former insurance building is the Central Bank of Ireland building on Dame Street. It is the most prominent example of modern

Building the new Central Bank on Dame Street in late 1970s. (Courtesy of Dublin Forums)

architecture in the area. It was designed by Sam Stephenson. Work started on the controversial building in 1971 and was completed six years later. It houses 1,600 staff. The site on which it was constructed was blitzed of its historic buildings and streets, with the resultant structure causing much debate as to whether the building is sympathetic to its location. Some would argue that it is too different to its surroundings and thus not in keeping with the character of Temple Bar. Supporters of the modern building argued that it is unique, being one of only a handful of buildings in the world to use suspensions held from its centre. During construction, each floor was built at ground level and then hoisted up with all the fittings and services already in place. Internally, the offices are lit by floor-to-ceiling glazing, which give the buildings its bold, striped appearance.[10]

The controversy surrounding the erection of this bunker-like building culminated in the discovery that the height conditions in the granted planning permission had been breached, so the top of the building had to be left incomplete and an iron girder-like structure left exposed on the roof.

THE INFLUENCE OF BERKELEY OR BACCHUS?

The Central Bank was again embroiled in controversy, this time in the first decade of the twenty-first century, for its failure to anticipate the collapse of the Irish economy in 2008. It was established by the Central Bank Act of 1942, which replaced the Currency Commission. It acts as a bank for the government and for other smaller banks. The bank is supposed to be the regulating body for

The Central Bank of Ireland on Dame Street. (Courtesy of Doyler79, Wikimedia Commons)

Central Bank of Ireland on Dame Street. (Courtesy of DubhEire, Wikimedia Commons)

the Irish financial sector; however, it was severely criticised from 2008 onwards and was accused of 'light touch regulation', which was a factor in the collapse of the Celtic Tiger and the subsequent bank bailout.

The Fianna Fáil-led government had to introduce a blanket bank guarantee to safeguard not only people's deposits but to prevent the bankruptcy of the country as it experienced one of the world's most destructive property crashes.[11]

In 2015, the bank decided that the building on Dame Street was no longer fit for purpose and opted to move into a new building on Dublin's quays – the former unfinished Anglo-Irish Bank Headquarters.

In the plaza in front of the building stands '*Crann an Oir*' (Tree of Gold), sculpted by Éamonn O'Doherty.

THE MARINER'S PLAQUE AND THE OUZEL

Beyond the Central Bank Plaza, there is a plaque on the wall next to the Commercial Buildings. This is the Ouzel Galley Society Plaque (or the Mariner's

Plaque) and it has a nautical theme. The name derived from a ship called the *Ouzel* that, under the command of Captain Eoghan Masey, disappeared at sea in 1695 and turned up five years later. Having been presumed lost at sea, insurance money had been paid out to the owners, Messrs Ferris, Twigg and Cash, after much dispute and debate. When the *Ouzel* sailed into Dublin port in 1700, the initial jubilation turned to consternation. The galley had been captured by pirates in the Mediterranean, under the leadership of an Algerine, but after a few years the captain and crew, with the pirates' loot and the original cargo, managed to escape.

The question then arose: who owned the ship and its contents? The owners had been compensated, so they could not claim it, and the insurers had contracted to insure it, so they had no claim on it either. It was finally agreed by all parties, including Dublin Corporation, that the money would be used for charitable purposes, including supporting poverty-stricken merchants in Dublin who had fallen on hard times. The saga motivated the Dublin merchants to form a society for the future arbitration of commercial disputes.[12]

The Ouzel Galley Society, founded in 1705, had its first meetings in the Rose and Bottle Tavern on Dame Street and the Eagle Tavern on Eustace Street until it found a permanent home in the Commercial Buildings. Its objectives were to promote the principles of arbitration in commercial disputes. It was decided that the new society would deal with ship insurance and arbitration. The organisation later evolved into the Dublin Chamber of Commerce (1783), although the society itself existed until 1888.

William Cope, a fleece merchant and prominent Dublin businessman, was a very important person on the board of both bodies. He achieved notoriety in 1798 for passing on critical information to an informer in the pay of Dublin Castle, an act that led to the suppression of the United Irishmen rebellion. Cope was awarded a pension by the government in 1798 for having persuaded the notorious Thomas Reynolds (a Catholic silk merchant and a brother-in-law of Wolfe Tone) to inform on the United Irishmen. Cope was deleted from the Royal Dublin's Society's membership list in 1820.[13]

'A most respectable meeting of merchants' was how the members described themselves in a journal article in 1820. United Irishmen Napper Tandy and Oliver Bond were members of the early Chamber of Commerce. Arthur Guinness, son of the founder of the famous brewery, was president for almost 20 years. The Chamber's lawyer at one time was Daniel O'Connell. William Martin Murphy, that stalwart businessman, was president during the 1913 Dublin Lockout.

THE COMMERCIAL BUILDINGS

The Ouzel Galley Society Plaque is the only remaining element of the original Commercial Buildings, a three-storey granite building by Edward Parke, completed in 1799 (the plaque is dated with the same year). The Commercial Buildings stood on the site now occupied by Central Bank at the Crown Alley side.

In 1837, the Commercial Buildings were described glowingly by Samuel Lewis in his *Topographical Dictionary*:

> The Commercial Buildings form a plain but substantial square of three stories, constituting the sides of a small quadrangle and wholly unornamented except in the principal front to College-green, which is of hewn stone and has a central entrance supported by Ionic columns. On the left of the grand entrance-hall and staircase is a news-room, 60 feet long and 28 feet wide, occupied by the members of the Chamber of Commerce (established to protect and improve the commerce of the city); and on the right is a handsome coffee-room, connected with that part of the building which is used as an hotel. The north side of the quadrangle is occupied by the Stock Exchange and merchants' offices, and on the east and west are offices for the brokers.[14]

One of the controversies that arose in relation to building the Central Bank was the threat to the Commercial Buildings. After much debate, in 1973 it was taken down (not demolished), with each stone numbered systematically to allow for reconstruction. However, despite the painstaking work, a replica was built instead. The plaque was kept, but the rest of the building is new. Moreover, it was rotated 90 degrees and moved off its former site to the edge of the Central Bank Plaza.

The building beside the wall bearing the Mariner's Plaque is the ornate former Patriotic Assurance Company building, which was constructed in late Victorian times. This is a further reminder of the Victorian grandeur in Dublin.

There are also buildings dating from the late eighteenth century, which were most likely residential properties. No. 38 dates from 1790 and was built on one of the original plots of Dame Street from the time when it was widened by the Wide Streets Commissioners. It also retains its original ground-floor façade. Many of the widened streets would have originally had similarly designed shopfronts at street level.[15]

THE OAK AND THE VIKING

Over the centuries, there were many taverns on Dame Street, including the Duke's Head, which was frequented by members of the ascendancy. There are some pubs from the nineteenth century still in business. At the corner of Dame Street and Crane Lane, The Oak bar, established in 1860, boasts a fascinating history. *Thom's Directory* for 1862 shows that the occupant of 81 Dame Street was P.J. Burke, a grocer and a home and foreign spirit dealer. In the early 1920s, the bar was bought by the Humphry family. To this day, you can see the original tiled-floor sign at the entrance reminding customers of its old name. After a redecoration in 1946, the name of the pub was changed to The Oak because the oak panelled interior of the bar was made with wood salvaged from the RMS *Mauretania*, the sister ship of the RMS *Lusitania*. The ship was withdrawn from service in 1934 and its furnishings and fittings were put up for auction. In the 1990s, an extension was built on the roof. It was nicknamed 'the yoke on the oak'.

The former Viking Inn, at 75 Dame Street, predated the George as Dublin's first 'exclusively gay bar'. Situated beside the Olympia Theatre, the pub was renamed Brogan's Bar in the early 1990s. Before it was a pub, the premises operated as a surgery for a 'mechanical dentist' by the name of John Egar in the 1850s. Towards the end of the nineteenth century, it was remodelled as a public house. Various names over the years have included O'Brien Bros. (1920s), Kerins (1940s), McCabe's (1950s), Leonards (1960s/1970s), the Crampton Court (late 1970s), The Viking Inn (1979–1987), The City Hall Inn (1989–1993) and finally Brogan's Bar (1993 to the present).

The entrance to the Oak pub on Dame Street. The Humphrys were former owners. (Courtesy of Humphry Family)

NICOS AND FRÈRES JACQUES

Among the many restaurants on Dame Street, two stand out – Nicos at 53 and Les Frères Jacques at 74 Dame Street (two doors from the Olympia Theatre), which is run by the Caillabet family. Both have been on the street for approximately thirty years. The latter changed its name in recent years and is now named 'Jules', after the son of one of the original founders, who now runs the restaurant. Shortly after opening, it was recognised as one of Dublin's finest restaurants and became synonymous with authentic, high-quality French cuisine. Nicos has been in business slightly longer and also has an excellent reputation, specialising in Italian food.

The building beside Nicos at No. 52 is an impressive structure with squared bay windows on the first and second floors. This short terrace of four houses survives from the Wide Streets Commissioners activity on the street in the late eighteenth century. Nearby, there are more ornate buildings on the Dame Street/ Temple Lane South corner from No. 51 to No. 56, particularly when one takes in the whole building, from the first floor to the rooftops. Near the Olympia Theatre, Nos 68 and 69 were at one time one building, but separated and having finely decorated twin doors with carved heads as a feature.

Douglas Hyde (in back of the car holding a top hat), leaving Dublin Castle in 1938 with a cavalry escort following his inauguration as Ireland's first President. The car has just turned out onto Cork Hill/Dame Street at this point. (Courtesy of NLI Commons Collection)

Every building on Dame Street is different to its neighbour in so many ways. The architectural variations are noticeable and create an unusual but pleasing effect. The undulating street seems to sweep, swirl, and swoop from Cork Hill to Trinity College.

FROM HOGGEN TO COLLEGE

College Green is Dublin's great architectural treasure. It is often regarded as the real centre of Dublin because of its splendour and magnificence and its panoply of important buildings. Today, the area it is a major public space of outstanding significance, an historic area very much part of the city's showpiece. However, it is only when it is free of traffic at certain times of the day that one can really appreciate the beauty and grandeur of the space and the surrounding historic buildings, which have evolved as centres of business, education and politics over the centuries.

College Green, formerly Hoggen Green, takes its name from a green field that covered a large area in front of Trinity College Dublin (1592), which stretched halfway up the present Dame Street. 'Hoggen' comes from a Norse word meaning 'mound'. A medieval order of nuns, St Mary de Hogge, was located on the site for hundreds of years. There was also a hospital on the green that later became a court and then converted into Chichester House when it was bought by the government in the late 1680s to be used a meeting place for the Irish parliament. It was subsequently demolished and the new Parliament House (now Bank of Ireland) was built. Daly's Club occupied a nearby premises on College Green. By the end of the nineteenth century, the area was the banking and insurance centre of Dublin.

With the extension of Temple Bar eastwards towards the college, the Dame Street/Foster Place/College Green nexus was the location for the houses of the ascendancy, which surrounded a statue of King William of Orange. The statue was located in the middle of College Green (opposite Foster Place) from 1701 until 1929, when it was blown up (not for the first time). It was built by the Orange ascendancy in Dublin to commemorate his famous Battle of the Boyne victory in 1690. There had been many attempts over the years to destroy it. On one occasion, a local gunsmith, Walter Cox, attempted to file off the king's head, but had not anticipated that the figure was made of brass and was forced to abandon his task, leaving marks on the neck. On another occasion, it was covered in a combination of tar and grease, which proved difficult to remove. There were many attempts, some

College Green late 1920s/early 1930s. (Courtesy of NLI (Commons) collection)

successful (1836), to blow it up, but it was always reinstated until its final destruction in 1929.[16]

In the twentieth century, the Thomas Davis memorial was built near the site. Not too far from the memorial was the first office of *The Nation* newspaper of the Young Ireland movement, which grew out of Daniel O'Connell's Repeal Association (i.e repeal of the Act of Union). The newspaper was located at No. 12 Trinity Street in the early 1840s before it moved to D'Olier Street.

Another statue dominating this part of College Green is of the great orator and parliamentarian Henry Grattan. It is near the former Irish Parliament building, where the powerful orator saw his dream of an independent Irish parliament (often known as 'Grattan's Parliament') come to fruition in 1782. It faces Trinity College.

THE OLD JURYS HOTEL

Jurys Commercial & Family Hotel, at the junction of Dame Street/Anglesea Street and College Green, was also part of old Dublin. Known simply as Jurys Hotel, it started as a commercial lodgings business at No. 7 College Green in 1839 and over the years developed a reputation as one of Dublin's premier

The old
Jurys Hotel,
Dame Street.
(Courtesy of
Archiseek)

hotels. The name came from William Jury, a former commercial traveller who set up an inn that became so successful that by the middle of the century it had become known as the Commercial and Family Hotel. In 1866, Jurys Hotel became part of the partnership responsible for building the city's Shelbourne Hotel. After that hotel opened, Jury sold his business to a cousin, Henry James Jury, who further expanded the College Green hotel site. The renowned Victorian architect E.H. Carson was responsible for unifying the various Wide Streets Commissioners buildings with stucco additions, including Jurys Hotel. In 1859, he designed the new coffee and smoking rooms.

The hotel was one of several Temple Bar locations featured in James Joyce's *Ulysses*, hence the name of the hotel behind it, Blooms, which was originally part of the Jurys Hotel premises. The British forces requisitioned the hotel in 1918 during Ireland's War of Independence.

In 1924, after the hotel had been vacant for some two years, a group of Dublin businessmen bought the property and reopened it. In 1963, the company added a new eighty-room wing to the original College Green property. However, in the 1970s it closed down and was demolished. The site is now an office building, but the name lives on in other Jurys hotels in Dublin. Despite the closure of the main part of the hotel, the extension was reopened as Bloom's Hotel on Anglesea Street.[17]

Another prominent building that survived is the former Daly's Club, between Anglesea Street and Foster Place. The building has retained its granite façade. The buildings at each side of Daly's are later replacements of earlier structures. Other impressive Victorian buildings that grace this street include the Ulster Bank, the Northern Bank, Allied Irish Bank and the Hibernian Bank buildings, the latter three now occupied by different businesses (see above). These buildings are a fine legacy of mercantile architecture.[18]

FOSTER PLACE – BANKS AND WAXWORKS

Foster Place is one of Temple Bar's, and Dublin's, most unappreciated enclaves, hidden away behind an array of mature broadleaf trees with the added distraction of a cluttering taxi rank. For hundreds of years, it was possible for Dubliners to cross from College Green to Fleet Street via Turnstile Lane and Alley. In the 1780s, Turnstile Lane was widened considerably and renamed Foster Place after John Foster, last Speaker of the Irish House of Commons (and Wide Streets Commissioner) before the Irish parliament was abolished in 1800. He was an outspoken critic of the Act of Union. Turnstile

The Armoury Building on Foster Place. (Courtesy of DubhEire, Wikimedia Commons)

Alley was renamed Parliament Row in around 1775. A narrow alleyway still linked College Green to Fleet Street until 1928, when it was closed due to the construction of the Bank of Ireland armoury.

Today, Foster Place is partially hidden among the many trees, with the imposing Bank of Ireland on one side. There was once a row of fashionable houses in this cul-de-sac, but over time it gradually became commercial. Two of the residential dwellings survive at the end of the leafy cul-de-sac. The Van Homrigh family lived in one of the fashionable residences in the early eighteenth century. Bartholomew Van Homrigh was a Dutch Huguenot who, in 1697, became Lord Mayor of Dublin.

There was a bank located on Foster Place from the late 1790s, with various names, including Sir Thomas Leighton's Bank, Shaws, the Royal Bank and Allied Irish Bank (AIB). Allied Irish Bank was an amalgamation of the Royal Bank, the Muster and Leinster Bank, and the Provincial Bank of Ireland. The entrance to the former AIB, an imposing Portland stone building in classical design, was completed in 1868 and incorporates part of one of the original houses. Trinity College Dublin now uses the building for lectures. The interior remains intact and it is regarded as one of the finest Victorian banking halls in Dublin. The ornate interior, with its fine plasterwork, its twelve ornamented pillars supporting the lantern roof, the old cash desk and the two marble fireplaces, is still intact. There is also a wall clock that is 3ft in diameter, with a frame of plasterwork foliage.[19]

At the northern end of Foster Place, the former guard house of the Bank of Ireland, which was later the armoury, is now occupied by the Waxworks Museum. The entrance is striking as it has large doors above which there are sculpted figures of arms and armour, created by the celebrated sculptor Joseph Kirk. The building was used for the Currency Commission and later the Central Bank before the latter's move to the new Central Bank building on Dame Street in 1978.

FROM IRISH PARLIAMENT HOUSE TO BANK OF IRELAND

Perhaps the most striking of the buildings in the Temple Bar area is the Bank of Ireland on College Green, which contained the Irish Houses of Parliament until 1800. According to local historian Pat Liddy, 'Parliament House [building commenced in 1728] was the single most important architectural achievement in the first half of the eighteenth century, not only in Temple Bar but in the whole country'.[20]

US President Barack Obama and First Lady Michelle Obama outside Bank of Ireland before their speech at College Green during their visit to Ireland, May 2011. (Courtesy of Pete Souza, Executive Office of the President of the United States)

The wealthy and privileged Protestant ascendancy was determined to build to reflect the prosperity of Dublin and their increased confidence as the colonial overlords.

The Irish Houses of Parliament was the world's first purpose-built, two-chamber parliament house and it was the seat of the House of Lords and the House of Commons. It served as the Irish parliament of the Kingdom of Ireland for most of the eighteenth century until the Act of Union of 1800 abolished that parliament, corruptly. Ireland then became part of the United Kingdom of Great Britain and Ireland, a relationship that lasted until 1921.

DUBLIN'S NOBLEST STRUCTURE

In the seventeenth century, before the construction of the building, the parliament of the Kingdom of Ireland met in Chichester House, a large town house on the same site that was previously owned by George Carew, President of Munster and Treasurer of Ireland. It was later given the name Chichester House after a subsequent owner, Sir Arthur Chichester, who leased the house to the Irish parliament. The Members of Parliament were once described by the Speaker, Sir Audley Mervyn, in the late seventeenth century as 'a choice collection of Protestant fruit'.[21] The house itself had been built on the site of a convent forfeited during the Reformation of the mid-1500s. Chichester House was of sufficient importance for the Law Courts to temporarily reside there in the early 1600s. The legal documentation facilitating the Plantation of Ulster was signed in this house on 16 November 1612.

By the end of the seventeenth century Chichester House was regarded as no longer fit for purpose to house the Irish Houses of Parliament. The foundation stone of the replacement building was laid in 1729, during the administration of Lord Carteret, and the new building was constructed under the supervision of Sir Edward Lovett Pearce, engineer and Surveyor General, between 1729 and 1739. Later, the renowned architect of the present custom house, James Gandon, had a significant input. The original building designed by Pearce is only part of the existing structure consisting of the central section, with its huge colonnades overlooking College Green. Pearce's design for the new Irish Houses of Parliament was revolutionary. The building was effectively semi-circular in shape, occupying nearly 6,000m² (1.5 acres) of ground. Unlike Chichester House, which was set far back from College Green, the new building was to open directly on to the green. The principal entrance consisted of a colonnade of Ionic columns extending around three sides of the entrance quadrangle, forming the letter 'E'. Three statues, representing Hibernia (the Latin name for Ireland), Fidelity and Commerce, stood above the portico. Over the main entrance, the royal coat of arms was cut in stone. The building has no windows on its façade because of the window tax that existed during the building phase in the 1730s. Consequently, the architects did include windows, but had them covered in so that it would be easier to glaze the windows at some future date.[22]

This truly beautiful and magnificent building was described by the famous artist and illustrator James Malton as 'The noblest structure Dublin has to boast; that it is no hyperbole to advance, that this edifice in the entire, is the grandest, most convenient, and most extensive of the kind in Europe.

It derives all its beauty from a simple impulse of fine art; and is one of the few instances of form only, expressing true symmetry.'[23]

After the 1800 Act of Union put an end to the Irish Houses of Parliament, the building was bought by the Bank of Ireland in 1803 on the condition that it was never again to be used as a parliamentary building and that the structure inside be altered to ensure this.

Despite the conversion work that was effected, it is still possible to see the old House of Lords chamber, with its impressive, barrel-vaulted chamber and a large, coffered, lantern-lit ceiling. There is Irish oak woodwork, including the carved oak mantelpiece, a mahogany longcase parliament clock and the splendid 1788 Dublin crystal chandelier made of 1,223 pieces. Two huge, original wall tapestries depicting the Battle of the Boyne and the Siege of Derry (made by John van Beaver, the famous tapestry maker who lived on World's End Lane, which is now Foley Street). The main banking hall, the former House of Commons, is similarly impressive. Some of the most important legislation affecting the history of Ireland was enacted or rescinded in this building. Consequently, it remains Ireland's most architecturally significant and historic eighteenth-century public building.

WESTMORELAND STREET – BESHOFF, BEWLEY AND THE WALDORF

Following the curve of this building brings us to Westmoreland Street, which was laid down in the 1790s thanks to the Wide Streets Commissioners. Prior to that, there was a narrow alleyway here called Fleet Lane, which dated from the early 1700s. The plan was to link College Green to Sackville Street (O'Connell Street) via a new wide street and a new bridge, Carlisle Bridge. Two of the commissioners were Luke Gardiner Junior and John Beresford, who both had substantial property holdings on the north side of the River Liffey. It may be presumed that the work of the WSC was carried out with an awareness of their speculative endeavours on the north side of the River Liffey. The plan was to their advantage, as was the moving of the old custom house from Wellington Quay farther downstream to its present location. The street is named after John Fane, 10th Earl of Westmoreland, who was Lord Lieutenant of Ireland from 1789 to 1794.

The first building to catch one's attention upon entering Temple Bar from Westmoreland Street is the building on the corner of Fleet Street and Westmoreland Street (No. 7). Designed by G.C. Ashlin to resemble a French Renaissance corner pavilion, this striking building was the result of an architectural competition for offices for the Northern Fire and Life Assurance

The former EBS office on Westmoreland Street facing the Fleet Street entrance to Temple Bar. (Courtesy of Psyberartist, Wikimedia Commons)

View of Lafayette Building on Westmoreland Street from Aston Quay. (Courtesy of Psyberartist, Wikimedia Commons)

Company. The winning design was published in the *Building News* in 19 November 1886.

On the front elevation of the building next door there is an old, carved, stone sign that reads 'Fitzgerald's Wholesale Tea & Wine Merchants 1861–1931'. The short terrace of tall, ornate buildings are of different architectural styles, Italian and Gothic, a part of late Victorian Dublin. On the opposite side of Westmoreland Street, there are three outstanding buildings – the landmark Lafayette Building overlooking O'Connell Bridge (Lafayette were *the* photographers in Dublin for generations), the former Hyam's Building (later EBS) facing Temple Bar (Hyam's were men's outfitters and tailors) and the former AIB building (now the Westin Hotel). The Lafayette Building was originally designed for the London & Lancashire Insurance Company by the famous architect J.J. O'Callaghan (who also designed the Dolphin Hotel on Essex Street East). Both buildings have Gothic and Ruskin influences.

Thomas Moore's famous *Irish Melodies* (known as Moore's Melodies) was published at Power's music publishers at No. 4 Westmoreland Street. The business was located there from the late 1790s until the mid-1830s. Subsequently the premises was occupied by Marcus Moses, who had a pianoforte, harp and music warehouse. Other recent businesses near this entrance to Temple Bar included Beshoff's, the fish-and-chips family business operating in Dublin since 1913, and the equally famous Bewley's Café. Another long-established business is the Waldorf Barbershop, which has been operating there since 1919.

Rowan's Seed Merchants were located next door to the Bank of Ireland building. The family was involved in a long-running battle in the early 1970s over what the Rowans regarded as unfair banking practices. Their protest received widespread media coverage and public sympathy.

CARLISLE BRIDGE AND THE BALLAST OFFICE

There was no bridge spanning the River Liffey near the corner of Westmoreland Street and Aston Quay until 1798 when Carlisle (now O'Connell) Bridge was constructed. On the corner, there is the old Ballast Office, a reminder of former days and activities in Dublin Port. The present building is a modern version of the original Ballast Office that was built in the early 1800s and performed an important function regulating shipping in Dublin Port. Formed in around 1707, the Ballast Office made its money by providing ballast to ships and cleaning and dredging the mouth of the River Liffey to enable the smooth movement of ships. The clock on the building, dating from 1870, was regarded as an indispensable aid to the activities of the Ballast Office – precise timing was of great importance and the clock was linked to Dunsink Observatory.[24]

THE QUAYS

The quays on the border of Temple Bar have survived into the twenty-first century against the odds. In the closing decades of the twentieth century, they were threatened by a plan put forward to build a car park from Butt Bridge to the Ha'penny Bridge, covering this part of the River Liffey. Another plan to build two motorways would also have involved demolishing the quays at each side of the river. Luckily neither plan was carried out. However, the building of Heuston Station and Collins Barracks involved the demolition of many of the old quayside houses, which were then replaced with apartment blocks. Transport and housing rather than history or heritage seem to have been the primary concern for some officials.[25]

Today, we take the quays for granted, but Temple Bar and the rest of the city might easily have ended up with a completely different appearance were it not for the vision of James Butler, 12th Earl of Ormonde.[26]

Woodprint of Merchant's Quay and the Ha'penny Bridge by artist Harry Kernoff. (Courtesy of Appollo Gallery)

Aston Quay is called after a former Lord Mayor of Dublin, Henry Aston, a prominent Dublin merchant in the first decade of the eighteenth century. It was he who helped reclaim some land from the River Liffey and, with the support of the city, built the quay wall in the early 1700s to protect his land. This act facilitated building on much of the quay and the land behind as far as Fleet Street.

McBirney's department store was for many years one of Dublin's most famous stores. It started business in the early nineteenth century as McBirney, Collis & Co., Silk Merchants and Drapers and subsequently prospered.

As shopping habits changed, McBirney's location, away from the main shopping areas of Grafton and Henry streets, and adverse trading conditions forced it to close in 1984. All that remains today is the old name, McBirney & Co. Ltd, which still adorns the entrance. Above the name is smaller print and carved around a shamrock is the name of the building – Hibernian House. A later owner of the building was Virgin Megastore.

Next door to McBirney's was the former premises of the coach house for the Dublin-to-Cork coach link. Hodges Hardware later occupied the premises. In the twentieth century, Irish Shipping, the Irish Continental Line and the Union of Students of Ireland (USIT) have occupied the building at various times.

CRAMPTON QUAY

This quay, along with the adjoining Aston Quay, was once famous for the number of outside second-hand bookstalls that lined the quays. This is perhaps not surprising considering the name of the quay derived from Philip Crampton, a wealthy bookseller who bought the land in the early seventeenth century, built and developed the quays and operated his business there.

George Webb Booksellers was a famous browsing spot for generations of Dubliners from the late nineteenth century until the closing years of the twentieth century. Another famous bookseller, Fred Hanna of Nassau Street, took over Webb's in the 1940s and continued trading there, under the old name, for the next fifty years. Many of Ireland's famous literary giants frequented Webb's over the years. The late nineteenth-century artist Walter F. Osborne painted an expressive oil-on-canvas picture entitled *Dublin Streets – A Vendor of Books* (1889), which is held in the National Gallery of Ireland. It depicts a book vendor on the cobblestone Aston Quay, with the newly widened O'Connell Bridge in the background. Beside the browsers, a barefooted child is selling daffodils. The painting captures much of daily life in Dublin at that time.

In the 1940s, No. 2 was occupied by Fred Moore, a trunk, bag and portmanteau maker and athletic outfitter. George Webb also ran a tobacconist and confectioner in No. 7, while the same building housed Laurence Campbell, a military and ladies' bootmaker.

WELLINGTON QUAY AND THE IRON DUKE

This was the last of the city quays to be constructed. It was built sometime between 1812 and 1816 and replaced a row of houses that had been on the river's edge. The quay was named after Arthur Wellesley (1769–1852), later Duke of Wellington, victor at the Battle of Waterloo in 1815, who was born on Merrion Street. It was constructed thanks to the Wide Streets Commissioners, who wished to continue building the Liffey wall and connect Essex and Crampton quays. When it was completed, it was the final link in the major reconstruction project that saw much of the embankment of the old Liffey tidal estuary below Essex (Grattan) Bridge reclaimed and walled. The rubble from the demolition of the old custom house was used as dry filling for the construction of Wellington Quay.

The Wellington Quay boundary of Temple Bar. (Courtesy of Psyberartist, Wikimedia Commons)

HA'PENNY BRIDGE – DIFFERENT NAMES, DIFFERENT STORIES

Since May 1816, Dubliners have been walking over what is now popularly known as the Ha'penny Bridge, though the bridge was originally known as the Liffey Bridge. It is one of the main access points to Temple Bar. The bridge and Merchant's Arch have become an iconic entrance to the area. The Ha'penny Bridge was cast at Coalbrookdale in Shropshire in England. The bridge was the only pedestrian bridge on the Liffey until the Millennium Bridge was opened in late 1999. (It was built to relieve congestion on the Ha'penny Bridge. This 134ft bridge was built in Carlow, transported to Dublin and lowered into position by crane.)[27]

Once a toll bridge, besides the above names, over the years the Ha'penny Bridge was also called the Wellington Bridge and the Metal Bridge. The Ha'penny Bridge name eventually stuck because of the halfpenny it once cost to cross it. Before the pedestrian bridge was built, people used to use the ferries to cross but over time the cost of maintaining these ferries proved prohibitive and the company's owner, William Walsh, decided on a pedestrian bridge. Wellington Bridge opened to the public in 1816.

According to a newspaper report at the time of unveiling, 'it has a light and picturesque appearance, and adds much to the convenience and embellishment of the river'. At £3,000, the bridge was a costly replacement for the ferry service that had moored at Bagnio Slip. The costs of building the bridge were recouped through the halfpenny toll that Walsh was allowed to collect. The toll was charged until 1917 when Dublin Corporation abolished it.[28]

The bridge is believed to be one of the world's first iron bridges. The *Dublin Evening Post*, full of enthusiasm for the new spectacle, also reported on the opening of the bridge, 'This Arch, spanning the Liffey, is one of the most beautiful in Europe: the excellence of its composition, the architectural correctness of its form, the taste with which it has been executed, and the general airiness of its appearance, renders it an object of unmixed admiration.'[29]

Certainly it is an iconic bridge in Dublin and it has attracted not only pedestrians, visitors and admirers, but also all sorts of merchants, beggars, musicians and singers. For generations, there were different stalls and hucksters at either end of the bridge, particularly at the open space outside the famous Dublin Woollen Mills (1888) on the north side of the bridge. Individuals such as Hector Grey, who started the tradition of Sunday selling at the bridge, sold his wares here for over fifty years in the twentieth century. He sold quality items at affordable prices. Paddy Slattery was famous for glass and tile cutters and enthralled people with the simplicity of the art.

The Ha'penny Bridge and the Merchant's Arch entrance to Temple Bar. (Courtesy of Psyberartist, Wikimedia Commons)

Busker in the 1950s at Ha'penny Bridge. (Courtesy of Brian Browne Walker)

Another famous stall was Joe Clarke's bookstall. On Saturday afternoons, the open space at the bridge was occupied by sideshows and variety acts. Famous acts included Blondini the Sword Swallower, the Cart Wheel Man and the Whip Man, who could whip a cigarette out of his wife's mouth from 20ft away. Other stalls included the Magic Soap Man, whose own brand of soap only needed a drop of water to remove the worst stains. Grain the Hall Door Man sold items to improve your front door.[30]

THE MERCHANT'S HALL AND ARCH

Merchant's Hall, built in 1821/2, was originally designed as a guildhall for the important craftspeople of Dublin who were members of various guilds, e.g. tanners, tailors, coopers, jewellers and cutlers. It was located in Temple Bar, which was appropriate given the variety of crafts in the area. It is one of only two surviving guildhalls in Dublin (the other being the nearby Tailor's Hall at Back Lane in the Liberties).

Frederick Darley, the third generation of a family of architects and quarry owners, designed the building. It was leased from the Wide Streets Commissioners by the Merchants' Guild as a meeting house. The Merchants' Guild was ranked the most important of Dublin's five guilds at a time (stretching back to medieval times) when the trades of Dublin were run by the powerful guilds. These merchants had also lobbied for the building of the Royal Exchange on Cork Hill and the Commercial Buildings on Dame Street.

Merchant's Arch, the passage through the building, was a stipulation of the Wide Streets Commissioners when they supported the plan to build the hall. It provides access to Temple Bar via the Ha'penny Bridge for those coming from north of the River Liffey.

The merchants' tenure on the new building was short-lived. The 1841 Municipal Reform Act curtailed the legal rights and power of the guilds and set up an elected body, which would be known as Dublin Corporation. Members of Dublin Corporation were directly elected rather than achieving office through the influence of the guilds. The building became superfluous as the old medieval guilds were wound up. The power and influence of the guilds (and the Dublin Liberties) had been a bone of contention for the city's authorities for generations and there had often been clashes over legal rights, extending back to the charter of Henry II in 1171, which granted the city of Dublin to the men of Bristol and established autonomous Liberties in the process.

Following the disbandment of the guilds, the building has been used for many different purposes, including as a shirt-and-poplin factory for most of the twentieth century and a Protestant boys' school. Many of the original fixtures have survived, including the restored, cantilevered, granite staircase in the oval-shaped room already mentioned. The high ceilings, original beams and elegant Georgian sash windows have also survived.

The hall has had various commercial uses over the years and the arch (and the bridge) has featured in many of the photographs of music groups, including U2, The Chieftains and Thin Lizzy. There is a memorial plaque on the wall inside the arch dedicated to the great Thin Lizzy lead singer Phil Lynott, who had made a video in the vicinity for one of his albums. Mojo's Record Store is still going strong and its owner, George Murray, who has been operating in the Arch since the 1950's, also sells 78s. At the National Gallery of Ireland, a painting of the arch entitled *Merchant's Arch, Temple Bar* (*c.* 1909) by William Orpen (1878–1931) shows the alley festooned with loaded washing lines. The artist used watercolours, black and red chalk, and graphite. It relates to an oil painting called *The Knackers Yard* that Orpen painted in 1909. The artist Maurice MacGonigal (1900–1979) made a drawing called *Merchants' Arch, Wellington Quay*, also in the early years of the twentieth century. In the middle of the twentieth century, another prominent artist,

Could it be U2 taking a rest in Merchant's Arch in the early 1970s? (Courtesy of IHI)

Merchant's Arch by William Orpen. (Courtesy of NGI)

Harry Kernoff (1900–1974), captured the essence and atmosphere of the location when he drew a sketch of Merchant's Arch.[31]

FROM THE CUSTOM TO THE CLARENCE

The old custom house, erected in 1707, was located on the site of what is now the Clarence Hotel. The old custom house was a three-storey building with a mansard roof. After its closure, the building was used as a barracks until it was demolished.

The present Clarence Hotel is a fifty-room, four-star hotel, dating from 1939. There was an older Clarence Hotel on the site from 1852. Before that, the site was the location of a few quayside houses. They were reconstructed to fit together and some façade stucco decoration was added to form the hotel. Some of the more expensive rooms had their own fireplaces. The terrazzo flooring in the hotel, dating from the 1930s, is one of its many attractive features. The hotel's Tea Room and Octagon Bar are noteworthy. The former was designed like a church, with a soaring ceiling and double-height windows. Over the years, the hotel has had an eclectic clientele, including visiting clergymen and bawdy musicians. Towards the end of the twentieth century, the hotel had become tired and shabby but was soon to take on a new lease of life as 'the original rock and roll hotel'. The hotel was modernised and extended upwards in the early 1990s when U2 band members Bono, the Edge and their business partners bought the hotel and refurbished it. In 2000, shortly before the release of a U2 album, U2 played on the roof of the hotel, as the Beatles had once done on the rooftop of a London building. The stunt was not a novel occurrence in Dublin as Jack Hilton and his band had played on the roof of Independent House on Middle Abbey Street in May 1933. Nonetheless, the act had a resounding impact.[32]

Next door to the Clarence, fronting on to the quays, the former Dollard's Printworks is now offices. The Dollard's building, with its arched entrances and dormer windows, is reminiscent of the work of Thomas Burgh, who designed the old custom house located nearby. Other important activities along this quay included the City of Dublin Workingmen's Club (now with a public bar at ground level and also used as a music and art centre). This building dates from early Victorian times and the club has been there since 1888. The former Bassi's shop (run by an Italian family and known as an 'Art Framing and Bona Crux' business) was renowned for its religious statues and picture-frame manufacturing. For decades during the late nineteenth

Dublin's original Custom House, by Thomas Burgh, on Essex Quay, built in 1707. It was pulled down in the late eighteenth century to make way for Gandon's version further downstream. (Courtesy of Archiseek)

Page 473

THE CUSTOM HOUSE

and for most of the twentieth century, there were always crucifixes and statues in the shop window. James Joyce mentioned the shop in *Ulysses* – 'By Bassi's blessed virgins Bloom's dark eyes went by'. The business also published Irish-made prayer books and other standard books of Catholic piety. Bassi's closed in the later twentieth century but Mulvany Brothers, also a famous family of picture framers and print sellers, have been in the business since 1885 and operated from various locations before settling at No. 9 Wellington Quay in 1961. Thirty-four years later, the business transferred to Clondalkin, where it continues to prosper. Grattan House on the corner of the quay with Parliament Street has a striking, marble-pillared, curved entrance.

The famous publisher James Duffy was located at No. 7 Wellington Quay for much of the nineteenth and twentieth centuries. In the 1940s, No. 1 was occupied by Macaulay's, vestment makers and church linen. Nos 13-14 were occupied by Patrick Cahill, described as 'opticians to H.H. Pius XI'. In Nos 18-19 were Fox's nickel and chrome plating works and foundry. No. 21 was the Dublin Smelting Company, bullion dealers and assayers. In No. 24 was an agent for Bush Radio a popular model for an increasing number of Irish households. Located in No. 26 was the Northlight Razor Blade Company. A flooring company occupied part No. 34, specialising in linoleum much used in Irish homes as an alternative to the more expensive carpets. No. 34a was the Liffey Bank Restaurant and next door, in No. 35, was the New Era Café. No. 41 housed Gallagher & Johnson, wholesale handkerchief and neckware specialists. In No. 42 was J. Costello, an ophthalmic optician, a business which had been established in 1840.

MALTON'S VIEW

Essex Quay, from Parliament Street/Grattan Bridge to Wood Quay, was built in the late 1600s. This quay and Wellington Quay were used as the main docking and unloading areas for Dublin port, with the old custom house located here from the early 1700s until the late eighteenth century. Prior to the opening of the Ha'penny Bridge, ships used to navigate up the Liffey and dock at the old Custom House Quay. James Malton's 1797 print of Essex Bridge from Capel Street, looking towards the Royal Exchange (City Hall), is important as Capel Street was one of Dublin's foremost shopping streets in the Georgian era. In Malton's print, you can clearly see the mast of a sailing ship close to the parapet of a bridge. The first bridge here was Essex Bridge, opened in 1676 and called after Arthur Capel, Earl of Essex and Lord Lieutenant for Ireland. Humphrey Jervis, one of Dublin's major landowners at the time, built the bridge to link the north side of the river and his land to the commercial part of Dublin. The building of Parliament Street added to the importance of the bridge by directly linking Capel Street to Dublin Castle and later the Royal Exchange via the bridge. For nearly two hundred years, Essex Bridge was the easterly crossing point of the River Liffey. The bridge was particularly important for Temple Bar as it further enhanced the area's role as the commercial heart of the city.

The Temple Bar merchants fought vigorously against the building of any additional bridges across the river and it was not until 1795 that Carlisle Bridge

Crossing Grattan Bridge from Parliament Street in the 1920s. (Courtesy of IHI)

Grattan Bridge and Temple Bar. (Courtesy of Psyberartist, Wikimedia Commons)

(O'Connell) was opened. The merchants feared an erosion of their powerful and dominant position in the commercial life of Dublin. Essex Bridge itself was rebuilt in each subsequent century and was renamed Grattan Bridge in 1874 after further remodelling. This work included widening the bridge and was undertaken by an Irish engineer, Bindon Blood Stoney (1828–1909), often described as the man who made modern Dublin and the 'Father of Irish Concrete'. He was a creative engineer with a flair for new ideas and a habit of pushing techniques to their limits. He made his name designing the Boyne Railway Viaduct (thereby linking Dublin and Belfast by rail) and subsequently by helping deepen Dublin Port with the invention of a new dredger called a diving bell, using precast concrete blocks and a steel container that could hold six men working under water. This diving bell, weighing 80 tons, was instrumental in the process of refurbishing and building the quay walls and turning the port into a deep-sea port, which was so important for Dublin's economic development.[33]

With the building of the new custom house downstream at its present location on the north bank of the river, the importance of Essex and Wellington quays and Temple Bar itself somewhat diminished, as predicted by the local merchants.

THE STORY OF SOAP – THE SUNLIGHT CHAMBERS

One of the most beautiful and unique landmarks in Temple Bar, the Sunlight Chambers, is located on the corner of Essex Quay and Parliament Street. With its curious, eye-catching façade, this building dates from the early twentieth century and replaced a number of old shops. Designed by the Liverpool architect Edward Ould, it was built in a romantic Italian Renaissance palace style, with attractive Art Nouveau frieze work and wide, overhanging eaves, a red-tiled roof and arcaded upper floors. The building boasts one of the most unusual architectural features in Dublin – two multi-coloured terracotta/ceramic friezes on its exterior, illustrating the story of soap and the importance of hygiene and washing. The building project met with resistance from architects in Dublin at the time because a foreign architect had been hired. Upon its completion, the *Irish Builder* referred to it as the ugliest building in Dublin (referring to its plain interior presumably) and a few years later the same journal called it 'pretentious and mean'.[34]

The building was designed as the Irish offices for Lord Leverhulme (of Lever Brothers), who saw opportunities to sell Sunlight Soap (hence the name of the building) in Ireland as it was the age when the soap bar became a necessary household item. Lever Brothers was an original company when it came to advertising its product. The company was in an ideal location and so it used the building's façade to educate the public about its product. On the upper layers,

The Sunlight Chambers on corner of Parliament Street and Essex Quay. (Courtesy of Psyberartist, Wikimedia Commons)

the frieze shows merchants haggling over the original oil product, then the manufacture of soap itself. Builders and farmers ploughing fields are shown working, in the process getting their clothes dirty. On the layers below them, the panels show soap being used for everyday washing, with women drawing water from a well, using scrubbing boards and visiting washing rooms. It has been suggested that the work captures an era when the prevailing view of the sexes was that men made clothes dirty and women washed them. The many little, colourful images include what architectural historian Christine Casey memorably described as 'shiny naked children'. Conrad Dressler, a German sculptor and potter, was engaged to design and craft the series of four roundels and twelve panels around the three faces of the building. The glazed ceramic friezes were made in Dressler's own pottery works in Buckinghamshire.[35]

Until recently, these friezes were quite dirty but restoration works have returned the building to its former multicoloured splendour.

For many years, Mason's Opticians and Photographers was located next door to the Sunlight Chambers. Operating since the early nineteenth century, the business sold magic lanterns, spirit levels, spectacles, compasses, sundials, brewer's gauges, rulers, barometers and goggles. It was the leading photographic firm in Dublin. The business moved to Dame Street in the twentieth century and operated there until the 1970s.[36]

William Walsh (1841-1921), later the Archbishop of Dublin (1885-1921), was born at No. 11 Essex Quay. In the 1940s at No. 28, a company called Smyth's were umbrella and walking-stick manufacturers. In No. 13 was Henry Philips who was a gold and silver leaf manufacturer. Nos 15 & 16 was the Grattan Hotel and Restaurant.

Farther along Essex Quay, in complete contrast to the Sunlight Chambers, is the Bookend Building near the corner with Lower Exchange Street and facing Dublin City Council's Wood Quay office. This small block of apartments, built in 1999 by Arthur Gibney, has been described by Archiseek as 'uncompromisingly modern with stark white render and sharp detailing'. This is part of the character of Temple Bar – mixing the old, the new and the curious, layer upon layer.[37]

15

FROM THE SMOCK TO THE PROJECT – THEATRE TIMES AND RIVAL TYPES

Temple Bar is home to one of Europe's oldest theatres (the Smock Alley Theatre), one of Ireland's smallest theatres (The New Theatre), one of the best examples of a Victorian theatre (The Olympia) and one of Ireland's best-known modern theatre spaces and arts centres (Project Arts Centre). Moreover, some of Europe's most famous actors and actresses of the eighteenth century graced the stages of the Smock Alley Theatre and Crow Street's Theatre Royal.

The world of Irish theatre from the eighteenth century onwards was vibrant and the actors were home-grown, with visiting companies providing variety. Three of Dublin's most important theatres were located in Temple Bar from the eighteenth century – the Fishamble Street Music Hall, the Smock Alley Theatre and the Theatre Royal in Crow Street, also known as the Crow Street Theatre. These three theatres were part of the social round of the golden circle in Irish upper-class or ascendancy life. The first theatre in Dublin was opened in the mid-1660s in Werburgh Street by a John Ogilby. There were also a few other smaller theatres operating at different times in the Temple Bar area, including Madame Violante's in Fownes Court in 1732, but they did not have the long-lasting appeal of the larger theatres. The eighteenth and nineteenth centuries were great times for Dublin theatregoers as the theatres in Temple Bar were in full swing and drew huge audiences.

Today, we are so used to the impressive designer lighting which is now de rigueur in theatres that we forget how it was in the eighteenth century.

Temple Bar theatres were lit with tallow candles, stuck into tin circles, hanging from the middle of the stage. Every now and then, they were snuffed out or lit by a performer. From the end of the eighteenth century onwards, the new Irish Romanticism that was coming into vogue was adapted for the stage and provided audience with an impressive spectacle that included elaborate scenery, music and an idealised rural landscape with stock characters. This became very popular and was a style that dominated in Irish theatres until well into the twentieth century. Dion Boucicault's *The Colleen Bawn* (1860) is a good example of a play from this time.

Theatre provided an opportunity for a cross-section of society, from the Lord Lieutenant to the artisan or shopkeeper, to sit in the same building and enjoy the same production in which issues such as loyalty, justice and identity were debated in plays ranging from the tragic to the comic and often combining both, as, for example, in Thomas Sheridan's *The Brave Irishman* (1743). Such was the emotional impact of plays on Dublin's theatre-going public that there were often riots in theatres and so two soldiers with fixed bayonets always stood like statues on each side of the stage, close to the boxes, to keep the audience in order. Theatres were boisterous places where the actors frequently came under attack from disgruntled audiences, who threw things such as rotten oranges at them. The soldiers were called upon on many occasions and sometimes people were actually killed during riots. The galleries of the theatres were usually noisy whereas the ladies and gentlemen in the boxes nearly always dressed smartly, with the emphasis being on etiquette and decorum.[1]

With the decline of these major theatres in the late nineteenth century, the Star of Erin (Olympia Theatre) on Dame Street/Crampton Court took over and became the most important theatre in Temple Bar.

THE SMOCK ALLEY THEATRE

Smock Alley is significant in the history of Irish theatre as it was the site of the principal theatre in Ireland for more than a century. The Smock Alley Theatre originally opened its doors in 1662 under the name Theatre Royal, as King Charles II had been restored to the English throne in 1660. The theatre was dependent on the patronage of Dublin Castle for many years after its foundation. Many of the early actors were officers from the regiments based at Dublin Castle. It was the first custom-built theatre in the city and remains in much the same form as it did then, making it one of the most important sites in

European theatre history. It was a large building with a pit and three galleries, with the viceregal box on the lowest for the Lord Lieutenant, a green room and the manager's house next door. It was built on unsure foundations, on land reclaimed from the River Liffey, which led to partial collapse (and killing 'a poor girlie', according to a contemporary account) and subsequent rebuilding in 1735. Thomas Sheridan was manager in the 1740s/'50s and made many improvements.

From its early days, the theatre gave the world the plays of George Farquhar, including *The Recruiting Officer*, Oliver Goldsmith's *She Stoops to Conquer* and Richard Brinsley Sheridan's, *The Rivals* and *The School for Scandal* (Richard was the son of Thomas Sheridan). The brilliant performances of Peg Woffington, George Ann Bellamy, Thomas Sheridan himself, Spranger Barry and Charles Macklin enthralled Dublin audiences. In the 1690s, a young George Farquhar accidentally stabbed a fellow actor in a duel scene on stage, using a real sword rather than a silver foil, and decided to give up acting for playwriting. In addition, it was at this theatre that the greatest actor of the eighteenth century, David Garrick, first played Hamlet in 1741.[2]

For nearly twenty-five years after its closure in 1787, the Smock served as a whiskey warehouse. Then a Catholic church was built on the site. In the early twenty-first century, when the then closed church was excavated by archaeologists, they discovered that the old theatre had never been completely demolished, as had been long believed. The 1662 foundations and much of the post-1735 walls remained. During the course of renovations, builders discovered the old burial vaults of the former church, which appeared to have been in the original pit of the old Smock Alley Theatre. In 2012, after extensive renovations undertaken by the new owner, Patrick Sutton, Smock Alley Theatre reopened. The building still boasts ornate stained-glass windows, the original ceiling plasterwork with carefully carved angels and the famous freedom bell over the entrance. These features remain (as stipulated by the planning permission) part of the refurbished theatre as a reminder of its time as a church.

Scenes from *Strumpet City*, the famous story of the Dublin Lockout of 1913, based on the book by James Plunkett, were filmed here and particular use was made of the former presbytery beside the theatre. The Gaiety School of Acting is located in one of the former schools beside the theatre.[3]

SPARKS AND SHERIDAN'S

Certain names stand out in the early history of the theatre. As noted, the famous playwright Richard Brinsley Sheridan (1751–1816) has strong connections with the theatre. It was said that his confidence in his genius was justified by his success. It was also said that no one was better able to ridicule others than him. Like his father, he was much involved in theatre life and, building on his success, he purchased the Drury Lane Theatre in London.

Isaac Sparks (1719–1776) was a celebrated comedian frequently seen on the Smock stage and was regarded as was one of the most popular comedians on the Dublin stage in the eighteenth century. The *Hibernian Magazine* stated towards the end of his career that 'despite his double chins and his comic vocation, his person was always majestic and commanding'. Born in College Street, he returned to the Dublin stage from Drury Lane in London in 1749. He played old men, clowns in pantomimes and Irish peasants until his death. In these roles, he was regarded as the most talented comic actor of his generation. He was described as 'a large fat man, and such a favourite that a nod and a wink from him was reckoned a bon mot, and produced a mirthful peal. His looks were so whimsical, that he had little trouble to do this.'[4] Another name associated with the Smock was Charlotte Melmoth, later to become the 'Grand Dame of Tragedy on the American Stage', who began her acting career in this theatre.

MADAME VIOLANTE'S

In 1729, a small theatre opened in Fownes Court, Fownes Street, in the former mansion of Sir William Fownes. Madame Violante, an Italian rope dancer and pantomime artiste, ran it. Her success was based on the unusual nature of her fare, which involved extraordinary feats of strength and agility and high-rope dancing. She provided many thrills for her audiences, including dancing with a person standing upright on her shoulders or with a basket containing a small child tied to each foot. The theatre also achieved some measure of success with its company of tumblers and ropedancers. Advertisements at the time hailed her as 'the most famous Rope-Dancer now living'. After a time, the public grew weary of looking at acrobats whirling around the stage and Madame Violante started to put on plays and farces, which again achieved a measure of success, but only for a short while.

Refusing to accept failure, she found inspiration in Swift's *Gulliver's Travels* and formed a Lilliputian theatre company of children to perform *The Beggar's Opera* (1732). The Dublin public was so enraptured by the novelty and originality of the Lilliputian troop, with its tiny geniuses, that the theatre drew huge crowds. Some of Dublin's greatest eighteenth-century actors and actresses came out of the company, including Peg Woffington (her stage debut at age 10 as Polly Peachum) and Isaac Sparks, who both went on to greater glories in the Smock and elsewhere on the Irish stage.[5]

It was said of Peg Woffington (1714–1760), who had become Dublin's leading actress by 1740, that to establish her origin would challenge a genealogist. It was known that her mother sold fruit in the vicinity of the theatre at one time. Madame Violante had seen the shabbily dressed girl drawing water from the River Liffey for her mother's washtubs. Despite her humble beginnings, or maybe because of them, she went on to become a celebrated actress and a favourite with many of the ascendancy. Her Sylvia in George Farquhar's *Recruiting Officer* and her Sir Harry Wildair in the same author's *The Constant Couple* made her Dublin's darling. She enjoyed not only professional success but also the celebrity that came

A portrait miniature of the famous Irish actress Peg Woffington. (Courtesy of Best Antiquarian)

with it. Such was her fame that she was set fashions in clothing and much else. Thomas Sheridan of the Smock Alley Theatre founded the Beefsteak Club, which used to meet next door. The only woman invited to some of the weekly dinners was Peg Woffington. It was said that she preferred the company of men to that of women as she found that her own sex talked of nothing but silks and scandal. The great writer, actor and producer David Garrick was the most important man in her life until 1745, but she is said to have rejected his efforts to direct her in plays, as well as in bed. Edmund Burke was also an admirer and was suspected of being one of her lovers. She collapsed on stage in 1757 during Shakespeare's *As You Like It*, after which she retired.[6]

Another interesting character associated with this theatre was one John Magill, who rose to prominence in Dublin society and even became a member of the Irish parliament. His career was recounted in his autobiographical *Life and Adventures of Buttermilk Jack*. The young John Magill began his working life as a helper with Madame Violante around the time the young Peg Woffington started. He then became a carpenter and worked on the new parliament building on College Green. While there, he ingratiated himself with government officials, achieving high office overseeing property management, and continued his rise to prominence.[7] Madame Violante's theatre had closed long before and the building had been converted into a chocolate house by Peter Bardin of the Smock Alley Theatre.

THE CROW STREET THEATRE

The Crow Street Music Hall dates from 1731. It was built by the newly established Dublin Academy of Music for the promotion and enjoyment of Italian music. Its opening was attended by the principal nobility and gentry of Dublin. However, it was not open long when a riot broke out and the army was called in. They opened fire on the audience, killing some. The Music Hall stayed open for the next twenty years or so, until the Irish-born actor, Spranger Barry (1719–1777) formerly of London's Covent Garden Theatre, returned to Dublin in 1753, looking for a site for a theatre. In 1757, he bought and demolished the building on Crow Street, purchased some adjacent sites and replaced the old Music Hall with a magnificent and much expanded 2,000-seat theatre, which he renamed the Theatre Royal. It had an impressive interior with a rectangular auditorium with four galleries. It was so large that there were at times pony races around a central pit.

Barry was born at Skinner's Row, beside Fishamble Street, so he would have known the area well. He had been a silversmith until he began his acting career on the Smock Alley stage in 1744. He then moved to London and achieved fame and fortune there. He acted at the same time as the legendary David Garrick and London society was divided when it came to the merits of the great rivals. It was said that Barry's masterpiece was his portrayal of Othello, described as a performance 'which could not be transcended', and it was also said that if any player deserved to be described as 'unique' or 'genius' it was Barry.[8]

Opening in October 1758, the Theatre Royal achieved a Europe-wide reputation for the eminence of its actors and the standard of its productions. The company of actors organised by Barry was supposed to have been the most numerous and most expensive company ever collected in Dublin. In the long term, however, this led to financial problems for Barry.

Over the years, there was much rivalry and controversy between the new theatre and the well-established Smock Alley, which had opposed the original plans to build the new theatre. One of the best actors with the Theatre Royal, Henry Mossop, left the company and took over the management of the Smock Alley Theatre, thereby precipitating an intense and disastrous rivalry for both venues. On many occasions, both theatres presented the same play at the same time, vying with each other to be the public's favourite. An example was the tragedy *The Orphan of China*, written by Arthur Murphy, which had received much acclaim in London. Smock Alley kept their intention of presenting the play secret whereas the Theatre Royal went to great lengths to publicise the play, emphasising that their production would be on a par with

The famous Irish actor Spranger Barry, also owner of the Theatre Royal, Crow Street, Temple Bar. Here he is playing Romeo in 1759. (Courtesy of Dublin Forums)

the showing in Drury Lane in London. On Monday morning, 5 January 1761, when the expectations of Dublin were raised to fever pitch, Smock Alley, only a few days before the Theatre Royal's presentation, announced that it was presenting the play with even superior costumes. Rehearsals were held three times a day and the play was presented in the Smock Alley to full houses, much to the dismay and financial loss of the Theatre Royal. This was just one example of the rivalry. Another was Mossop trumping Barry by engaging a top actor called Charles Macklin, who was famous in the eighteenth century for revolutionising theatre by introducing a 'natural style' of acting. He was renowned for his portrayal of Shylock in *The Merchant of Venice*.[9]

However, it was in the area of pantomimes that Crow Street's Theatre Royal managed to temporarily achieve the upper hand as it decided to specialise in this form of entertainment. The Dublin public became entangled in the rivalry, with the Countess of Bandon and her entourage only visiting the Smock Alley venue. However, such was the impression made by Spranger Barry in many of his performances that the countess was eventually won over by the Theatre Royal. Besides pantomimes, Crow Street was unsurpassed when it came to 'Grotesque Dancing' (acrobatic), which was popular and included using dancing dogs and monkeys. The theatre also had the advantage of having a young Simon Slingsby, whose incredible agility astounded Dublin audiences and later European audiences. He moved so quickly that his human figure practically disappeared during his acrobatic dancing.

The rivalry continued between what became known as the 'Barryists' and the 'Mossopians' and it seemed neither manager was prepared to come to his senses. After seven years of bitter rivalry, the financial costs were starting to be felt, first at Crow Street. In 1767 when Spranger Barry was forced to hand over a lease to Henry Mossop, who then retained control until 1770. Spranger Barry died in 1777. Such was the esteem in which he was held that he was buried in Westminster Abbey. It was a pyrrhic victory for Mossop as within five years he was forced to retire by another rival theatre in Capel Street, which was attracting the public's attention and custom.[10]

There followed a litany of speculative owners over the succeeding decades, well into the nineteenth century. Most eventually retired, beggared by their investment. One such owner was Richard Daly. It was reputed that he allowed there to be a brothel in the overhead apartment, which opened in the mornings and was transformed into a gambling den at night. Ownership of Crow Street changed hands again in the late eighteenth century when one of the wealthy young 'bucks', Frederick Jones, who frequented Daly's Club (he had a fine house, Clonliffe House, on what is now Jones's Road/ Clonliffe Road), bought and refurbished it. *The Merchant of Venice* was performed on what was said to have been a splendid opening night. However, Jones was soon embroiled in difficulties. For example, when the theatre was putting on a show called *The Forest of Bondy*, based on the story of the dog of Montargis, the owner of the trained Newfoundland dog demanded on opening night an advance of the salary for his animal. Jones was stubborn in his refusal and the dog's owner was just as obstinate. Jones cancelled the performance and quickly substituted it with *The Miller and his Men*, but the disappointed audience insisted on the advertised programme. Jones was proud and would neither apologise nor explain, so the audience rioted and severely damaged the theatre. One particular riot in 1820 in the Crow Street Theatre, known as the Bottle Riot, made legal history when twelve men were arrested and unsuccessfully charged with conspiracy to murder for throwing bottles at the Viceroy. The judge, Charles Bushe, ruled that once heckling was not premeditated, and was in the heat of the moment, it was not illegal. However, if it was premeditated, then it was conspiracy.

The change in the political and economic fortunes of the ascendancy due to the 1800 Act of Union resulted in an exodus of many of the well-to-do in Dublin society. The theatre struggled on with mixed fortunes (including more rioting) and finally closed in 1820.

The Theatre Royal name lived on for many more years and in 1820 a new theatre, the Albany, opened in Hawkins Street, a short stroll from Temple Bar. It subsequently changed its name to the Theatre Royal, which survived until 1962. Over the years, it acquired legendary status, particularly in the twentieth century.

In 1836, part of the old Theatre Royal site was bought by the Company of the Apothecaries' Hall of Dublin. They built a number of lecture rooms and a laboratory for their Medical School. The premises were sold in 1852 to John Henry Newman's Catholic University of Ireland. Some of its property became the site of the university's Medical School (1855–1931).

THE FISHAMBLE STREET MUSIC HALL

The Fishamble Street Music Hall (originally Neal's Music Hall) is famous for being the venue where George Frederick Handel's *Messiah* was first performed. It was founded in 1741 by the Bull's Head Musical Society to be used as a music hall for gentlemen's music clubs, concerts and oratorios for charity.[12] It was designed by the architect Richard Cassels. The arch we see on the street today was the original entrance. More than one hundred years later, the historian John Gilbert wrote of the arrival of Handel to Dublin, 'Handel, driven by the goddess of dullness to the Hibernian shore, arrived in Dublin on the 18th of November, 1741, six weeks after the opening of the Music Hall and gave notice of his first Dublin public performance for 23 December 1741.' He remained in Dublin for ten months. He had been invited to Dublin to help raise funds for the poor who were languishing in debtor's prisons.[13]

His success in Dublin culminated on 13 April 1742 when *Messiah* was first presented to the music-loving world. To accommodate the 700-strong audience clamouring to hear Handel's latest work, ladies were requested to come 'without hoops' in their skirts, and men 'without swords'. Jonathan Swift, Dean of St Patrick's Cathedral, suggested to the organisers that the choirs of his cathedral and that of Christ Church Cathedral participate in the concert. However, he was less keen upon hearing the venue of the proposed performance (as it was in such a disreputable area and the organisers had their meetings in the Bull's Head Tavern, which Swift regarded as 'a club of fiddlers'). He promised to 'punish such vicars for their rebellion, disobedience, perfidy and ingratitude'. Another reason for this change of heart was that his physical and mental health was in serious decline at this time. However, his warning was ignored. The concert went ahead and at midday on 13 April 1742 *Messiah* was publicly performed for the first time in the Music Hall .

The oratorio was an instant success – 'The sublime, the grand and the tender, adapted to the most elevated and moving words, conspired to transport and charm the ravished heart and ear,' wrote one enthusiastic critic – and *Messiah*'s popularity has endured. Twenty players and the choirs of St Patrick's Cathedral and the nearby Christ Church Cathedral did justice to one of the most impressive pieces of music ever composed.

Handel was somewhat taken aback by the quietness of the audience as he was used to rowdy crowds. He said at the time that he had never come across such a polite audience. The audience had actually listened to his playing, which was unusual in theatres. The celebrated work is now performed in Dublin annually, close to the original location.[14]

Before he left Ireland, Handel paid a visit to the dying Jonathan Swift in his deanery at St Patrick's Close, in the shadow of the famous cathedral. When those who were looking after Swift managed to make him understand who his visitor was, he exclaimed, 'O! A German and a Genius! A Prodigy! Admit him.' And so it was that the author of *Gulliver's Travels* and the composer of *Messiah* met.[15]

After Handel's departure, entertainment of various kinds continued to be performed in the Music Hall, including concerts of the Charitable Musical Society to raise funds for civic and private charities. Balls were also held, including the first masquerade ball to be held in Ireland in 1776. These proved popular with the ascendancy, including the Duke of Leinster, who came dressed as a fruit woman. The following year the Music Hall reopened as a theatre after major refurbishment. In 1780, the first Irish State Lottery was drawn at the theatre. The numbers were chosen from a mahogany wheel turned by two boys from the Blue-Coat School. For the remainder of the century it was managed by Frederick Jones, who later became the owner of the Theatre Royal on Crow Street.[16] It remained the most fashionable place for public entertainment in Dublin until the late eighteenth century. It stayed in business for most of the nineteenth century until it was taken over in 1868 by Kennan's ironworks. The building was a small steel assembly plant until the late 1970s and was demolished in the 1990s. The entrance arch is the only reminder of the famous Music Hall.

Appropriately, the present-day Contemporary Music Centre of Ireland is located at No. 19 Fishamble Street, beside the old arched entrance to the Music Hall. This is Ireland's national archive and resource centre for new music and supports the work of composers. The centre contains the only collection in existence of music by Irish composers. A bronze plaque on No. 19 commemorates 'the first performance of George Frederic Handel's oratorio *Messiah*, given in the old Music Hall in Fishamble Street at noon on Tuesday April 13th 1742'.

FROM THE STAR OF ERIN TO THE OLYMPIA

Music of a different kind was played in another of Temple Bar's famous theatres. The Olympia Theatre on Dame Street began life as Dan Lowry's 'Star of Erin Music Hall' and officially opened on Monday, 22 December 1879. Such was the crowd in attendance at the opening that soldiers were called to be on standby. A variety show was put on, with song and dance, trapeze artistes, contortionists, weightlifters and a Punch and Judy show. The richly decorated Music Hall had its main entrance on Crampton Court. It had three levels and many private boxes. For decades, it echoed with the sounds of singing, jokes, speciality acts and comic songs reflecting everyday life . It was built on a large site previously occupied by a bakehouse and various businesses, including gunmakers, watchmakers, boot and shoemakers, engravers, sundry stores and a tavern. It was not until the 1890s that a new and elaborate entrance was built on Dame Street. The theatre, with its late Victorian interior, is a joy to behold and visit. Interestingly, it has unusually small seats, perhaps because they are from a time when people were physically smaller than they are today.

Dan Lowrey (1823–1890) was born in Roscrea, County Tipperary. His parents emigrated to England and he ended up running a tavern in Liverpool before coming to Dublin in 1878, whereupon he purchased the site of an old military barracks in Crampton Court. This had also been the site of a tavern and the Monster Saloon Music Hall. In 1881, Dan assigned the running of the Star of Erin to his son, also Daniel, who changed the name to Dan Lowrey's Music Hall. In 1889, the theatre's name was changed again, this time to Dan Lowrey's Palace of Varieties. In July 1890, Dan senior died at the age of 66 and was buried in Glasnevin Cemetery.

In 1915, during the First World War, the composer of the Irish national anthem, Peadar Kearney, made an unannounced stage appearance and turned the fire hoses on the orchestra in the pit. Apparently, he took great umbrage at them playing the British anthem. It was never played again in the Olympia. In 1917, following renovations, the entrance was moved to its present position on Dame Street, with a new canopy, and theatre was renamed the Empire Theatre of Varieties and then the Empire Palace Theatre. After a few years, the name was changed to the Olympia Theatre. Famous actors on the Olympia stage included the legendary Jimmy O'Dea (famous for performing the song 'Biddy Mulligan the Pride of the Coombe') from 1932 onwards and Jack Cruise. The famous comic duo Laurel and Hardy, as well as Charlie Chaplin, appeared at the theatre during their visits to Ireland. For many years in the second half of the twentieth century in Dublin, Jack Cruise was the star actor in the Christmas offering at the Olympia. Maureen Potter was the same at the Gaiety.[17]

The old Victorian coloured glass canopy that projects out on to the pavement was replaced in the 1980s, but in 2004 it was hit by a reversing truck and badly damaged. Luckily, early photographs of the theatre were used to construct an exact replica of the original and the new canopy bears all the hallmarks of its Victorian predecessor.

Near the Olympia, on Dame Street, was the firm of theatrical costumiers, P.J. Bourke's, which operated from 1934. P.J. himself was a man of many talents and the Irish Film Institute on Eustace Street has a copy of a film made by him in 1914 called *Ireland a Nation*. The film blends drama and newsreels to tell of Ireland's struggle for independence from 1798 to the promise of home rule in 1914. It was not shown in Dublin until 1917, nine months after the Easter Rising, but was quickly banned by the military authorities. The actor Barry O'Brien played Robert Emmet.[18]

SIVE AND A WHISTLE IN THE DARK

One of the theatre's great strengths is its willingness to move with the changing times and to anticipate change. The Olympia Theatre has presented different

fare to its usual variety and pantomimes. Two names stand out in this respect:
John B. Keane and Tom Murphy. *Sive* by the Listowel playwright John B. Keane
was shown in 1958, having been rejected by the Abbey Theatre. This was
Keane's first and most famous play, written when he was a 30-year-old publican
in Listowel, County Kerry. He had recently returned from England. On one level,
the play is about an evil matchmaker who sells a young girl to an old farmer.
On another level, the story depicts the conflict between the forces of darkness and
light, the conflict between the ideas of the old extended family and the modern
nuclear family, mixing melodrama and myth. It proved hugely controversial in
late-1950s, conservative Ireland.[19] Another great Irish playwright, Tom Murphy,
also had his challenging, landmark play *A Whistle in the Dark* rejected by the
Abbey Theatre. It was shown in the Olympia in 1962. A powerful play, it has
been described as a work telling Ireland what the country did not wish to hear
and reflecting a culture caught between the old and the new.[20]

THE PROJECT ARTS CENTRE

One of the early anchors in the 1980s struggle for the survival of Temple Bar
was the Project Theatre. After the Olympia it is the oldest cultural organisation
in Temple Bar and one of Ireland's leading arts centres. Now called the
Project Arts Centre, it operates from that outstanding modern building on
Essex Street East. It began life in November 1966 as an artists' collective
on Lower Abbey Street. It moved to its present site in 1974, operating from
what was a converted old factory-cum-garage, and adopted the Project
Theatre name. It was the first such arts centre in Ireland and was at the
forefront of innovative, alternative theatre in its early years, as it still is.
Some productions – for example, *The Sweatshop*, *The Gay Detective* and plays
involving nudity – precipitated strong protests outside the theatre. A Robert
Ballagh exhibition showed his response to Bloody Sunday in Derry in 1972
with chalk outlines of thirteen bodies and chicken blood. Directors such
as the Sheridans and Neil Jordan made use of the centre. Playwright Tom
Murphy's first work, *On the Outside*, was premiered at the centre and actors
such as Liam Neeson and Gabriel Byrne honed their acting skills on its stage.

The original building was demolished in 1998 and a purpose-built theatre
was developed by Temple Bar Properties. It was designed by Shay Cleary
and its design and style (e.g. huge metal door on the exterior of building)
acknowledge the garage that once stood on the site. Since then, the theatre has
broadened its range and become the Project Arts Centre, a multidisciplinary

arts centre that hosts theatre, dance and performance. Music also found a place in the centre, with the twenty-four-hour Dark Space Festival at which U2, the Virgin Prunes and the Boomtown Rats all played. The centre's stage was moveable and sometimes appeared in the middle or to one side of the auditorium, depending on the performance. Thus, the seating arrangement invited the audience to be participants in the drama being enacted. This was radical, challenging, and very different to the mainstream theatres. It pushed the boundaries of performance work in Ireland. The Rough Magic Theatre Company fitted in well and became the Project's flagship theatre company.

The centre has been the venue for many of Dublin's performing arts festivals, including the Dublin Dance Festival, the Dublin Writers' Festival, the Dublin Fringe Festival and the Dublin Theatre Festival. As with Temple Bar itself, the theatre has had an eventful history, which has reflected political and cultural changes.[21]

THE NEW THEATRE

A relatively recent addition to Dublin's theatre world is the New Theatre, also on Essex Street East, over Connolly's Books. Despite its name, it has been in operation for twenty years. It is Ireland's only 'new writing' theatre that supports new and emerging writers. It provides its sixty-six-seat theatre as well as technical and professional expertise, for artists, performers, writers, directors and technicians to enable them to develop artistically in a professional setting. It has a substantial and impressive catalogue of productions.

16

SCRIBES OF THE TEMPLE – FROM SWIFT TO SMYLLIE

BY THE SIGN OF THE LEATHER BOTTLE

Before the building of Lord Edward Street in the late nineteenth century, Fishamble Street extended to the top of Castle Street and to Skinner's Row (now Christ Church Place). It was here, in 1551, that the *Book of Common Prayer* was printed, the first book to be printed in Ireland. In 1685, the *Dublin News-Letter* appeared, published by Robert Thornton at the Sign of the Leather Bottle tavern. It consisted of a single leaf of small size, printed on both sides and written in the form of a letter. Each one was dated and commenced with the word 'Sir'. The location was significant as it was near the seat of power in Ireland, Dublin Castle. In addition, the seat of local officialdom in Dublin, the Tholsel, was right next door on Skinner's Row. According to historian Hugh Oram, 'The intimate entanglement between the newspaper industry and the vintner's trade that continued unabashed to the present day was established in Ireland by Thornton. By setting up business so near the Castle, he also highlighted the relationship between newspapers and political authority, alternately subservient and symbiotic.'[1]

This area, from Skinners Row to College Green, through Temple Bar, was the centre of the newspaper publishing industry in Dublin for many years and many of Dublin's first newspapers were printed and published there. Furthermore, there was a considerable concentration of booksellers and publishers – possibly thirty-five or so – around 1730, an extraordinary number at that time for a city the size of Dublin. By 1760, 160 titles had been published in the area. The eighteenth century proved to be the most successful period in the history of the Irish publishing, printing, book- and newspaper-selling industry and Temple Bar was the epicentre of this success.[2] The British Copyright Act of 1709 did not extend to Ireland and so pirated editions of works first published in London, including books, music and newspaper reports, were commonplace.[3] It was common practice to buy books in London, reprint them and then sell them cheaply in Dublin.

Near Thornton's, Richard (Dick) Pue had his coffee house on the site of what is now Jurys Inn, where auctions of books, land, and property took place in the eighteenth-century. Pue published a paper called the *Flying Post* in 1699. This was followed by *Impartial Occurrences* (later *Pue's Occurrences*) in December 1703, in partnership with Edward Lloyd. It was regarded as the official organ of Dublin, i.e. effectively subsidised by Dublin Castle. As well as social and political news, it specialised in sales notices for country estates. It ceased publication in the 1790s, but was predominant among Dublin newspapers during most of the eighteenth century.

THE GOLDEN AGE OF PUBLISHING AND BOOKSELLING

Fishamble Street, Parliament Street and Essex Street were the hub of the bookselling and newspaper trade in Dublin in the eighteenth century. Newspapers continued to be published in Temple Bar until well into the twentieth century. Thomas Hume published the *Dublin Gazetteer* in Essex Street from 1703. Thomas MacDonnell at No. 50 Essex Street East originally published the *Hibernian Journal or Chronicle of Liberty* in the latter decades of that century. A regular contributor was Wolfe Tone. George Faulkner's early eighteenth-century newspaper, the influential *Dublin Journal*, was published at No. 27 Parliament Street.[4] Most newspapers of the era included news of war and politics, as well as local news, court cases, robberies, visitors to Dublin and entertainment.[5]

In the nineteenth century, No. 12 Parliament Street was the premises of *The Irish People*, a Fenian newspaper. Charles Stewart Parnell's sister, Fanny, was a frequent contributor. Other contributors included John O'Leary and Charles Kickham, a patriot and author of the bestselling book *Knocknagow*. In the early twentieth century, the *Daily Express* had offices at Nos 39 and 40 and the *Evening Mail* was located on the corner of Parliament and Dame streets. Also in the twentieth century, Arthur Griffith, the founder of Sinn

Féin, had offices at Fownes Street, where the *United Irishman* newspaper was published.

An important printer on Essex Street was George Grierson, among whose publications was William Petty's *Maps of Ireland*, following his infamous *Down Survey*. In 1727, he was made King's Printer for Ireland. His business was called the Sign of the Two Bibles. It is still possible to see his headstone in Rathfarnham's old Church of Ireland graveyard (in the village). Reference to Grierson's position as King's Printer of Ireland is included on the memorial.[6]

Such was the high standard of Dublin decorative bookbinding, which had begun in the early eighteenth century, that, according to historian Maurice Craig, by the end of that century, 'it had flowered in a school of extraordinary loveliness, distinguished by Morocco inlays of various colours including white, in panels based mainly on the lozenge shape.'[7]

If you wanted a book with luxury binding and gold lettering, McKenzie's at the College Arms on Dame Street had the best variety of ornamentation. They would do a floral design with urns wreathed in garlands and maybe

Example of the golden age of booksellers and bookbinding in Temple Bar in the eighteenth century. The coat-of-arms of the Putland family. Notice the elephant motif. (Courtesy Irish Antiquarian Books/TCD)

include some insects or birds. John Archer in Crampton Court would have a different range of ornamentation to choose from. Some of the booksellers would also offer the addition of sumptuous endpapers of marbled paper, or even watered silk, to give the finished product a touch of class. Gilt edges added a sense of luxury, too; they looked good and were effective early dust deflectors. In later years, the famous Greene's bookshop on Clare Street, dating from the 1840s (it remained in business for 164 years, until 2007), was able to trace its roots directly to some of these earlier fine bookshops and publishers.[8]

FROM TEMPLE TO CATHEDRAL – DEAN SWIFT

In 1725, the *Dublin Journal* was published by George Faulkner (1699–1775), printer, publisher and friend of Jonathan Swift. The *Dublin Journal* was originally published near Castle Street and shortly afterwards moved to Essex Street East. It then moved around the corner to Parliament Street, where it remained until it ceased trading in 1825. It was immensely popular as it contained not only political news items, but also gossipy news such as robberies, births, deaths and marriages. Faulkner used woodcuts to illustrate his stories, which was unprecedented at the time.[9]

Jonathan Swift provided a great stimulus to publishing in Temple Bar and had strong links with the industry in the area. Born at Hoey's Court, Werburgh Street, beside Fishamble Street, his father died before he was born and he was brought up in the care of his uncle Godwin, a close friend of Sir John Temple, son of Sir William Temple, who had settled in Dublin prior to becoming provost of Trinity College Dublin. In later years, Swift, prior to becoming Dean of St Patrick's Cathedral, acted as secretary to Sir William Temple (1628–1699), the grandson of the original William Temple. Swift worked for Temple at the latter's home in England for about ten years from 1689. It was there that he met Esther Johnson, who became a lifelong love and whom he immortalised with the nickname 'Stella'. She was acting as a companion to Temple's sister, Lady Giffard.

He was unable to find suitable employment in England following Temple's death and had made some enemies (particularly Lady Giffard) writing Temple's memoirs, so he returned to Ireland disappointed. He often returned to England in the hope of finding work there. In 1713, he became Dean of St Patrick's Cathedral. One of his good friends in Dublin was the actor and playwright Thomas Sheridan of the Smock Alley Theatre. A second great friend was another Esther – Esther Van Homrigh, whom he had met in London and who had then followed him to Dublin. The Van Homrighs were Dutch Huguenots who had settled in Dublin and had a house in Temple Bar at Foster Place. Swift immortalised this Esther as 'Vanessa'. Theirs was a tempestuous relationship. Vanessa died at the age of 35, but not before destroying the will she had made in his favour. It was a one-time friend of Swift's who was made a co-heir in her alternative will: the philosopher George Berkeley, who was studying and attending the Dublin Philosophical Society meetings in Temple Bar. Esther was buried across the road in the cemetery adjoining St Andrew's church.

When he finally settled in Dublin, Swift began to develop a reputation as a writer, using satire to convey his message. His exile from England, as he saw it, drove him to pamphleteering and fighting for the cause of Ireland. Some of his greatest works were written, printed and published in Temple Bar, including *The Drapier's Letters*, *Gulliver's Travels*, *A Tale of a Tub* and *A Modest Proposal*, all of which reflected his political views. *Gulliver's Travels* was originally printed in London, but the Dublin version was a superior and better-quality printed version, with George Faulkner as printer and publisher. Swift's writings annoyed the government, which made clumsy attempts to silence him, including arresting and imprisoning his Temple Bar printers and publishers.[10]

COBWEBS, WASPS AND SLAVERY

In 1720, Edward Waters, who had his printing works on the corner of Essex Street East and Sycamore Alley, was prosecuted for having attempted to interfere with the interest of English traders by publishing Swift's pamphlet *Proposal for the Universal Use of Irish Manufacture, in clothes and furniture of houses, and utterly rejecting and renouncing everything wearable that comes from England*. This pamphlet encouraged the Irish to wear Irish clothes instead of imports. The export of these Irish products had been prohibited in order to protect English exports. At his trial, the jury found him not guilty but was sent back nine times by the judge in the (failed) hope of changing the verdict.

The saga was turned into a song by Swift, who wrote, in reference to English imports, 'Who'er will not wear them is not the King's lover' and 'Our true Irish hearts from old England to wean'. He also noted, 'Laws are like cobwebs, which catch small flies, but wasps and hornets may break through.' As regards the suppression of independent opinion, Swift added, '... for those who have used suppression to cramp liberty have gone so far as to resent even the liberty of complaining; although a man upon the rack was never known to be refused the liberty of roaring as loud as he thought fit'.[11]

The pamphlet was an important statement on free trade, the right to export Irish commodities to England and the right of the Irish to use their own products rather than English imports. The question of Ireland's right to free trade subsequently became one of the central issues of the Patriot Party's movement for Irish legislative independence in the late eighteenth century. Henry Grattan later acknowledged Swift's influence.

Waters' arrest was followed by that of John Harding, based at Molesworth Court, Fishamble Street, who was imprisoned for printing Swift's *Drapier's Letters*. These were seven pamphlets written anonymously between 1724 and 1725 and signed by M.B. Drapier, each criticising the government over the imposition on Ireland of privately minted copper coinage that Swift believed to be of inferior quality and would consequently damage the economy. Swift represented Ireland as constitutionally and financially independent of Britain. He noted in one pamphlet that, 'For in reason, all government without the consent of the governed is the very definition of slavery.' Swift's pamphlets inspired popular support and a boycott against the coin, which was withdrawn. His patriotism earned him huge respect and he was called the 'Hibernian Patriot'.[12]

Waters' and Harding's arrests were followed by that of George Faulkner, who had his printing works at Essex Street East and a house and shop on Parliament Street. He was one of the most important publishers and booksellers of his era. Such was the esteem in which he was held that he was chosen as the preferred publisher of the *Works* of Swift, but this resulted in a short imprisonment in Newgate Gaol in 1735. Swift responded quickly and censured the Irish House of Commons:

Better we all were in our graves
Than live in slavery as slaves.[13]

This experience further enhanced Faulkner's career. However, Harding paid the ultimate price for publishing Swift's pamphlets when he died in prison. After his death, George Faulkner became Swift's main printer and publisher. The many arrests and imprisonment were not unusual at the time; printers and publishers who were not obedient to Dublin Castle paid the price.[14]

SWIFT'S MODEST PROPOSAL

In 1729, Sarah Harding, John Harding's widow, took the courageous decision to publish Swift's famous satire, *A Modest Proposal for Preventing the Children of*

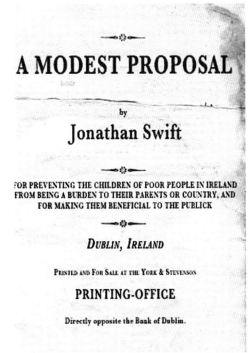

—◦✿◦—

A MODEST PROPOSAL

by

Jonathan Swift

—◦✿◦—

**FOR PREVENTING THE CHILDREN OF POOR PEOPLE IN IRELAND
FROM BEING A BURDEN TO THEIR PARENTS OR COUNTRY, AND
FOR MAKING THEM BENEFICIAL TO THE PUBLICK**

—◦✿◦—

DUBLIN, IRELAND

PRINTED AND FOR SALE AT THE YORK & STEVENSON

PRINTING-OFFICE

Directly opposite the Bank of Dublin.

Inside title page of Swift's *Modest Proposal*.

Poor People from being a Burthen to their Parents or the Country, and for making them beneficial to the Publick. This had a huge impact on the public and further enhanced Swift's reputation. His solution to the poverty in the country was, in his own words, 'I have been assured by a very knowing American of my acquaintance in London, that a young healthy child well nursed is at a year old a most delicious, nourishing, and wholesome food, whether stewed, roasted, baked, or boiled; and I make no doubt that it will equally serve in a fricassee or a ragout.'[15]

THE PRINCE OF PRINTERS

Upon his release from prison, George Faulkner's fame grew. His controversial newspaper, the *Dublin Journal*, continued to challenge the government and he was frequently arrested because of articles that appeared in it. Swift greatly admired Faulkner's courage and Faulkner remained Swift's publisher for the rest of his life. It was he who published Swift's *Works* in twenty volumes. The first complete collection of the *Drapier's Letters* appeared in the 1734 George Faulkner edition of the *Works*, along with a frontispiece offering praise and thanks from the Irish people.

Faulkner was also a major publisher in his own right, having published over 1,000 titles by 1748, but he was accused by his rivals of being a 'pirate' (of works from England). 'George Faulkner's Pamphlet Shop' at 27 Parliament Street could be depended on for the latest bestsellers direct from London or in better-value editions published by himself in Dublin.[16]

However, despite some criticism, for most of his life he was revered in Dublin and England as 'the Prince of Dublin Printers'. He was also known as a character in Dublin (and a wealthy one at that). He had an accident that required the amputation of one leg. Thereafter, he was often ridiculed for having 'one leg in the grave' or having a 'wooden understanding', which was in reference also to the statue in the vicinity of Essex Street known as the Wooden Man. Another story relates how his rivals would sometimes send him misinformation relating to accounts of births, deaths, marriages or robberies, which had never occurred. One irate reader tackled Faulkner personally on the issue, having been enraged to find himself dead in the previous edition of his newspaper. Faulkner replied, 'Sir, tis impossible for me to tell whether you are alive or dead, but I'm sure I gave you a very good character in my Journal.' The accuser was quite pleased with this response.[17]

The monument to Dean Jonathan Swift in St Patrick's Cathedral from the *Hibernian Magazine*, June 1802.

Through his connection with Swift and as the publisher of the *Dublin Journal* (later brought out three times a week), Faulkner's shop became the meeting place for the chief literary and political characters of the day. Like Swift, he had his patriotic side and was highly regarded for advocating the relaxation of the Penal Laws against Catholics. It was said that Faulkner's name 'deserves to be handed down to posterity as the first Protestant who stretched his hand to the prostrate Catholic, recognised him as a fellow Christian and a brother, and endeavoured to raise him to the rank of a subject and a freeman'.[18]

He was also one of the early members of the Dublin Society, founded at Dame Street.

Today it is possible to see a bust of Jonathan Swift in St Patrick's Cathedral created by the renowned sculptor Peter Cunningham for George Faulkner. It was placed over the entrance of George Faulkner's publishing business on the corner of Parliament Street and Essex Street (where Turk's Head pub is now) until 1760, when his nephew T. Faulkner donated it to the cathedral, hence the letter T rather than G in the inscription.

Another important inscription is the one on Swift's burial monument in the cathedral, located beside Faulkner's bust of Swift. It was described by W.B. Yeats as 'the greatest epitaph in history'. It reads:

Bust of Jonathan Swift in St Patrick's Cathedral, Dublin. Notice the wording – 'a gift from T. Faulkner'. He was a nephew of George Faulkner, Swift's printer in Temple Bar.

Swift has sailed into his rest,
Savage indignation there
Cannot lacerate his breast.
Imitate him if you dare,
Word-besotted traveller, he
Served human liberty.[19]

In later years, the *Dublin Journal*, under new ownership and called *Faulkner's Dublin Journal*, became a government-subsidised evening newspaper. This was published each Monday, Wednesday and Friday, sold at 5*d* per copy and was produced at No. 15 Parliament Street. It was the predecessor to *The Irish Times*.

THE FREEMAN'S JOURNAL AND THE 'SHAM SQUIRE'

Another prominent character in the Temple Bar publishing world was Francis Higgins (1750–1802), the notorious 'Sham Squire', who at one time in the history of the *Freeman's Journal* managed to become its owner. The newspaper had a number of homes in Temple Bar, including in the tower over St Audoen's Arch, on Blind Quay, at No. 4 Essex Quay, at No. 4 Crane Lane and later on Trinity Street, off Dame Street.[20]

It is regarded as one of the oldest nationalist newspapers in Ireland, having been co-founded in 1763 by the politician Charles Lucas, and was identified with radical, eighteenth-century Protestant patriot politicians such as Henry Grattan and Henry Flood. Lucas protested at length against the assumption of England that it had a right to legislate for Ireland. For Lucas, the experience of Ireland in this respect was 'a more severe bondage than the Israelites suffered in Egypt'. Besides political news items, it also covered robberies of both the highway and house varieties.[21]

The paper was unique, not only due to its nationalism, but also because it upheld liberal principles at a time when, according to Hugh Oram, 'no other publication in the country dared follow suit'.[22]

This changed dramatically in 1784 when it was taken over by Francis Higgins. Under his ownership, the paper published many proclamations and notices from Dublin Castle. As it was put, 'all pretension to liberalism vanished despite his claims of impartiality'.[23]

Higgins had a varied career as a messenger boy, a 'shoeblack' and a waiter in a porterhouse (tavern), a proprietor of a public house and a hosier (selling stockings). He became a highly controversial figure in his day, having acquired the nickname by which he is generally known (the 'Sham Squire') by impersonating a gentleman of landed property and gaining the confidence and then the hand of a wealthy lady. As part of his strategy, he was introduced to her family by a priest, to whom he had pretended that he wished to convert to Catholicism. He failed to tell him that he had already been christened a Catholic. When it was discovered that he was an imposter, he was jailed and the lady died of grief. While in jail, he studied for the legal profession to advance his career when he was released. He became an attorney. In his spare time, he visited

Late eighteenth-century image of the infamous 'Sham Squire', Francis Higgins, proprietor of the *Freeman's Journal*. (Courtesy of Fotofinish)

the brothels and gaming tables of Temple Bar. Conveniently, the premises of the *Freeman's Journal* on Crane Lane also fronted as a notorious brothel run by Margaret Molly. He operated a large gambling den that could be accessed via Parliament Street, Essex Street and Crane Lane. Two of his good friends included Buck Whaley and John ('copper-faced Jack') Scott.[24]

Motivated by the desire for wealth and influence, he wrote for the *Freeman's Journal* from the early 1780s. He was an opportunistic man and readily took advantage of his employer's weaknesses by lending him money, with the result that within a very short time he became the owner of the paper. He acquired it at a quarter of its value when he called in the debt he was owed in 1783. The *Freeman's Journal* had long been associated with the Patriot interest in the Irish parliament. Once Higgins became involved with the paper, this began to change. Proclamations and other official notices began appearing in the paper in 1782 and by 1784 the paper began to profess itself 'impartial', with government advertisements appearing regularly in its pages. This was his nature – he wormed his way into the confidence of people of rank, importance and fortune in the country and was ready for any job at a price. An old Dublin expression characterises him well – 'Elegance and ease, like a shoeblack in a noddy' (carriage).

He had a distinctive fashion sense. He was once described as 'dressed in the pink of fashion as he daily displayed himself'. He wore a 'three cocked hat, fringed with swan's down, a canary-coloured vest, with breeches to match, a bright green body-coat, with very deep tails, spangled with highly burnished buttons, and he was the only buck in Dublin who carried gold tassels on his Hessian boots; violet gloves concealed his chubby fingers, richly decorated with rings. A stiff stock, fastened with a diamond brooch, elevated still more his already pompous chin.'[25]

The *Dublin Evening Post*, a rival newspaper owned by John Magee, had little time for Higgins and ran several articles implicating him in dubious dealings, including seducing a merchant's daughter, having a suspect background and being a staunch friend of Dublin Castle. This, of course, was all wonderful and exciting for the Dublin reading public. However, Higgins had a good friend of the judge John ('copper-faced Jack') Scott, who fined Magee heavily in the hope of putting him out of business. Magee was unable to pay the fine (more than £7,000) and was imprisoned. Following this, in the early 1790s, an Act was passed to prevent such large fines and Scott became a figure of public ridicule. Magee rented a field opposite Scott's land and advertised a regular pig hunt. This brought thousands of people on to the land, damaging Scott's property in the process.[26]

Besides becoming proprietor of the *Freeman's Journal*, Higgins also began to practise as an attorney and held a variety of other posts, including deputy coroner of Dublin, under-sheriff and then Justice of the Peace for County Dublin. He is also suspected of having provided intelligence on the United Irishmen to Dublin Castle in the late 1790s for the sum of £1,000. It is alleged that is was he who betrayed Lord Edward Fitzgerald during the 1798 Rebellion.

When Higgins died in 1802, the *Freeman's Journal* was left to Frances Tracy, who was possibly his illegitimate daughter. Under the care of Tracy's husband, Philip Whitfield Harvey, the paper regained some independence from government influence, but it was not until the middle of the nineteenth century that it became a nationalist and Catholic newspaper. It was taken over by Independent Newspapers in 1924.[27]

THE DUBLIN EVENING MAIL – JIGGS AND MAGGIE

The *Dublin Evening Mail* was launched on 3 February 1823, with Joseph Timothy Haydn as its first editor. With its offices on the corner of

The *Evening Mail* offices on corner of Cork Hill and Parliament Street, 1952. (Courtesy of Bureau of Military History)

Parliament Street and Cork Hill, it proved to be the longest-surviving evening paper in Ireland (surviving until 10 July 1962). From 1823 until 1828, it was known as the *Dublin Evening Mail* and from 1928 until 1962 it was the *Evening Mail*. Within a month of being launched, it had become the city's bestselling newspaper; 2,500 copies of each issue were printed and sold mainly to the gentry and the aristocracy (at a time when few could read). Its success quickly undermined competing newspapers, including the *Dublin Journal*, founded by George Faulkner.[28]

The *Dublin Evening Mail* was always a Protestant newspaper. In its early years, under Haydn, it was popular because it was a sensationalist newspaper with much anti-Catholic bigotry, which appealed to its niche readership. However, the paper's owners became concerned in later years because of the increase in libel actions and they bought Haydn out.[29]

According to Hugh Oram, 'under its later name [*Evening Mail*] it was required reading at teatime for generations of Dubliners, a surprisingly homely, almost innocent, mix of news and features. Jottings by "Man About Town" and cartoons, including Jiggs and Maggie and Mandrake the Magician, were very popular.'[30] The paper carried regular progress reports about people in isolation hospitals, such as the old Cork Street Fever Hospital (in the Liberties) and Cherry Orchard. Patients could be 'satisfactory' or 'not so well' and were listed not by name, but by number. It also printed An Óige hostelling and cycling notes, a 'Lost and Found' column, limericks, notices about missing animals and even a lonely hearts section. It was the paper with the best 'Situations Vacant' columns. The most widely read part of the paper was 'Letters to the Editor'. For years, if somebody had a grievance, a well-known encouragement in Dublin was, 'Write to the *Mail* about it'. This unchanging formula yielded a solid circulation of some 100,000 copies per issue in the twentieth century.[31]

The newspaper itself made headlines in 1898 when it received reports, via wireless telegraphy, on the Kingstown (Dún Laoghaire) yachting regatta. This was the first time any newspaper in the world had used a wireless for news. Marconi had taken up a position in the harbour master's house and relayed the information from there to the *Mail*, which was the sponsor of the event.[32] Two years later, the Guinness brewing company took over the newspaper. In April of the same year, Queen Victoria visited Dublin. As part of her visit, some of the royal party sailed up the River Liffey, accompanied by festooned yachts from various clubs. The crowds enjoyed the spectacle. In a notorious typographical error, the *Dublin Evening Mail* reported that Her Majesty had 'pissed over O'Connell Bridge'.[33]

In June 1923, the paper ran a competition to select an Irish national anthem, though 'Amhrán na bhFiann' ('The Soldiers' Song') was used informally, it had not been officially adopted. W.T. Cosgrave's Irish Free State government was under pressure to choose whether to use this or 'God Save the King' for functions and events abroad. W.B. Yeats, Lennox Robinson and James Stephens were appointed as adjudicators and there was a prize of 50 guineas for the winning entry. However, the judges decided that the entries were not of the standard required and five years later, in 1928, the Irish Free State adopted 'Amhrán na bhFiann' as its anthem.

For many years, '*Herald* and *Mail*!' – or 'Herrelly Mail!', to be more precise – was the traditional cry of newspaper sellers on the capital's streets. Both had been features of Irish (or in the case of the *Mail*, Dublin) life since the previous century. However, the year 1954 (sometimes referred to as 'the Marian Year') brought new, and deadly, competition for the *Mail* in the form of the *Evening Press*. Both the editorial content of the *Evening Press* and its ability to attract small advertisements away from the *Mail* meant that the latter was soon in difficulties. A slogan for many years was '*Evening Press*, Best for Small Ads'; if you were looking for a bedsit, a flat, a second-hand car or a job, you would first try the *Evening Press.*

When there was a fire at *The Irish Times* building in 1951, David Allen, the general manager of the *Evening Mail*, arranged for the newspaper to be printed on the presses of the *Mail* in Parliament Street. Perhaps this was an omen as the newspaper was bought by *The Irish Times* in 1960 and closed in 1962, after 139 years of publication.[34]

DUBLIN'S INVISIBLE PRINCE

Certain individuals in the long history of the newspaper stand out. One of the co-owners of the *Dublin Evening Mail* in the 1840s and 1850s was Joseph Sheridan Le Fanu (1814–1873), best known for his mystery and horror fiction. He was regarded in the nineteenth century as one of Europe's foremost ghost-story writers. However, before gaining this reputation, he was one of Dublin's most influential newspaper owners and editors. He took over the *Mail* in 1842 and, according to Éamonn MacThomáis, 'Whether you agreed or not the *Mail* always spoke out in the honest Huguenot tradition of its famous owner-editor, Joseph Sheridan Le Fanu.'[35]

His roots were in Temple Bar. According to historian Maurice Craig, 'he had a share of the brilliant blood of the Sheridans'.[36] His father was Joseph Le Fanu (of Huguenot descent) and his mother Alicia Sheridan, who was related to the famous dramatist and politician Richard Brinsley Sheridan. As such, he would also have been connected to Thomas Sheridan of the Smock Alley Theatre. He named his son 'Brinsley'. His mother used to tell him stories about the 1798 Rebellion. He had kept the dagger belonging to Lord Edward Fitzgerald (which his mother had acquired) and a letter belonging to another United Irishman, John Sheares, written just before his execution. It seems clear that some of the seeds of his later interest in the macabre were sown in his childhood.

Le Fanu was part of the vanguard of the nineteenth-century Gothic literature enthusiasts. In 1838, while studying law at Trinity College, he began writing stories for the *Dublin University Magazine*. His first published ghost story was 'The Ghost and the Bone Setter'. Shortly afterwards, he wrote stories about demonic visitation and Satanic possession: 'The Fortunes of Sir Robert Ardagh' and 'Schalken the Painter'. However, despite studying the law, as soon as he graduated he quickly discarded the wig and the gown in favour of the pen and ink of newspaper publishing. Business matters took up a lot of his time in subsequent years (including the *Mail*), although he retained his interest in writing stories. His early stories were set and published in Dublin. He later changed the locations to English ones, which further enhanced their popularity.[37]

Joseph Sheridan Le Fanu, 1870.
(Courtesy of Dublin Forums)

His stories were influenced by years of supernatural stories, superstitions and traditions. He specialised in the unexplained and mysterious, using tone and nuance to create an undercurrent of the Gothic and the macabre. His ghost stories and tales of mystery have been described as 'reaching a crescendo of terror, while his use of nature and the supernatural made the terror all too believable'.[38]

He also wrote novels that pushed the boundaries of Victorian ghost stories and he has been described as Dublin's Edgar Alan Poe. Some of these include stories *The House by the Churchyard* (1863), one of his best known, set in Chapelizod, County Dublin, and *Wylder's Hand* (1864). One of Le Fanu's greatest known works is his Gothic horror novel *Uncle Silas* (1864), which was made into the 1987 film *The Dark Angel*, starring Peter O'Toole. It tells the story of a wealthy heiress who survives a murder plot against her by her uncle, her cousin and an evil governess. Other popular novels of his included *The Cook and the Anchor* (one of his first, in 1845; the novel depicts a colourful Dublin, with its alehouses and duels), *All in the Dark*, and *Haunted Lives*.[39]

Twenty-six years before Bram Stoker gave us *Dracula*, Le Fanu wrote his 1871 novella *Carmilla* about a sexually charged lesbian vampire. The story would go on to inspire several films, including Hammer Horror's *The Vampire Lovers* (1970). Excerpts of *Carmilla* were first published in the magazine the *Dark Blue* and later incorporated into Le Fanu's *In a Glass Darkly*. This was a collection of five chilling horror stories written as the case histories of

'Funeral', illustration by Michael Fitzgerald for *Carmilla* in the *Dark Blue*, January 1872.

Dr Martin Hesselius, one of the first occult detectives in literature.

Following the death of his wife Susan Bennett in 1858, Le Fanu turned into somewhat of a recluse and it was around this time that he produced some of his best writings. He became known as 'the invisible prince' because of his wanderings around the city at night (he lived in Merrion Square). He is buried in Mount Jerome cemetery in the shadow of one of the boundary walls with the Hospice for the Dying, alongside a path called the Nun's Walk. In recent years, his tombstone, a limestone slab on a granite vault, has been cleaned up and a plaque installed on it in his memory. It states:

Illustration by D.H. Friston in *Carmilla*, Joseph Sheridan Le Fanu's vampire story.

Here Lies Dublin's Invisible Prince
Joseph Sheridan Le Fanu
28th August 1814 – 7th February 1873
Novelist and Writer of Ghost Stories.[40]

THE PRINCE OF DARKNESS

Le Fanu's writings had an undoubted influence on another individual associated with the *Dublin Evening Mail*. Approximately twenty-five years after Le Fanu introduced the world to his version of Gothic horror, Bram Stoker (1847–1912) was working as an unpaid theatre critic for the newspaper.[41] He did this in a part-time capacity as he was working full-time across the road from the *Evening Mail* in Dublin Castle as an inspector for petty sessions. He spent twelve years working there. One of his first books was called *Duties of Clerks of the Petty Sessions*, which he later described as 'dry as dust'.

Stoker was always interested in theatre and was respected for his incisive reviews for the *Mail*. After seeing Henry Irving, the greatest actor of his generation, play Hamlet in the Theatre Royal (Hawkins Street), he wrote a review that the actor liked. The two met for dinner in the Shelbourne Hotel. Irving invited him to London to run the Lyceum Theatre (which he owned) and be his business manager. Stoker and his wife Florence (who had previously been Oscar Wilde's girlfriend) moved there in 1878. He worked for Irving until the actor's death in 1905. It was while working in London that he found time to write *Dracula*, first published in 1897. He had written many other novels already, including *The Snake's Pass* (1890), *Lady of the Shroud* (1909) and *The Lair of the White Worm* (1911). Interestingly, Bram Stoker seems to be more recognised in Romania, which he never visited, than in his home in Dublin, all because of his use of the place name Transylvania.[42]

Sheridan Le Fanu's lesser-known novel *Carmilla* may have been an influence for Stoker's *Dracula* since both deal with

Bram Stoker in 1906. He never visited Romania and *Dracula* was only published for the first time in Romanian in 1990. (Courtesy of Romanian Tourism/Dublin Forums)

vampires and occult doctors and both are set in a dark, remote Gothic castles in some faraway, wild and mountainous country. Was Stoker's success founded on recognising and expanding upon the work of prior authors such as Joseph Sheridan Le Fanu? Either way, it was not Stoker who invented the vampire; Le Fanu deserves this accolade.

Both authors found their inspiration on the corner of Parliament Street in Temple Bar.

THE MAN IN THE CLOAK – JAMES CLARENCE MANGAN

There has been speculation from time to time as to whether Bram Stoker also found inspiration in Dublin from the man widely known in Temple Bar and the Liberties 'as the man in the cloak'. The 'cloak' has always been a hallmark of Dracula's persona and apparel. The Dublin 'man in the cloak' was the nineteenth-century poet James Clarence Mangan (1803–1849), Ireland's prolific poet and author of over 1,000 poems. He was born at No. 3 Fishamble Street on 1 May 1803. He left school prematurely to help his impoverished family. While working in a scrivener's office, he began studying European languages. He had been baptised as James, but he used the adopted 'Clarence' constantly to sign

Cover of a booklet containing songs, ballads and poems of James Clarence Mangan. (Courtesy of Walton's)

Commemorative stamp for James Clarence Mangan. (Courtesy of Dublin Forums)

his poems, quoting Shakespeare's *Richard III*, 'Clarence is come, false, fleeting, perjured Clarence'.[43]

His poetry appeared in *The Comet*, the *Dublin Penny Journal*, the *United Irishman* and in the first and subsequent editions of the Young Irelander's *The Nation* newspaper. In 1859, the Young Irelander John Mitchell edited Mangan's poetry, including his 'My Dark Rosaleen' (his most famous poem, which begins with the lines, 'O my dark Rosaleen, do not sigh, do not weep ...') and 'Woman of Three Cows', for a New York edition. An eccentric in dress and habits, Mangan was frequently seen in the streets of Dublin dressed in a large pointed hat and a cloak. A pair of dark green spectacles emphasised the paleness of his features. He was said to have carried two umbrellas, even in the warmest weather. W.B. Yeats admitted that Mangan had been an important influence. James Joyce was also influenced by him and read a paper on Mangan to the Literary and Historical Society of UCD in 1902.

Mangan began drinking heavily early in life and became addicted to opium. He often lay in the gutters of Bride Street and Peter Street, totally debilitated. He fell victim to the cholera epidemic during the Great Famine (1845–9) and died in the Meath Hospital. His last writings, which he was carrying in his hat when brought to hospital, were unfortunately destroyed by a ward orderly. There is a memorial to the great poet in St Stephen's Green. It was the last work completed by James H. Pearse, the father of 1916 Rising leader, Pádraig Pearse. It is an unusual sculpture as it has two heads: one of the poet and the other, below this, of '*Róisín Dubh*', his 'Dark Rosaleen'.[44]

MOORE'S MELODIES

In the nineteenth century, the poet, singer and raconteur Thomas Moore (1779–1852) became hugely popular. He was born at No. 12 Aungier Street, a stone's throw from Temple Bar, the son of a wealthy tea merchant. He is often considered Ireland's national bard and has long been associated in the public's mind with Moore's Melodies.

Sometime in the early nineteenth century, he was invited to visit No. 4 Westmoreland Street, the offices of Power's Publishers. Power's Publishers were in business from 1797 until 1831. That visit was to have a significant influence on his subsequent career and fame. James and William Power specialised in music publishing and had invited Moore (known then more as a poet) to collaborate with them on a projected edition of Irish airs and to write lyrics to a series of Irish tunes. The first volume, *Selection of Irish Melodies*,

Early twentieth-century image of the statue of Thomas Moore on Westmoreland Street.
(Lawrence Collection, courtesy of NLI (Commons) collection)

was published in around 1807/08. There followed nine additional issues and
a supplement, containing 124 airs. The airs proved to be enormously popular
and Moore consequently became best known for these *Irish Melodies* (often
just called Moore's Melodies). Famous pieces included 'The Meeting of the
Waters', 'The Minstrel Boy', 'She Move's Through the Fair', 'The Last Rose of
Summer' and 'Oft in the Stilly Night'.

Moore moved in upper-class social and political circles and would have known
Lord Edward Fitzgerald and Robert Emmet. He was a strong advocate of Catholic
Emancipation, citing its absence as the cause of the 1798 Rebellion. He later
wrote biographies of Lord Edward Fitzgerald and Richard Brinsley Sheridan.

Today, there is a bronze statue of Thomas Moore on Westmoreland Street,
facing Temple Bar and erected in 1857.[45]

THE PALACE BAR AND THE LITERATURE SET

The Palace Bar on Temple Bar's Fleet Street is one of Dublin's most historic
literary pubs. In the words of one of Ireland's most famous poets, Patrick
Kavanagh, 'When I first came to Dublin in 1939, I thought The Palace the
most wonderful temple of art.'[46]

When Bill Aherne, the 'mountainy-man' from Rearcross in County Tipperary, acquired the Palace Bar during the post-war economic gloom of 1946, he could not have known that this premises was about to enter its golden literary age. In fact, there were two such ages: one in the 1930s, which lasted until around the time of the death of owner George Ryan in 1938, and another in the 1940s and '50s and beyond, though this was not as dramatic as the first. The novelty wore away with time and custom was lost to the nearby Pearl Bar on the opposite end of Fleet Street.

While these years were intellectually and culturally bright (against a backdrop of draconian censorship), they were frequently impoverished times for the literary set. Today the pub holds a returned cheque for £1 10s 0d presented by a famous rural poet. Bill Aherne's son Liam succeeded him in the 1970s and today the third generation of this family, including William, steeped in licensed trade tradition, are involved in the day-to-day operations of this famous Victorian jewel.

The Fleet Street area was a haven for the Irish literati and the arts community, perhaps unsurprisingly as *The Irish Times* was published nearby on D'Olier Street. The Palace became the nexus for the literary set, even before Bill Aherne took over from George Ryan. It was, in the words of Flann O'Brien, 'the main resort of newspapermen, writers, painters, and every known breed of artist and intellectual'. One frequenter of The Palace opined, 'The Palace Bar was perhaps the last place of its kind in Europe, a Café Littéraire, where one could walk in to have an intelligent discussion with a stranger, listen to Seamus O'Sullivan on the early days of Joyce, or discuss the national problem with the giant Hemingwayesque editor of the *Irish Times*.' He wrote that it was 'like a warm alligator tank'. It was also known as the 'branch office of *The Irish Times*', a magic circle from which outsiders were scrupulously barred.[47]

That the pub became the favoured pub of the fourth estate was due in no small measure to the imperious, Chestertonian figure of Robert Marie Smyllie, then editor of *The Irish Times* (1934–54). He cut an extraordinary figure around Dublin – hugely overweight, wearing a green sombrero and an overcoat like a cape, often followed by a coterie of hangers-on. It was said that Smyllie ('call me Bertie') could read proofs using one hand while playing dominoes with the other.[48]

A famous cartoon appeared in *Dublin Opinion* magazine in 1940 depicting Smyllie in the company of Brian O'Nolan, Patrick Kavanagh and others. Cartoonist Alan Reeve drew the Palace Bar with a who's who of the Irish literary and artistic figures that frequented the establishment, including Maurice Walsh, Harry Kernoff, Lynn Doyle, Padraic Fallon, Donagh MacDonagh, M.J. MacManus and many more. Smyllie had a lot of time for books and authors, whom he encouraged to write for *The Irish Times*, even during the Emergency when paper was rationed. There was a Dublin saying at one time, 'If you miss *The Irish Times*, you miss part of the day and if you go into the Palace Bar you'll miss the whole bloody day!'[49]

Smyllie, who had a passionate affinity with Bill Aherne's Palace Bar whiskey, had the power to publish or dismiss emerging Irish literary talent, so night after night hordes of aspiring literary artists came to pay homage and, hopefully, gain favour with Smyllie. Each night, the back room contained more literary talent than had hitherto passed through the gates of nearby Trinity College. Austin Clarke, Patrick Kavanagh, Francis Stuart, Brendan Behan and Brian O'Nolan were invariably there. The latter was once found hiding in a telephone box on the premises during a raid on the pub for after-hours drinking.

Poets, writers, sculptors and artists all came to discuss their work and get inspiration from their peers. Much whiskey, ale and porter were consumed as the night wore on and voices became increasingly raised and passionate. Sometimes Behan would dissolve the intensity by unleashing a ballad on unwelcoming ears – unwelcoming because if it was nationalistic in sentiment, Smyllie would promptly depart. Today, those living literary traditions are recalled by various annual, commemorative events and the Palace's literary legacy has been perpetuated in recent decades by the patronage of such regulars as the late Seamus Heaney and Con Houlihan.[50]

PALACE REGULARS – FLANN O'BRIEN

One of the many famous Dublin writers who visited the Palace Bar was Brian O'Nolan (1911–1966), who wrote under the name Flann O'Brien. O'Nolan was at his satiric best in his 'Cruiskeen Lawn' column for *The Irish Times*. Written from 1940 to 1966 under the pseudonym Myles na gCopaleen ('Miles of the Little Horses'), the column introduced readers to the archetypal Dublin man, 'the Brother', whose homespun philosophy served as a balm to most of life's problems. O'Nolan was a respectable civil servant who was unfortunately overly fond of alcohol. By 1953, his office drinking had become such a problem that he was forcibly 'retired'. 'You were seen coming out of the Scotch House at 2.30 p.m.', his superiors challenged him, to which O'Brien replied tartly, 'You mean I was seen coming in.'[51]

The centenary of the birth of Brian O'Nolan was celebrated on 5 October 2011, inside and outside the Palace Bar. Four bronze pavement plaques were unveiled. The plaques depict four great Irish literary figures: Patrick Kavanagh, Brendan

Flann O'Brien (on the right) in the Palace Bar, Fleet Street, in the 1950s. (Courtesy of Hulton Archive/Getty)

Behan, Flann O'Brien and Con Houlihan, all frequenters of the Palace. Jarlath Daly is the artist who created the casts. As well as an image of the writer, each plaque has words of wisdom attributed to the individual in question: Flann O'Brien – 'All over my garden I have tiny wooden houses stuck on poles. I call them tantrums because the birds fly into them'; Con Houlihan – 'Whenever my county are in the All-Ireland Final, my head says Kerry and my heart says the Kingdom'; Patrick Kavanagh, from his poem 'Sanctity' – 'To be a poet and not know the trade, to be a lover and repel all women; Twin ironies by which great saints are made. The agonising pincer-jaws of Heaven'; and Brendan Behan – 'Critics are like eunuchs in a harem; They know how it's done, they see it done every day, but they are unable to do it themselves.'

JAMES JOYCE AND TEMPLE BAR

James Joyce makes reference to many of Temple Bar's buildings, alleys, arches and streets in his work. Joyce is celebrated today in various ways. There is a statue of him with Oliver St John Gogarty on Anglesea Street and a hotel, Blooms, called after one of his most famous characters, Leopold Bloom. Today the work of designer James Earley is boldly painted all over the exterior of Blooms Hotel on Anglesea Street, depicting the lead characters of *Ulysses* (Bloom, Molly, Stephen, Blazes, and Buck Mulligan). While he was working on the project, Earley noted that he was 'new to *Ulysses* and it's the forever peeling onion with a million layers!' He added, 'In between the character panels are graphic representations of various themes in the book. The illustrative style is inspired by graphic illustrator Alphonse Mucha. The Art Nouveau style is in keeping with the era the book was based. I have added in my own twist on the style, but the basis is still all there.'[52]

Another hotel in *Ulysses* is the famous Dolphin Hotel on Essex Street East. On his way through Temple Bar to cross the River Liffey, McCoy stops outside the Dolphin Hotel to allow the ambulance to gallop past, dodges a banana peel and goes up the steps under Merchant's Arch. A reference to Temple Bar in 'Counterparts' in *Dubliners* captures an attitude to the area at the turn of the century when it was in decline, a place to pass through on the way to somewhere else. 'He went through the narrow alley of Temple Bar quickly, muttering to himself that they could all go to hell because he was going to have a good night of it.'[53]

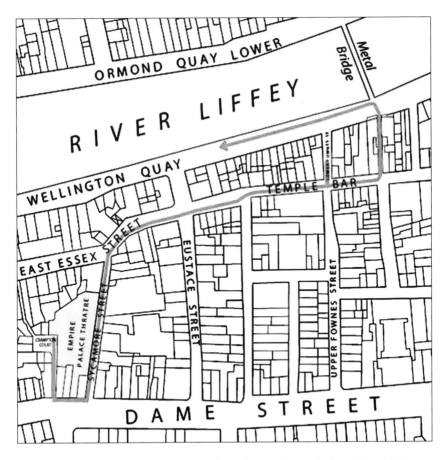

The route taken by Lenehan and M'Coy in *Ulysses* from the Empire Palace (Olympia) Theatre at Crampton Court

Bedford Row, off Fleet Street, is also mentioned in *Ulysses*. Clohissy's bookshop was located at Nos 10 and 11 and it was there that Stephen Dedalus rummaged through the books looking for one of his school prizes. Wellington Quay features in *Ulysses*, too: Leopold Bloom buys a copy of the book *The Sweets of Sin* for his wife Molly from one of the second-hand bookstalls lining the Merchant's Arch passageway.[54]

As already noted, Bassi's religious goods shop on Wellington Quay is mentioned, 'by Bassi's blessed virgins Bloom's dark eyes went by. Blue robed, white under, come to me. God they believe she is: or goddess ... by went his eyes. The sweets of sin.' No. 20 Essex Street East features in Joyce's *A Portrait of the Artist as a Young Man*. The character Cranly is based on a friend of Joyce's from his student days, John F. Byrne, who had lived in that house on Essex Street. Fitzgerald's Pub, formerly J.J. O'Neill's (and now The Norseman on Eustace Street), was mentioned in the 'Wandering Rocks' episode of *Ulysses* and is also mentioned in 'Counterparts' in *Dubliners*.

ALL IN THE GUTTER

Two gentlemen admire the statue of Edmund Burke outside Trinity College Dublin, c. 1869. (Courtesy of National Library of Ireland (NLI) Commons Collection)

Other writers associated with Temple Bar include Standish O'Grady, who lived for a time in Eustace Street. Maria Edgeworth of *Castle Rackrent* fame has links with the area. Edmund Burke and Oliver Goldsmith hold pride of place in front of Trinity College Dublin, facing Temple Bar. The Young Irelander Thomas Davis, a poet, a patriot and one of the founders of *The Nation* newspaper, is celebrated with a statue on College Green. Moreover, the Gutter Bookshop on Cow's Lane takes its name from the famous line in Oscar Wilde's *Lady Windermere's Fan*, 'We are all in the gutter, but some of us are looking at the stars.'

17

LINEN AND LIPSTICK – RESURGENCE AND RENEWAL

During the late nineteenth century, Temple Bar slowly declined in popularity as other parts of the city centre developed and grew in importance. Historian Peter Pearson quotes a piece from an 1879 issue of the *Irish Builder*:

> Alas, there is nothing sweet or pleasant in the Temple Bar of our day! There are plenty of foul-smelling drains, dilapidated dwellings, back yards seething in filth, and poverty and rags from basements to attics out and about. There is still some life and huckstering trade in Temple Bar but its wealthy merchants and big and prosperous shopkeepers of forty or fifty years ago are all dead and gone, or if any of them still live, they know the place no longer. Poor Temple Bar! Ruin – black, ghastly and deadly has rained upon you in torrents![1]

There was not much improvement in the twentieth century. The toll of urban decay had set in by the 1950s as the city's commercial core contracted, with many derelict or rundown buildings and there was a significant property slump in the mid- to late 1980s, with interest rates in double figures. In his classic work, *The Destruction of Dublin* (1985), Frank McDonald noted, 'Dublin is probably the shabbiest, most derelict city in Europe, chaotic and disorderly like the capital of some Third World country. The tourists, no more than the inhabitants, cannot walk more than a few hundred yards without being confronted by shocking evidence of urban blight.'[2]

Dublin was a rundown city, with derelict sites and abandoned buildings everywhere. Temple Bar was particularly dilapidated. Frank McDonald suggested that the poor attitude towards preservation was a 'cultural problem'. For many Irish people, Georgian buildings were a symbol of the colonial past. 'It is tied up with the idea of 800 years of oppression and the like. The Georgian heritage wasn't really seen as Irish despite the fact that it was all built in Ireland by Irish workmen.'[3] Consequently, the rush to eradicate the colonial past saw the destruction of much of Georgian Dublin and its replacement with modern, generic buildings in the American corporate style.

Temple Bar retained a little importance until the mid-twentieth century, with banks and insurance companies still on Dame Street and sundry small businesses operating in the area. But many businesses, shoppers and residents were moving elsewhere. Today there is only a handful of small businesses that have survived the vagaries of time and tide. Yet, they have survived and provide an indispensable link with the historic identity of the area.

Temple Bar of the late 1970s and '80s was a place of narrow streets lined mostly with nineteenth-century industrial, commercial and domestic structures. Signs of neglect and urban decay were everywhere, engendered by the intention to develop the area as a major bus transportation hub. The building stock was allowed to slip into disrepair and a significant number of structures were removed altogether. On top of that, the overall city centre population (those living within the boundaries of the canals) had declined to approximately 75,000 people. Frank McDonald said during the Dublin Millennium Year of 1988, 'We don't really have a city to celebrate. A total of 160 acres in the centre of Dublin are derelict, in addition to a host of tumble-down buildings and vacant and potentially vacant buildings. The inner city has essentially been abandoned. The population of the inner city has been halved in the last 25 years.'[4]

SUBURBAN VERSUS URBAN

It seemed that suburban values had triumphed over urban values and there was little interest in preserving or supporting the inner city. The neglect of Temple Bar was only a part of the terrible destruction of some of the most historic parts of the city centre. In the late 1970s, there were major protests against the plans of the city authorities to erect civic offices on Wood Quay (known to all and sundry as 'bunkers'). Today these buildings are seen as a physical expression of the mentality of Dublin Corporation at the time. A Dublin taxi driver described the whole project in 1985 as 'a real Guns of Navarone job'.[5]

Conversely, the availability of buildings – however rundown – on cheap, short-term leases had brought an increasingly bohemian fusion of culture, cafés and small-scale commerce to Temple Bar. Speaking in the mid-1980s, Christine Bond, chairman of the board at Temple Bar Studios, the only low-rent studio space for artists in the city, said, 'Rents are cheap and it is a place where lots of younger people could get in and get something going.' Out of this eclectic mixture, an alternative vision for the future of the area emerged.[6]

Meanwhile, starting in the late 1970s, Córas Iompair Éireann (CIÉ), the state transport company, had started buying many buildings in central Temple Bar, with a view of building a large, modern central bus station on the site. Plans were drawn up by Skidmore Owings & Merrill, which included a vast shopping centre. From 1981 onwards, CIÉ began to purchase more and more property to build the huge transport hub. Its renting of properties was paradoxically transformative as its massive building project and proposal generated huge divisions, eventually triggering a rejuvenation process.

While CIÉ was dealing with the planning process, it leased properties at low rents to artists, musicians, co-ops and other cultural bodies. Short-term, cheap leases also led to the appearance of small restaurants, art galleries, studios, rehearsal facilities, clothes shops and so on. The Square Wheel Bicycle Shop (with its psychedelic shopfront), Borderline Records (like Mojo's in Merchant's Arch), the Green Party offices and many resource centres all found a home in the area. The Temple Bar Gallery and Studios, The Project Theatre, Black Church Print Studios, the Gallery of Photography, the Graphic Studio, Claddagh Records and Temple Bar Music Centre (now the Button Factory) also established themselves in Temple Bar during this period. This lent the area an alternative, bohemian atmosphere and residents began to appreciate the value of Temple Bar. The influx of young people and 'arty' types led to the Temple Bar area being dubbed Dublin's 'Left Bank', adding an interesting and hitherto poorly developed side to the city. The increasing vibrancy of the area resulted in demands for its preservation. A committee known as the Temple Bar Development Council was founded in 1988 to oppose CIÉ's plans for the bus depot and resistance against CIÉ plans to demolish Temple Bar grew.[7]

In the midst of the opposition to the transport hub plan, members of An Taisce (the National Trust for Ireland) had begun to examine the architectural heritage and streetscapes of Temple Bar. In a report published in 1985, the association advised that this quarter of Dublin had a unique architectural heritage, which had survived virtually intact for over 200 years.

The report recommended that preservation was the way forward and that the plan for a bus station should be abandoned.[8]

A POLITICAL PROJECT?

The cumulative effect of protests by An Taisce, conservationists, urbanists, residents, traders and the indigenous arts community, combined with the media's increased awareness of the situation eventually led to the cancellation of the bus station project. Other external factors, such as the 1988 Dublin's Millennium Celebrations and the designation of Dublin as the European Capital of Culture in 1991, did much to focus attention not only on Dublin's history and heritage but also on Temple Bar itself. The campaign had successfully lobbied Dublin Corporation and various government departments, including the Department of An Taoiseach. Finally, in what was to prove a turning point, Taoiseach Charles Haughey pledged during the general election campaign of 1987 that Temple Bar would be preserved. He described Temple Bar as 'one of the most important, traditional, historic, attractive and interesting parts of Dublin'.[9]

This promise was kept and funding and tax incentives were put in place. The most remarkable project of urban renewal in the State's history had begun.[10]

1991 – THE YEAR OF CHANGE

On 14 December 1991, Taoiseach Charles Haughey and Dublin's Lord Mayor Sean Kenny inaugurated the Temple Bar Street Improvements Scheme. This was given legislative effect with the Temple Bar Area Renewal and Development Act, 1991. This Act led to the creation of Temple Bar Properties (TBP), a newly constituted development company (and a State agency) established on behalf of the Department of An Taoiseach to oversee the regeneration of the area as Dublin's designated cultural quarter and to carry through the scheme of conservation and renewal. It was mandated to 'develop a bustling cultural, residential and small-business precinct that will attract visitors in significant numbers'. Temple Bar Renewal (TBR) was a sister company, charged with overseeing applications for projects hoping to avail of tax incentives to locate in the area.

With offices in a refurbished Georgian house on Eustace Street, an extremely talented, energetic, far-seeing, pro-active and creatively driven team spearheaded the work of TBP (two outstanding individuals were known as the 'linen and lipstick sisters'). Paddy Teahon, assistant secretary in the Department of An Taoiseach, was appointed TBP's first managing director and Pat Kenny, an accountant, its first chairman. Owen Hickey, a chartered surveyor was also on the board. He had previously been in charge of CIÉ's property portfolio. Laura Magahy, who was previously an administrator with the International Financial Services Centre (the IFSC), Patricia Quinn, another administrator and later head of the Arts Council, and John Quinlivan, involved in the save Temple Bar campaign, were also hugely and successfully involved in the work of TBP (and its successor the Temple Bar Cultural Trust). Their task was to develop Temple Bar as Dublin's cultural quarter and to build on what was taking place 'spontaneously' in the area.

They were ably assisted by a youthful and dynamic team that had great understanding of the spirit of the area and the demands of the task, including the commercial aspects. Individuals such as Maeve Jennings, Eve Ann Cullinan, Pat Walsh and Joe Melvin threw themselves into the job with relish. Others, such as the Dublin Corporation's Michael Gough, a senior planner, made significant contributions to the project.

The board and team faced marathon challenges, including at times being regarded as somewhat of 'an alien being' by some in Dublin Corporation not content with a perceived erosion of its autonomy. There were many battles over TBP's choice of architecture and there was hostility and friction with planners, politicians and publicans, and, at times, nearly insurmountable legal and archaeological obstacles, not to mention the power play between extraordinarily driven personalities and organisations from such diverse administrative, political and professional backgrounds, who all had to work together or against each other.[11]

THE '91 ACHIEVEMENT – PRESERVING AND TRANSFORMING

In 1991, CIÉ sold its land bank to Temple Bar Properties, which then organised the 1991 Framework Plan competition, an important stage in deciding the future of the area. The idea was to come up with a plan to rehabilitate the area by promoting a network of urban spaces with residential and cultural uses. The project required the retention of existing buildings/structures/streetscape and the use of vacant sites for building or urban space. The competition was won by Group '91 Architects, a collective of eight Irish architectural practices – Shay Cleary Architects, Grafton Architects, Paul Keogh Architects, McCullough

Mulvin Architects, McGarry Ní Éanaigh Architects, O'Donnell and Tuomey Architects, Shane O'Toole Architects and Derek Tynan Architects.[12]

Group '91 looked to European tradition for inspiration and so brought something radically new to the table. They were particularly influenced by Aldo Rossi, an Italian architect. He believed that cities were comprised of layers to be revealed and not destroyed or replaced. Group '91 envisaged a new approach that would see new buildings talking to old buildings – an evolving historic area, with each generation creating a new layer.[13]

This framework plan, which Frank McDonald described as 'so startlingly new and different that Temple Bar came to be featured in architectural and lifestyle magazines across the world', shaped the changes to the area in the decade following the competition. The built environment was transformed by the reintroduction of cobblestones, the creation of public spaces, the pedestrianisation of the core area and the new businesses and residents. The area became a vibrant entertainment district also, although concerns have been raised about the dominance of this entertainment aspect to the detriment of cultural activities. However, the area's vibrancy and creativity cannot be doubted. While the steel, glass, brick and concrete of contemporary Temple Bar may differ in finished detail from the 1991 proposals, they are largely where the plan indicated they should be. Central to the framework plan was a recognition of the need to preserve as well as transform. Consequently, much of what stood in 1985 still stands, despite the upheaval, mistakes, problems and issues that invariably go hand in hand with such a major project of urban regeneration. Temple Bar has its critics as well as its admirers, which is perhaps inevitable when such diverse groups and vocations are involved, all with the goal of regenerating Temple Bar. Despite this (and possibly because of it), Temple Bar is a byword for urban regeneration, restoration and cultural development.

The days of dystopian urban decline in the area are gone. Instead, Temple Bar has been transformed into an iconic district in Dublin. The story is a remarkable one of gentrification, involving a positive and enlightened process, the results of which are now obvious to natives and visitors alike. After decades of decline, the process culminated in the dramatic renaissance of Temple Bar. It now presents us with a veritable statement about Ireland past, present and future.

In the words of Frank McDonald, 'the development of Temple Bar was an extraordinary achievement'. In 1996, TBP published a work-in-progress report of its first five years, *The Power of an Idea*, which succinctly captures the essence of that achievement.[14]

EPILOGUE

Temple Bar had become more 'skewed' towards the hospitality sector and other interests, according to a report commissioned by the Project Arts Centre in late 2015 (and published in 2016). The report, *Unity of Purpose and Sustaining Futures*, drew on the experiences and views of twenty-four cultural organisations. 'A casual stroller entering and walking through Temple Bar might rightly wonder why it is designated Dublin's cultural quarter. The brand that is Temple Bar has been commercialised at the expense of culture.' It said that Temple Bar had become 'besieged by antisocial behaviour', while 'the visibility of culture in the area is barely apparent'. The Report, compiled by Arthur Lappin of Kilspin Ltd, made the case for a new arts-driven organisation in place of TBCT, which had administered the area until early 2016. 'The ultimate objective is to see Temple Bar restored to a vibrant cultural quarter where the cultural needs of people who reside, work, and visit Temple Bar are not eclipsed and compromised by a burgeoning commercial sector', the report advised. Temple Bar's inability to become a 'vibrant and thriving' corner of the city was the greatest failure of the disbanding TBCT, it noted. 'The cultural organisations in Temple Bar have been, unwittingly or otherwise, complicit in this failure.' 'Debate and collaboration will be essential to defining future policy and reclaiming Temple Bar as Dublin's cultural quarter.' Mark Hilliard, 'Temple Bar Commercialised at Expense of Culture, Report Finds', *The Irish Times*, 26 January 2016.

NOTES

INTRODUCTION

1. Pat Liddy, *The Changing Landscapes of Dublin* (Dublin City Info: Artane, Dublin, 2003)

1. MONKS OF THE TEMPLE – EARLY HISTORY

1. Maurice Curtis, *The Liberties: A History* (Dublin: The History Press, 2013), p.143
2. Howard Clarke (ed.), *Medieval Dublin: The Making of a Metropolis* (Dublin: The Irish Academic Press, 1990), pp.183–200
3. Niall McCullough, *Dublin: An Urban History* (Dublin: Ann Street Press, 1989), p.24; F.X. Martin, 'The Augustinian Friaries in Pre-Reformation Ireland' in *Augustiniana*, Augustinian Historical Institute (Belgium), VI (1956), pp.347–384; Robert Somerville-Woodward & Nicola Morris, *17 Eustace Street: A History* (Dublin: IFI/Timeline Research, 2007), p.5.
4. Hiram Morgan, 'Sir William Brabazon' in S.J. Connolly (ed.), *The Oxford Companion to Irish History* (Oxford: Oxford University Press, 1998), p.56; Maurice Curtis, *The Liberties: A History* (Dublin: The History Press Ireland, 2013), pp.26–8
5. Maurice Curtis, *The Liberties: A History* (Dublin: The History Press Ireland, 2013), p.29

2. CROMWELL, THE CROW'S NEST AND FAMILIES OF FORTUNE

1. John McCavitt, 'Chichester, Arthur, Baron Chichester (1563–1625)', *Dictionary of National Biography* (Oxford: Oxford University Press, 2004), p.291
2. Niall McCullough, *Dublin: An Urban History* (Dublin: Ann Street Press, 1989), p.24
3. Peter Pearson, *The Heart of Dublin* (Dublin: The O'Brien Press, 2000), p.34
4. Colm Lennon & John Montague, *John Rocque's Dublin* (Dublin: RIA, 2010), p.xvii.
5. John Gilbert, *History of the City of Dublin*, Three vols (Dublin: Gill & MacMillan, 1978), Vol. I, p.93
6. John Gilbert, *History of the City of Dublin*, Three vols (Dublin: Gill & MacMillan, 1978), Vol. II, pp. 170–180
7. Ibid.; Hiram Morgan, 'The Adventurer's Act' in S.J. Connolly (ed.), *The Oxford Companion to Irish History* (Oxford: Oxford University Press, 1998), p.4

8. Maurice Craig, *Dublin 1660–1860* (Dublin: Liberties Press, 2006 (reprint of 1952 edition)), pp.79–80; Toby Barnard, 'Petty, William' in *Oxford Dictionary of National Biography* (Oxford: Oxford University Press, 2004); Margaret Anne Cusack, *An Illustrated History of Ireland* (London: MacMillan, 1868), Ch. 31

9. John Gilbert, *History of the City of Dublin*, Three vols (Dublin: Gill & MacMillan, 1978), Vol. II, pp.170–80; Hiram Morgan, 'Cromwellian Land Settlement' in S.J. Connolly (ed.), *The Oxford Companion to Irish History* (Oxford: Oxford University Press, 1998), pp.128, 483

10. Maurice Craig, *Dublin 1660–1860* (Dublin: Liberties Press, 2006 (reprint of 1952 edition)), pp. 78–80; Eric Strauss, *Sir William Petty, Portrait of a Genius* (London: Glencoe, 1954), p.iii; *The Dictionary of National Biography*, new ed., XV, pp.999–1005; Sean O'Domhnaill, 'The Maps of the Down Survey' in *Irish Historical Studies* 3 (1943), pp. 381–392; John Gilbert, *History of the City of Dublin*, Three vols (Dublin: Gill & MacMillan, 1978), Vol. II, pp. 171–172

11. John Gilbert, *History of the City of Dublin*, Three vols (Dublin: Gill & MacMillan, 1978), Vol. II, p.5.

12. Hiram Morgan, 'Richard Boyle' in S.J. Connolly (ed.), *The Oxford Companion to Irish History* (Oxford, Oxford University Press: 1998), p.55; 'The Boyle Monument' in *Guide to St Patrick's Cathedral* (2013).

13. John Gilbert, *History of the City of Dublin*, Three vols (Dublin: Gill & MacMillan, 1978), Vol. II, pp.3–7; George Smith in *Concise Dictionary of National Biography*, Part 1–1900 (London: Smith, Elder & Co., 1882), p.133; Nicholas P. Canny, *The Upstart Earl: Richard Boyle, Earl of Cork* (Cambridge: Cambridge University Press, 1982). Thanks also to Turtle Bunbury; R.F.Foster, *Modern Ireland 1600-1972* (London: Penguin, 1988), p.8

14. F. Elrington Ball, *The Judges in Ireland 1221–1921* (London: John Murray, 1926), pp.271–77; John Gilbert, *History of the City of Dublin*, Three vols (Dublin: Gill & MacMillan, 1978), Vol. II, pp.310–313.

15 'Arthur Annesley, 1st Earl of Anglesey' in *Encyclopædia Britannica*, 11th ed., Vol. II (Cambridge: Cambridge University Press, 1911), p. 15; Maurice Curtis, *To Hell or Monto* (Dublin: The History Press Ireland, 2015), p.41

16. David Dickson, *Dublin: The Making of a Capital City* (London: Profile Books, 2014), p.183

17. Osmun Airy, 'Capel, Arthur (1631–1683)' in Leslie Stephen, *Dictionary of National Biography* 9 (London: Smith, Elder & Co. 1887), pp.12–17

3. RECLAMATION AND EXPANSION

1. Speed's Map of Dublin, 1610. Dublin City Council, *The Bridges of Dublin* (www.bridgesofdublin.ie)

2. O'Connell/Mahon Architects; Speed's Map of Dublin, 1610; John Rocque, *Exact Survey of the City and Suburbs of Dublin* (Dublin: George Faulkner, 1756)

3. Niall McCullough, *Dublin: An Urban History* (Dublin: Ann Street Press, 1989), p.33

4. Nuala Burke, 'Dublin's north-eastern city wall: early reclamation and development at the Poddle-Liffey confluence' in Howard Clarke (ed.), *Medieval Dublin: The Making of a Metropolis* (Dublin: Irish Academic Press, 2012), p.160

5. Niall McCullough, *Dublin: An Urban History* (Dublin: Ann Street Press, 1989), p.33

6. Maurice Craig, *Dublin: 1660–1860* (Dublin: Liberties Press, 2006 (reprint of 1952 edition)), p.53; Niall McCullough, *Dublin: An Urban History* (Dublin: Ann Street Press, 1989), p.24

7. Niall McCullough, *Dublin: An Urban History* (Dublin: Ann Street Press, 1989), p.32

8. Ibid., p.29

9. Ibid., p.32

10. Nuala Burke in Howard Clarke (ed.), *Medieval Dublin: The Making of a Metropolis*, pp.142–161; Niall McCullough, *Dublin: An Urban History*, pp.24–37
11. Pat Liddy, *Temple Bar – Dublin: An Illustrated History* (Dublin: Temple Bar Properties, 1992), pp.28–31
12. Nuala Burke in Howard Clarke (ed.), *Medieval Dublin: The Making of a Metropolis*, pp.142–161; National Library of Ireland, *Historic Dublin Maps* (Dublin: NLI, 1998); Hugh Oram, 'An Irishman's Diary', *The Irish Times*, 17 November 2003

4. CUSTOM HOUSES AND WIDE STREETS

1. Colm Lennon & John Montague, *John Rocque's Dublin* (Dublin: Royal Irish Academy, 2010), p.21
2. John Gilbert, *History of the City of Dublin*, Three vols (Dublin: Gill & MacMillan, 1978), Vol. II, pp.132–147; Niall McCullough, *Dublin: An Urban History* (Dublin: Ann Street Press, 1989), p.127
3. John Gilbert, *History of the City of Dublin*, Three vols (Dublin: Gill & MacMillan, 1978), Vol. II, p.139
4. John Gilbert, *History of the City of Dublin*, Three vols (Dublin: Gill & MacMillan, 1978), Vol. II, p.146
5. Dublin City Archives, Records and Maps of the Wide Streets Commissioners; Maurice Curtis, *The Liberties: A History* (Dublin: The History Press Ireland, 2013), p.34
6. Maurice Curtis, *The Liberties: A History* (Dublin: The History Press Ireland, 2013), p.34

5. BUCKS, BLASTERS AND CLUBS

1. David Dickson, 'Dublin' in S.J. Connolly (ed.), *The Oxford Companion to Irish History* (Oxford: Oxford University Press, 1998), p.161; Constantia Maxwell, *Dublin Under the Georges 1714–1830* (London: Faber & Faber, 1956 (original edition, 1937)), p.101
2. Patrick Geoghegan, *The Irish Times*, 8 October 2008
3. Maurice Curtis, *To Hell or Monto* (Dublin: The History Press Ireland, 2015), pp.86–87
4. Constantia Maxwell, *Dublin Under the Georges 1714–1830* (London: Faber & Faber, 1956 (original edition, 1937)), p.224;
   Diarmuid Ó Gráda, *Georgian Dublin* (Cork: Cork University Press, 2015), p.294
5. Ibid.
6. Valerie Shanley, *The Irish Independent* (14 June 2015); James Kelly, 'Duelling' in S.J. Connolly (ed.), *The Oxford Companion to Irish History* (Oxford: Oxford University Press, 1998), p.164
7. John Gilbert, *History of the City of Dublin*, Three vols (Dublin: Gill & MacMillan, 1978), Vol. II, p.308
8. John Gilbert, *History of the City of Dublin*, Three vols (Dublin: Gill & MacMillan, 1978), Vol. II, p.334
9. Constantia Maxwell, *Dublin Under the Georges 1714–1830* (London: Faber & Faber, 1956 (original edition, 1937)), p.119; John Gilbert, *History of the City of Dublin*, Three vols (Dublin: Gill & MacMillan, 1978), Vol. II, pp.38–9
10. John Gilbert, *History of the City of Dublin*, Three vols (Dublin: Gill & MacMillan, 1978), Vol. II, pp.40, 305–308; R.E. Brooke, *Daly's Club and Kildare Street Club* (Dublin: George Healy, 1930)

11. Maurice Craig, *Dublin: 1660–1860* (Dublin, Liberties Press, 2006 (reprint of 1952 edition)), p.181

12. *Edinburgh magazine*, Vol. 8 (1841), p.319

13. Charles Dickens, *All the Year Round*, vol. 15 (1866), p.496; John Gilbert, *History of the City of Dublin*, Three vols (Dublin: Gill & MacMillan, 1978), Vol. III, pp.39–40; Geoffrey Ashe, *The Hell-Fire Clubs: Sex, Rakes and Libertines* (London: Sutton Publishing, 2nd edition, 2005), p.63

14. Maurice Curtis, *To Hell or Monto* (Dublin: The History Press Ireland, 2015), pp. 80–85

15. Margaret Leeson, *The Memoirs of Mrs Margaret Leeson, Written by Herself* 3 vols (Dublin: M.L., 1795–1797); Mary Lyons (ed.), *The Memoirs of Mrs Leeson, Madam, 1727–97* (Dublin: Lilliput Press, 1995), pp.vi-xix; Karyn Moynihan, 'Peg Plunkett', article from Women's Museum of Ireland, 2012; Niamh O'Reilly, 'Prostitutes and Three Hundred Years of Vice', article from *Estudios Irlandeses* – the Global Women's Studies Programme at NUI Galway, 2008; Bláthnaid Ní Chofaigh, 'The Scandal of Mrs Leeson', *The Lyric Feature*, Lyric FM, August, 2014

16. Niamh O'Reilly, 'Prostitutes and Three Hundred Years of Vice', *Estudios Irlandeses* – The Global Women's Studies Programme at NUI Galway, 2008

17. Mary Lyons (ed.), *The Memoirs of Mrs Leeson, Madam, 1727–97* (Dublin: Lilliput Press, 1995), pp.vi-xix

18. Margaret Leeson, *The Memoirs of Mrs Margaret Leeson, Written by Herself* (Dublin: M.L., 1795–1797)

19. Constantia Maxwell, *Dublin Under the Georges 1714–1830* (London: Faber & Faber, 1956 (original edition, 1937)), p.113

20. Margaret Leeson, *The Memoirs of Mrs Margaret Leeson, Written by Herself* (Dublin: M.L., 1795–1797); Marie Luddy, *Prostitution and Irish Society, 1800–1940* (Cambridge: Cambridge University Press, 2007), pp.33–45

21. Margaret Leeson, *The Memoirs of Mrs Margaret Leeson, Written by Herself* (Dublin: M.L., 1795–1797)

22. *Dublin Evening Post*, 17 May 1797; Joe Jackson, *The Irish Times*, 27 June 2015

23. James Kelly & Martyn J. Powell (eds), *Clubs and Societies in Eighteenth-Century Ireland* (Dublin: Four Courts Press, 2010)

24. Maurice Curtis, *To Hell or Monto* (Dublin: The History Press Ireland, 2015), pp.86–90

25. Maurice Craig *Dublin 1660–1860* (Dublin: Liberties Press, 2006 (reprint of 1952 edition)), p.180–181; John Gilbert, *History of the City of Dublin*, Three vols (Dublin: Gill & MacMillan, 1978), Vol. I, pp. 16–17

26. Michael Fewer, 'The Hellfire Club, Co. Dublin' in *History Ireland*, vol. 18, no. 3 (May-June 2010), p.29; David Ryan, *Blasphemers and Blackguards: The Irish Hellfire Clubs* (Dublin: Merrion, 2013), p.98; J.W. Hammond, *The Story of Kilakee House and the Hellfire Club* (N.D.); Evelyn Lord, *The Hellfire Club: Sex, Satanism and Secret Societies* (Yale: Yale University Press, 2008), p.90

27. Peter Somerville Large, *Dublin* (London: Hamish Hamilton, 1979), p.156

28. John Gilbert, *History of the City of Dublin*, Three vols (Dublin: Gill & MacMillan, 1978), Vol. I, pp. 16–17

29. John Gilbert, *History of the City of Dublin*, Three vols (Dublin: Gill & MacMillan, 1978), Vol. I, pp. 14–15; John Gilbert, *History of the City of Dublin*, Three vols (Dublin: Gill & MacMillan, 1978), Vol. III, pp.251–255; Michael Fewer, 'The Hellfire Club, Co. Dublin' in *History Ireland*, vol. 18, no. 3 (May-June 2010), p.29; David Ryan, *Blasphemers and Blackguards: The Irish Hellfire Clubs* (Dublin: Merrion, 2012), p.98; J.W. Hammond, *The Story of Kilakee House and the Hellfire Club* (N.D.); Evelyn Lord, *The Hellfire Club: Sex, Satanism and Secret Societies* (Yale: Yale University Press, 2008), p.90

30. Tracy, Frank, '"If Those Trees Could Speak": The Story of an Ascendancy Family in Ireland' (pdf) (Dublin: South Dublin Libraries, 2005), p.6

31. Maurice Craig, *Dublin: 1660–1860* (Dublin: Liberties Press, 2006 (reprint of 1952 edition)), p.248

32. Constantia Maxwell, *Dublin Under the Georges 1714–1830* (London: Faber & Faber, 1956 (original edition, 1937)), p.119

33. Patrick M. Geogheghan, 'Buck Whaley: Drinking, Dissipation and Destruction' in *History Ireland*, issue 2, vol. 15 (March/April 2007); Michael Fewer, 'The Hellfire Club, Co. Dublin' in *History Ireland*, vol. 18, no. 3 (May-June 2010), p.29; Maurice Craig, *Dublin: 1660–1860* (Dublin: Liberties Press, 2006 (reprint of 1952 edition)), p.248

6. BEGGARS, BAWDS AND BAGNIOS

1. Constantia Maxwell, *Dublin Under the Georges 1714 – 1830* (London: Faber & Faber, 1956 (original edition, 1937)), p.101

2. Ibid., p.102

3. Frank McDonald quoted in *The Canberra Times* (17 March 1988)

4. Maurice Craig, *Dublin: 1660–1860* (Dublin: Liberties Press, 2006 (reprint of 1952 edition)), p.175; Oliver O'Hanlon, 'An Irishman's Diary on Alexis de Tocqueville and Ireland in 1835' in *The Irish Times*, 29 December 2015

5. *Hibernian Journal* 22/25 March 1776; James Whitelaw, *An Essay on the Population of Dublin, 1798* (London: Graisberry & Campbell, 1805), p.50, cited in Kevin C. Kearns, *Dublin Tenement Life: An Oral History* (Dublin: Gill & MacMillan, 1994), p.1

6. Maurice Curtis, *The Liberties: A History* (Dublin: The History Press Ireland, 2013), pp.49–51, 146–147; Constantia Maxwell, *Dublin Under the Georges* (London: Harap, 1936), p.78; John Gilbert, *History of the City of Dublin*, Three vols (Dublin: Gill & MacMillan, 1978), Vol. I, pp.142–145; Frank McDonald, 'A Window into the Sordid Reality of a Grand Era' in *The Irish Times*, 5 December 2015; Diarmuid Ó Gráda, *Georgian Dublin* (Cork: Cork University Press, 2015), pp.46–48, 58–61, 125

7. Maurice Craig, *Dublin: 1660–1860* (Dublin: Liberties Press, 2006 (reprint of 1952 edition)), p.71

8. Robert Somerville-Woodward & Nicola Morris, *17 Eustace Street: A History* (Dublin: Timeline Research Ltd, 2007), p.2; Maurice Curtis, *The Liberties: A History* (Dublin: The History Press Ireland, 2013), p.169

9. Niall McCullough, *Dublin: An Urban History* (Dublin: Ann Street Press, 1989), pp.33, 37

10. Maurice Curtis, *To Hell or Monto* (Dublin: The History Press Ireland, 2015), pp.73–74

11. *Hibernian Journal*, 6 May 1776

12. *Daily Gazeteer*, October 1736; Diarmuid Ó Gráda, *Georgian Dublin* (Cork: Cork University Press, 2015), pp.195, 200, 293–97; Hugh Oram, *The Newspaper Book* (Dublin: MO Books, 1983), p.35

13. John Gilbert, *History of the City of Dublin*, Three vols (Dublin: Gill & MacMillan, 1978), Vol. II, p.111

14. Constantia Maxwell, *Dublin Under the Georges 1714–1830* (London: Faber & Faber, 1956 (original edition, 1937)), pp.24, 26,33, 101, 23, 233

15. John Gilbert, *History of the City of Dublin*, Three vols (Dublin: Gill & MacMillan, 1978), Vol. II, pp.112–113

16. Diarmuid Ó Gráda, *Georgian Dublin* (Cork: Cork University Press, 2015), pp.293–297; Maurice Curtis, *The Liberties: A History* (Dublin: The History Press Ireland, 2013), pp.141–142

17. Ibid.

18. John Gilbert, *History of the City of Dublin*, Three vols (Dublin: Gill & MacMillan, 1978), Vol. I, p.94; Maurice Curtis, *The Liberties: A History* (Dublin: The History Press Ireland, 2013), p.142

7. FROM PUE'S TO BEWLEY'S – THE COFFEE HOUSES

1. Colette Adanan, Dublin City Architects
2. Máirtín Mac Con Iomaire, 'Coffee Culture in Dublin: A Brief History' in *A Journal of Media and Culture*, vol. 15, no. 2 (2012)
3. Constantia Maxwell, *Dublin under the Georges 1714–1830* (London: Harap, 1936); Maurice Curtis, *The Liberties: A History* (Dublin: The History Press Ireland, 2013), pp.140–141
4. Maurice Curtis, *The Liberties: A History* (Dublin: The History Press Ireland, 2013), pp.140–141
5. John Gilbert, *History of the City of Dublin*, Three vols (Dublin: Gill & MacMillan, 1978), Vol. II, pp.9–10
6. Máire Kennedy, 'Politics, coffee and news: The Dublin book trade in the eighteenth century', *DHR*, LVIII (2005), pp. 76–85; Colette Adanan, *Dublin City Architects*
7. John Gilbert, *History of the City of Dublin*, Three vols (Dublin: Gill & MacMillan, 1978), Vol. II, pp.161–162
8. John Gilbert, *History of the City of Dublin*, Three vols (Dublin: Gill & MacMillan, 1978), Vol. II, pp.163–164

8. FROM GRATTAN'S PARLIAMENT TO THE EAGLE TAVERN

1. Maurice Curtis, *The Liberties: A History* (Dublin: The History Press Ireland, 2013), pp.35–38
2. John Gilbert, *History of the City of Dublin*, Three vols (Dublin: Gill & MacMillan, 1978), Vol. III, pp.60–61
3. Ibid. p.72
4. Ibid. p.85
5. Margaret Cusack, *An Illustrated History of Ireland* (Dublin: Longmans Green & Co., 1868), Ch. 34; R.B. McDowell, 'The Protestant Nation (1775–1800)' in T.W. Moody and F.X. Martin, (eds), *The Course of Irish History* (Cork: The Mercier Press, 1994), p.233
6. R.B. McDowell, 'The Protestant Nation (1775–1800)' in T.W. Moody and F.X. Martin, (eds), *The Course of Irish History*, (Cork: The Mercier Press, 1994), p.233
7. Gwynn, Stephen, *Henry Grattan and his Times* (Westport: Greenwood Press, 1971); John Gilbert, *History of the City of Dublin*, Three vols (Dublin: Gill & MacMillan, 1978), Vol. III, p.122
8. Martin Wallace & Ian McCullough, *A Little History of Ireland* (Dublin: Appletree Press, 1994), p. 46; The Oireachtas, *Irish Parliamentary Tradition, Dublin* (Dublin: The Oireachtas, 2015)
9. John Gilbert, *History of the City of Dublin*, Three vols (Dublin: Gill & MacMillan, 1978), Vol. II, p.112
10. S.J. Connolly (ed.), *The Oxford Companion to Irish History* (Oxford: Oxford University Press, 1998), p.154
11. Maurice Craig, *Dublin: 1660–1860* (Dublin: Liberties Press, 2006 (reprint of 1952 edition)), pp.289–291; John Gilbert, *History of the City of Dublin*, Three vols (Dublin: Gill & MacMillan, 1978), Vol. III, p.134

12. Kildare Local History Society; Pat Marshall, 'Major Sirr the Arresting Officer' in *History Ireland*, No. 3, Autumn 2003

13. John Gilbert, *History of the City of Dublin*, Three vols (Dublin: Gill & MacMillan, 1978), Vol. II, p.30

14. William Drennan, *Erin*, No. 1 (1795)

15. John Gilbert, *History of the City of Dublin*, Three vols (Dublin: Gill & MacMillan, 1978), Vol. III, pp.167–70; *The Dublin Gazette*, July–December 1800

16. John Gilbert, *History of the City of Dublin*, Three vols (Dublin: Gill & MacMillan, 1978), Vol. III, p.173

17. John Gilbert, *History of the City of Dublin*, Three vols (Dublin: Gill & MacMillan, 1978), Vol. III, p.174

18. Maurice Craig, *Dublin: 1660–1860* (Dublin: Liberties Press, 2006 (reprint of 1952 edition)), pp.297–298

19. Mary Daly, *The Deposed Capital: A Social and Economic History 1860–1914* (Cork: Cork University Press, 1984)

20. Maria Edgeworth, *The Absentee* (Oxford: Oxford University Press, 1988), p.x.; Constantia Maxwell, *Dublin Under the Georges 1714–1830* (London: Faber & Faber, 1956 (original edition, 1937)), p.117

9. THE FREEDOM BELL AND THE FENIANS

1. Moody, T.W. (ed.), *The Fenian Movement* (Cork: Mercier Press, 1968); James Loughlin, University of Ulster

2. Barry Kennerk, *Shadow of the Brotherhood: The Temple Bar Murders* (Cork: Mercier Press, 2010)

3. Brian Maye, 'Centenary of United Irishman', *The Irish Times* (14 April 1999); Tomás O'Riordan, 'Arthur Griffith: The Pursuit of Sovereignty' in UCC Multitext Project in Irish History (2015)

4. Dublin City Council/City Hall, Cork Hill, Dublin, 2015

5. Donal Fallon, *Come Here to Me!* (www.comeheretome.com), 2 September 2014

6. *The Irish Times*, 25 April 1921

7. John Ainsworth, 'Kevin Barry – The Incident at Monk's bakery and the Making of an Irish Republican Legend' in *History*, vol. 87, no. 287, July 2002, pp.380–384.

10. FROM THE SHAMBLES TO THE EXCHANGE – THE OLD CITY

1. John Gilbert, *History of the City of Dublin*, Three vols (Dublin: Gill & MacMillan, 1978), Vol. I, pp.47–97; Douglas Bennett, *Encyclopaedia of Dublin* (Dublin: Gill & MacMillan, 1991), p.75; Maurice Curtis, *To Hell or Monto* (Dublin: The History Press Ireland, 2015), pp. 65–72; Howard Clarke, 'The Layers Missing from Viking Dublin' in *The Irish Times*, 30 January 2016; Howard Clarke (ed.), *Medieval Dublin: The Making of a Metropolis* (Dublin: Irish Academic Press, 2012), p. 28, 46, 60, 71.

2. John Gilbert, *History of the City of Dublin*, Three vols (Dublin: Gill & MacMillan, 1978), Vol. I, p.91

3. Douglas Bennett, *Encyclopaedia of Dublin* (Dublin: Gill & MacMillan, 1991), p.75

4. John Gilbert, *History of the City of Dublin*, Three vols (Dublin: Gill & MacMillan, 1978), Vol. I, p.55, 58

5. John Gilbert, *History of the City of Dublin*, Three vols (Dublin: Gill & MacMillan, 1978), Vol. I, pp.47–97; Douglas Bennett, *The Encyclopaedia of Dublin* (Dublin: Gill & MacMillan, 1991), p.75

6. J.W. de Courcy, *The Liffey in Dublin* (Dublin: Gill & Macmillan, 1996), p. 468; Frank McDonald, Open House Walking Tour of Temple Bar, 18 October 2015; *The Canberra Times*, 17 March 1988

7. 'Tart with a cart? Older song shows Dublin's Molly Malone in new light', *Guardian*, 18 July 2010

8. Ibid.

9. John Gilbert, *History of the City of Dublin*, Three vols (Dublin: Gill & MacMillan, 1978), Vol. I, p.55–92; Siobhán Marie Kilfeather, *Dublin: A Cultural History* (Oxford University Press US, 2005), p.6; Maurice Curtis, *To Hell or Monto* (Dublin: The History Press Ireland, 2015), pp.73–80; Rachel Flaherty, 'Molly Malone statue wheeled away to make way for Luas' in *The Irish Times*, 1 May 2014

10. Douglas Bennett, *The Encyclopaedia of Dublin* (Dublin: Gill & MacMillan, 1991), p.45

11. John Gilbert, *History of the City of Dublin*, Three vols (Dublin: Gill & MacMillan, 1978), Vol. I, pp.93–4

12. Éamonn Mac Thomáis, *Me Jewel and Darling Dublin* (Dublin: The O'Brien Press, 1985), p.89

13. John Gilbert, *History of the City of Dublin*, Three vols (Dublin: Gill & MacMillan, 1978), Vol. II, p.149; Douglas Bennett, *The Encyclopaedia of Dublin* (Dublin: Gill & MacMillan, 1991), p.71

14. *The Independent*, 18 January 1995

15. Peter Pearson, *The Heart of Dublin* (Dublin: The O'Brien Press, 2000), pp.65–67

16. Frank McDonald, Open House Tour of Temple Bar, 17 October 2015

17. John Gilbert, *History of the City of Dublin*, Three vols (Dublin: Gill & MacMillan, 1978), Vol. II, pp.114–119

18. Dublin City Council, *The Walls of Dublin*, N.D.

19. Howard Clarke, Sarah Dent & Ruth Johnson, *Dublinia: The Story of Medieval Dublin* (Dublin: The O'Brien Press, 2002), p.37

20. John Gilbert, *History of the City of Dublin*, Three vols (Dublin: Gill & MacMillan, 1978), Vol. II, p.121

11. LORDS OF THE HILL – CORK HOUSE TO THE CATHEDRAL

1. Douglas Bennett, *Encyclopaedia of Dublin* (Dublin: Gill &MacMillan, 1991), p.71; C.T. McCready, *Dublin Street Names Dated and Explained* (Dublin: Hodges, Figgis & Co., 1892)

2. John Gilbert, *History of the City of Dublin*, Three vols (Dublin: Gill & MacMillan, 1978), Vol. II, pp.6, 23; Vol. III, pp.46, 252

3. John Gilbert, *History of the City of Dublin*, Three vols (Dublin: Gill & MacMillan, 1978), Vol. II. pp.55–65

4. Niall McCullough, *Dublin: An Urban History* (Dublin: Ann Street Press, 1989), p.127

5. John Gilbert, *History of the City of Dublin*, Three vols (Dublin: Gill & MacMillan, 1978), Vol. II, pp.57–59

6. John Gilbert, *History of the City of Dublin*, Three vols (Dublin: Gill & MacMillan, 1978), Vol. II, p.60

7. John Gilbert, *History of the City of Dublin*, Three vols (Dublin: Gill & MacMillan, 1978), Vol. II, p.13

8. Maurice Craig, *Dublin: 1660–1860* (Dublin: Liberties Press, 2006 (reprint of 1952 edition)), p.229; John Gilbert, *History of the City of Dublin*, Three vols (Dublin: Gill & MacMillan, 1978), Vol. II, pp.14–21

9. John Gilbert, *History of the City of Dublin*, Three vols (Dublin: Gill & MacMillan, 1978), Vol. II, pp.16–17; Paul Rouse, *Sport and Ireland: A History* (Oxford: Oxford University Press, 2015)

10. Thanks to *Archiseek*, 2015
11. Liam C. Martin & Violet Martin, *Medieval Dublin* (Dublin: Xpress Publishing, 2014), p.16

12. SWORD MAKERS AND ROPE DANCERS – PARLIAMENT STREET TO FOWNES STREET

1. John Gilbert, *History of the City of Dublin*, Three vols (Dublin: Gill & MacMillan, 1978), Vol. II, pp.25–53
2. Peter Pearson, *The Heart of Dublin* (Dublin: The O'Brien Press, 2000), p.58
3. Frank McDonald, Open House Tour of Temple Bar, 17 October 2015
4. Pat Liddy, *Temple Bar – Dublin: An Illustrated History* (Dublin: Temple Bar Properties, 1992), p.36
5. John Gilbert, *History of the City of Dublin*, Three vols (Dublin: Gill & MacMillan, 1978), Vol. II, pp.27–29
6. Pat Lidy, *Temple Bar – Dublin: An Illustrated History* (Dublin: Temple Bar Properties, 1992), p.136; Peter Pearson, *The Heart of Dublin* (Dublin: The O'Brien Press, 2000), p.60; Maurice Craig, *Dublin: 1660–1860* (Dublin: Liberties Press, 2006 (Reprint of 1952 edition)), p.238
7. Patrick Freyne, 'Craft Beer Goes Mainstream', *The Irish Times* (24 October 2015); Lonely Planet, 2015.
8. Joe Curtis, *Times, Chimes and Charms of Dublin* (Dublin: Verge Books, 1992), p.40
9. John Lee, *Old Dublin Town/Reads Cutlers* (Dublin: John Lee, 2014); James Kelly of Kelly & Cogan Conservation Architects; Peter Pearson, *The Heart of Dublin* (Dublin: The O'Brien Press, 2000), pp.59–61; Éamonn MacThomáis, *Me Jewel and Darling Dublin* (Dublin: The O'Brien Press, 1985), p.91.
10. Constantia Maxwell, *Dublin Under the Georges 1714–1830* (London: Faber & Faber, 1956 (original edition, 1937)), pp.106–107
11. John Lee, *Old Dublin Town/Reads Cutlers* (Dublin: John Lee, 2014); James Kelly of Kelly & Cogan Conservation Architects
12. John Gilbert, *History of the City of Dublin*, Three vols (Dublin: Gill & MacMillan, 1978), Vol. II, pp.151–165
13. John Gilbert, *History of the City of Dublin*, Three vols (Dublin: Gill & MacMillan, 1978), Vol. II, pp.151–165
14. Peter Pearson, *The Heart of Dublin* (Dublin: The O'Brien Press, 2000), p.51
15. Pat Liddy, *Temple Bar – Dublin: An Illustrated History* (Dublin: Temple Bar Properties, 1992), p.117; Maurice Curtis, *Rathgar: A History* (Dublin: The History Press Ireland, 2015), p.94
16. Connolly's Books, 2015; Maurice Curtis, *Challenge to Democracy: Militant Catholicism in Modern Ireland* (Dublin: The History Press, 2010); Frank McNally, 'An Irishman's Diary', *The Irish Times*, 21 August 2015
17. John Gilbert, *History of the City of Dublin*, Three vols (Dublin: Gill & MacMillan, 1978), Vol. II, p.167; Hugh Oram, *The Newspaper Book* (Dublin: MO Books, 1983), p.31
18. Paul Clerkin, *Dublin Street Names* (Dublin: Gill & Macmillan, 2001), p.48; Katherine Butler, 'Synagogues of Old Dublin', *Dublin Historical Record*, vol. 27, no. 4 (September 1974), pp.118–130; Pat Liddy, *Temple Bar – Dublin* (Dublin: Temple Bar Properties, 1991), p.93
19. John Gilbert, *History of the City of Dublin*, Three vols (Dublin: Gill & MacMillan, 1978), Vol. I, p.67
20. Douglas Bennett, *Encyclopaedia of Dublin* (Dublin: Gill & MacMillan, 1991), p.46
21. Peter Pearson, *The Heart of Dublin* (Dublin: The O'Brien Press, 2000), p.52

22. Donal Fallon/Flora Mitchell/Siobhan Bradford/Lydia Little on *Come Here to Me!* (www.comeheretome.com), 2015
23. *The Irish Times*, 23 May 1931
24. John Gilbert, *History of the City of Dublin*, Three vols (Dublin: Gill & MacMillan, 1978), Vol. II, p.168
25. Maurice Curtis, *Rathgar: A History* (Dublin: The History Press Ireland, 2015), p.132–133
26. Frank McDonald, *The Construction of Dublin* (Cork: Gandon Editions, 2000), pp.288–289; Shane O'Toole of Group '91 speaking on *Designing Ireland*, RTÉ, 12 November 2015
27. Peter Pearson, *The Heart of Dublin* (Dublin: The O'Brien Press, 2000), pp.42–43; Douglas Bennett, *Encyclopaedia of Dublin* (Dublin: Gill & MacMillan, 1991), p.71
28. John Gilbert, *History of the City of Dublin*, Three vols (Dublin: Gill & MacMillan, 1978), Vol. II, pp. 310–314
29. Frank McDonald, Open House Tour of Temple Bar, 17 October 2015
30. Irish Film Institute, 2015
31. Irish Architectural Archive; Temple Bar Properties; Dublin City Council; Group '91 Architects – Shane O'Toole and Michael Kelly
32. John Gilbert, *History of the City of Dublin*, Three vols (Dublin: Gill & MacMillan, 1978), Vol. II, pp.310–313
33. Niall McCullough, *Dublin: An Urban History* (Dublin: Ann Street Press, 1989), p.32; Mona Germaine-Dillon, 'The Huguenots' in *Irish Family History*, Vol. XIII (1997).
34. Irish Landmark Trust/Dublin Civic Trust; Peter Pearson, *The Heart of Dublin* (Dublin: The O'Brien Press, 2000), pp.42, 47; Frank McDonald, Open House Tour of Temple Bar, 17 October 2015
35. Courtesy of The Irish Landmark Trust
36. Robert Somerville-Woodward & Nicola Morris, *17 Eustace Street: A History* (Dublin: IFI/Timeline Research, 2007), p.12; Douglas Bennett, *Encyclopaedia of Dublin* (Dublin: Gill & MacMillan, 1991), p.71
37. Peter Pearson, *The Heart of Dublin* (Dublin: The O'Brien Press, 2000), p.41
38. Murray O'Laoire Associates/Irish Architectural Awards, 1995; Peter Pearson, *The Heart of Dublin* (Dublin: The O'Brien Press, 2000), p.43; Aidan Dunne in Patricia Quinn (ed.), *The Power of an Idea* (Dublin: Temple Bar Properties Ltd, 1996) p.75.
39. Irish Architecture Awards, 1994–1996
40. Frank McDonald, 'The Business End of the Bar', *The Irish Times*, 10 August 2010
41. Peter Pearson, *The Heart of Dublin* (Dublin: The O'Brien Press, 2000), p.39
42. Pat Liddy, *Temple Bar – Dublin: An Illustrated History* (Dublin: Temple Bar Properties, 1992), p.81; Muriel Bolger, *Dublin: City of Literature* (Dublin: The O'Brien Press, 2011)
43. Thanks to Claddagh Records, 2 Cecilia Street, 2015
44. John Gilbert, *History of the City of Dublin*, Three vols (Dublin: Gill & MacMillan, 1978), Vol. II, pp.171–173
45. Pat Liddy, *Temple Bar – Dublin: An Illustrated History* (Dublin: Temple Bar Properties, 1992), p.95
46. John Gilbert, *History of the City of Dublin*, Three vols (Dublin: Gill & MacMillan, 1978), Vol. I, pp.320–321
47. Sean Murphy, *A Short History of Dublin's Temple Bar* (Bray: Centre for Irish Genealogical and Historical Studies, 1994–2002); Peter Pearson, *The Heart of Dublin* (Dublin: The O'Brien Press, 2000), p.39
48. *The Irish Times*, 25 April 1979

13. THE HEART OF TEMPLE BAR – THE SQUARE, THE CROWN AND THE FLEET

1. John Gilbert, *History of the City of Dublin*, Three vols (Dublin: Gill & MacMillan, 1978), Vol. II, pp.314–316
2. John Gilbert, *History of the City of Dublin*, Three vols (Dublin: Gill & MacMillan, 1978), Vol. II, p.317; National Gallery of Ireland, *Aspects of Irish Art* (Dublin: National Gallery of Ireland/Cahill & Co., 1974), p.112
3. *The Irish Times*, 8 November 2006
4. Group '91/Crofton Architects, 2015
5. Pat Liddy, *Temple Bar – Dublin: An Illustrated History* (Dublin: Temple Bar Properties, 1992), p.63
6. Temple Bar Gallery and Studios, *TBG&S Generation: 30 Years of Creativity at Temple Bar Gallery and Studios* (Dublin: TBG&S, 2013)
7. Ibid.
8. Bad Ass Café, 2015
9. John Gilbert, *History of the City of Dublin*, Three vols (Dublin: Gill & MacMillan, 1978), Vol. II, p.303; Diarmuid Ó Gráda, *Georgian Dublin* (Cork: Cork University Press, 2015), p.258
10. Graphic Studio Dublin, 2015
11. Olivia Kelly, *The Irish Times*, 13 May 2012; Frank McDonald, Open House Tour of Temple Bar, 17 October 2015
12. John Gilbert, *History of the City of Dublin*, Three vols (Dublin: Gill & MacMillan, 1978), Vol. II, p.321
13. Maurice Curtis, *To Hell or Monto* (Dublin: The History Press Ireland, 2015)
14. John Gilbert, *History of the City of Dublin*, Three vols (Dublin: Gill & MacMillan, 1978), Vol. II, pp.142, 44, 310, 321–335
15. Pat Liddy, *Temple Bar – Dublin: An Illustrated History* (Dublin: Temple Bar Properties, 1992), p.61
16. Maurice Craig, *Dublin: 1660–1860* (Dublin: Liberties Press, 2006 (reprint of 1952 edition)), p.70
17. John Gilbert, *History of the City of Dublin*, Three vols (Dublin: Gill & MacMillan, 1978), Vol. II, pp.333, 364; Douglas Bennett, *Encyclopaedia of Dublin* (Dublin: Gill & MacMillan, 1991), p. 77; *Thom's Directory*
18. Maurice Curtis, *The Liberties: A History* (Dublin: The History Press Ireland, 2013), p.87
19. IWWU, *A Brief History of the Irish Women Workers' Union* (Dublin: IWWU/SIPTU, 2015); Mary Jones, *These Obstreperous Lassies* (Dublin: Gill & MacMillan, 1988)
20. Thanks to Teresa Ahern and Willie Ahern of The Palace Bar, Fleet Street, Temple Bar, 2015
21. The Icon Factory, Aston Place, Temple Bar; Frank McDonald, Open House Tour of Temple Bar, 17 October 2015
22. *The Irish Times* (30 May 1928)

14. FROM THE ROYAL MILE TO THE BOOKEND – PERIMETER PLACES

1. John Gilbert, *History of the City of Dublin*, Three vols (Dublin: Gill & MacMillan, 1978), Vol. II, pp.256–280; Diarmuid Ó Gráda, *Georgian Dublin* (Cork: Cork University Press, 2015), p.86
2. John Gilbert, *History of the City of Dublin*, Three vols (Dublin: Gill & MacMillan, 1978), Vol. II, pp.279–280
3. John Gilbert, *History of the City of Dublin*, Three vols (Dublin: Gill & MacMillan, 1978), Vol. II, pp.281–303

4. Constantia Maxwell, *Dublin Under the Georges 1714–1830* (London: Faber & Faber, 1956 (Original edition, 1937)), pp.253–254

5. Peter Pearson, *The Heart of Dublin* (Dublin: The O'Brien Press, 2000), p.82

6. Ibid., pp.79–81

7. Éamonn MacThomáis, *Me Jewel and Darling Dublin* (Dublin: The O'Brien Press, 1985), p.92

8. Peter Pearson, *The Heart of Dublin* (Dublin: The O'Brien Press, 2000), p.79; Joe Curtis, *Times, Chimes and Charms of Dublin* (Dublin: Verge Books, 1992), p.44

9. Peter Pearson, *The Heart of Dublin* (Dublin: The O'Brien Press, 2000), p.77

10. Courtesy of *Archiseek*/Central Bank, 2015

11. Arthur Beesley/Ciarán Hancock in *The Irish Times*, 21 October 2015

12. Maurice Craig, *Dublin: 1660–1860* (Dublin: The Liberties Press, 2006 (reprint of 1952 edition)), p.118; Éamonn MacThomáis, *Me Jewel and Darling Dublin* (Dublin: The O'Brien Press, 1985), pp.14–15

13. Maurice Craig, *Dublin: 1660–1860* (Dublin: The Liberties Press, 2006 (reprint of 1952 edition)), p.118; John Gilbert, *History of the City of Dublin*, Three vols (Dublin: Gill & MacMillan, 1978), Vol. II, p.305.

14. Samuel Lewis, *Topographical Dictionary of Ireland* (London: S. Lewis & Co., 1837)

15. Peter Pearson, *The Heart of Dublin* (Dublin: The O'Brien Press, 2000), pp.82–83

16. John Gilbert, *History of the City of Dublin*, Three vols (Dublin: Gill & MacMillan, 1978), Vol. III, pp.40–56, 247–248, 367

17. Jurys Hotel Group, 2015

18. Peter Pearson, *The Heart of Dublin* (Dublin: The O'Brien Press, 2000), p.76

19. Ibid., p.77

20. Pat Liddy, *Temple Bar – Dublin: An Illustrated History* (Dublin: Temple Bar Properties Ltd, 1992), p.33

21. Maurice Craig, *Dublin: 1660–1860* (Dublin: The Liberties Press, 2006 (reprint of 1952 edition)), p.69

22. John Gilbert, *History of the City of Dublin*, Three vols (Dublin: Gill & MacMillan, 1978), Vol. III, pp.77–83

23. Ibid., p, 77; *Dublin Penny Journal*, vol. 1, no. 25, 15 December 1832

24. Joe Curtis, *Times, Chimes and Charms of Dublin* (Dublin: Verge Books), p.55

25. Peter Pearson, *The Heart of Dublin* (Dublin: The O'Brien Press, 2000), p.31

26. Maurice Craig, *Dublin: 1660–1860* (Dublin: Liberties Press, 2006 (reprint of 1952 edition)), p.53

27. *Archiseek*, 2015

28. Pat Liddy, *Temple Bar – Dublin: An Illustrated History* (Dublin: Temple Bar Properties, 1992), p.66; Donal Fallon, *Come Here to Me!* (www.comeheretome.com), 2 September 2014

29. *Dublin Evening Post*, 24 May 1816; Dublin City Council, *The Bridges of Dublin*, 2015

30. Éamonn MacThomáis, *Me Jewel and Darling Dublin* (Dublin: The O'Brien Press, 1985), p.12

31. Arminta Wallace in *The Irish Times* (16 June 2012); Pat Liddy, *Temple Bar – Dublin: An Illustrated History* (Dublin: Temple Bar Properties, 1992), p.108

32. The Clarence Hotel, 2015; Hugh Oram, *The Newspaper Book* (Dublin: MO Books, 1983), p.186

33. Colm Lennon and John Montague, *John Rocque's Dublin* (Dublin: Royal Irish Academy, 2010), p.21; Eamon O'Reilly of Dublin Port Company

34. Peter Pearson, *The Heart of Dublin* (Dublin: The O'Brien Press, 2000), p.65

35. Pól Ó Conghaile, *Secret Dublin: An Unusual Guide* (Versailles: JonGlez, 2013), p.73

36. Peter Pearson, *The Heart of Dublin* (Dublin: The O'Brien Press, 2000), pp.63–64

37. *Archiseek*, 2015

15. FROM THE SMOCK TO THE PROJECT – THEATRE TIMES AND RIVAL TYPES

1. John Gilbert, *History of the City of Dublin*, Three vols (Dublin: Gill & MacMillan, 1978), Vol. II, p.196; Diarmuid Ó Gráda, *Georgian Dublin* (Cork: Cork University Press, 2015), p.24; Christopher Morash, School of English, TCD

2. John Gilbert, *History of the City of Dublin*, Three vols (Dublin: Gill & MacMillan, 1978), Vol. II, pp.66–110; Smock Alley Theatre, 2015

3. Smock Alley Theatre; Frank McNally, 'An Irishman's Diary', *The Irish Times*, 21 August 2015; Frank McNally, Open House Tour of Temple Bar, 17 October 2015

4. John Gilbert, *History of the City of Dublin*, Three vols (Dublin: Gill & MacMillan, 1978), Vol. II, pp.332–333

5. John Gilbert, *History of the City of Dublin*, Three vols (Dublin: Gill & MacMillan, 1978), Vol. II, pp.319–320

6. Constantia Maxwell, *Dublin Under the Georges 1714–1830* (London: Faber & Faber, 1956 (original edition, 1937)), p.229; Chisholm, Hugh, 'Woffington, Margaret', *Encyclopaedia Britannica* (11th ed.) (Cambridge: Cambridge University Press, 1911)

7. Maurice Craig, *Dublin: 1660–1860* (Dublin: Liberties Press, 2006 (reprint of 1952 edition)), pp.196–197

8. John Gilbert, *History of the City of Dublin*, Three vols (Dublin: Gill & MacMillan, 1978), Vol. II, pp.182–184

9. John Gilbert, *History of the City of Dublin*, Three vols (Dublin: Gill & MacMillan, 1978), Vol. II, p.188

10. John Gilbert, *History of the City of Dublin*, Three vols (Dublin: Gill & MacMillan, 1978), Vol. II, p.194

11. Diarmuid Ó Gráda, *Georgian Dublin* (Cork: Cork University Press, 2015), p.272; Pat Liddy, *Temple Bar – Dublin: An Illustrated History* (Dublin: Temple Bar Properties, 1992), p.82; John Gilbert, *History of the City of Dublin*, Three vols (Dublin: Gill & MacMillan, 1978), Vol. II, p.255

12. Niall McCullough, *Dublin: An Urban History* (Dublin: Ann Street Press, 1989), p.136

13. John Gilbert, *History of the City of Dublin*, Three vols (Dublin: Gill & MacMillan, 1978), Vol. I, pp.71–78

14. Maurice Craig, *Dublin: 1660–1860* (Dublin: Liberties Press, 2006 (reprint of 1952 edition)), pp.162–163; John Gilbert, *History of the City of Dublin*, Three vols (Dublin: Gill & MacMillan, 1978), Vol. I, pp.86–91

15. Maurice Craig, *Dublin: 1660–1860* (Dublin: Liberties Press, 2006 (reprint of 1852 edition)), p.164

16. John Gilbert, *History of the City of Dublin*, Three vols (Dublin: Gill & MacMillan, 1978), Vol. I, pp.71–78

17. Pat Liddy, *Temple Bar – Dublin: An Illustrated History* (Dublin: Temple Bar Properties, 1992), p.56; The Olympia Theatre, 2015

18. Irish Film Institute, 'Ireland's Films Lost and Found: Rediscovered Gems of Irish Cinema', blog on www.ifi.ie, 2015

19. Fintan O'Toole, *The Irish Times*, 12 September 2015

20. Ibid., 25 September 2015

21. Project Arts Centre, *About Us/History*, 12 October 2015; Frank McDonald, Open House Tour of Temple Bar, 17 October 2015

22. The New Theatre, 2015

16. SCRIBES OF THE TEMPLE – FROM SWIFT TO SMYLLIE

1. Hugh Oram, *The Newspaper Book* (Dublin: MO Books, 1983), pp.25–26

2. Vincent Kinnane, 'Printing and Publishing' in S.J. Connolly (ed.), *The Oxford Companion to Irish History* (Oxford: Oxford University Press, 1998), pp.461–463; Peter Pearson, *The Heart of Dublin* (Dublin: The O'Brien Press, 2000), p.37

3. Maurice Craig, *Dublin: 1660–1860* (Dublin: Liberties Press, 2006 (reprint of 1952 edition)), p.108

4. John Gilbert, *History of the City of Dublin*, Three vols (Dublin: Gill & MacMillan, 1978), Vol. II, p.155

5. John Gilbert, *History of the City of Dublin*, Three vols (Dublin: Gill & MacMillan, 1978), Vol. I, pp.172–175

6. Maurice Curtis, *Rathfarnham* (Dublin: The History Press, 2013), p.30

7. Maurice Craig, *Dublin: 1660–1860* (Dublin: Liberties Press, 2006 (reprint of 1952 edition)), pp.242–243

8. Máire Kennedy – Special Collections, Dublin City Archives; Maurice Craig, *Irish Bookbindings 1600–1800* (London: Cassells, 1954); Maurice Craig, *Irish Bookbinding*, Irish Heritage Series, 6 (Dublin: Eason, 1976)

9. Hugh Oram, *The Newspaper Book* (Dublin: MO Books, 1983), p.28

10. Maurice Curtis, *The Liberties: A History* (Dublin: The History Press Ireland, 2013), pp.93–96; Maurice Craig, *Dublin: 1660–1860* (Dublin: Liberties Press, 2006 (reprint of 1952 edition)), p.227; St Patrick's Cathedral, 2015

11. John Gilbert, *History of the City of Dublin*, Three vols (Dublin: Gill & MacMillan, 1978), Vol. III, p.72

12. Mason, William Monck, *History of St Patrick's Cathedral* (Dublin: W. Folds, 1820); Jonathan Swift, *Drapier's Letters* (Herbert Davis ed.) (Oxford: Oxford University Press, 1935); Maurice Curtis, *The Liberties: A History* (Dublin: The History Press Ireland, 2013), pp.93–96

13. John Gilbert, *History of the City of Dublin*, Three vols (Dublin: Gill & MacMillan, 1978), Vol. III, p.84

14. John Gilbert, *History of the City of Dublin*, Three vols (Dublin: Gill & MacMillan, 1978), Vol. II, pp.153–154

15. Jonathan Swift, *A Modest Proposal* (Dublin: Sara Harding, 1729), available from Project Gutenberg. Retrieved on 30 November 2015 at www.gutenberg.org/files/1080/1080–h/1080–h.htm

16. John Gilbert, *History of the City of Dublin*, Three vols (Dublin: Gill & MacMillan, 1978), Vol. II, pp.30–33, p. 53; Boylan, Henry (1998). *A Dictionary of Irish Biography*. 3rd Edition. Dublin: Gill and MacMillan. p.128

17. John Gilbert, *History of the City of Dublin*, Three vols (Dublin: Gill & MacMillan, 1978), Vol II, p.49

18. John Gilbert, *History of the City of Dublin*, Three vols (Dublin: Gill & MacMillan, 1978), Vol. II, p.39

19. Maurice Craig, *Dublin: 1660–1860*. Dublin: Liberties Press, 2006 (Reprint of 1952 edition, pp.164–165; St Patrick's Cathedral, 2015

20. John Gilbert, *History of the City of Dublin*, Three vols (Dublin: Gill & MacMillan, 1978). Vol. I, pp.294–295

21. John Gilbert, *History of the City of Dublin*, Three vols (Dublin: Gill & MacMillan, 1978). Vol. III, p.99

22. Hugh Oram, *The Newspaper Book* (Dublin: MO Books, 1983), p.36

23. Ibid.

24. John Gilbert, *History of the City of Dublin*, Three vols (Dublin: Gill & MacMillan, 1978), Vol. I, pp.294–295; Diarmuid Ó Gráda, *Georgian Dublin* (Cork: Cork University Press, 2015), p.206

25. Diarmuid Ó Gráda, *Georgian Dublin* (Cork: Cork University Press, 2015), p.206; William John Fitzpatrick, *Ireland Before the Union: With Extracts* (London: Forgotten Books, 2013 (originally published 1867)), pp.77–78; John Gilbert, *History of the City of Dublin*, Three vols (Dublin: Gill & MacMillan, 1978), Vol. I, pp.25–26

26. Rosemary Richey, 'From the Files of the DIB – Copper Faced Jack' in *History Ireland*, Issue 6, no. 14, November/December 2006

27. John Gilbert, *History of the City of Dublin*, Three vols (Dublin: Gill & MacMillan, 1978), Vol. I, pp.294–295; William J. Fitzpatrick, *The Sham Squire and the Informers of 1798* (Dublin: W.B. Kelly, 1872); Felix M. Larkin, 'A Great Daily Organ: The *Freeman's Journal*, 1763–1924' in *History Ireland* (May-June 2006), pp.44–49; Hugh Oram, *The Newspaper Book* (Dublin: MO Books, 1983), p.36

28. Hugh Oram, *The Newspaper Book* (Dublin: MO Books, 1983), pp.48–49

29. Ibid., p.49

30. Hugh Oram, *The Irish Times* (20 July 2002)

31. Ibid.; Éamonn MacThomáis, *Me Jewel and Darling Dublin* (Dublin: The O'Brien Press, 1985), p.50

32. Hugh Oram, *The Newspaper Book* (Dublin: MO Books, 1983), p.92

33. Ibid.

34. *The Irish Times*, 11 March 2000

35. Hugh Oram, *The Newspaper Book* (Dublin: MO Books, 1983), p.59; Éamonn MacThomáis, *Me Jewel and Darling Dublin* (Dublin: The O'Brien Press, 1985), p.50

36. Maurice Craig, *Dublin: 1660–1860* (Dublin: Liberties Press, 2006 (reprint of 1952 edition)), p.338

37. Ibid.

38. Joe Langtry and Nikki Carter (eds), *Mount Jerome: A Victorian Cemetery* (Dublin: Staybro Publications/Mount Jerome Historical Project, 1996/7), pp.31–32

39. Brian Maye, *The Irish Times* 26 August 2014; Éamonn MacThomáis, *Me Jewel and Darling Dublin* (Dublin: The O'Brien Press, 1985), p.50

40. Mount Jerome cemetery, Graves of Historical Interest 2015

41. Mark Lawlor/John Gallagher in *The Irish Independent*, 12 April 2012

42. Don Cameron, *Don's Dublin*, 10 September 2015; Maurice Curtis, *Rathmines* (Dublin: The History Press Ireland, 2011), p.117

43. Maurice Curtis, *The Liberties: A History* (Dublin: The History Press Ireland, 2013), pp.135–136.

44. Ibid.

45. John P. Gunning, *Moore: Poet and Patriot* (Dublin: M.H. Gill and Son, 1900; Dublin Music Trade), *William Power*, 2015

46. Willie Ahern of The Palace Bar, 2015

47. Hugh Oram, *The Newspaper Book* (Dublin: MO Books, Dublin: 1983), p.185; Peter Costello, *The Dublin Literary Pub Crawl* (Dublin: Irish Books and Media, 1996), pp.60–64; Willie Ahern of The Palace Bar, 2015

48. Hugh Oram, *The Irish Times*, 14 October 2006

49. Colm Quillagan, *Dublin Literary Pub Crawl* (Dublin: Writer's Island, 2008), pp.92–93; Hugh Oram, *The Newspaper Book* (Dublin: MO Books, 1983), p.283

50. Willie Ahern of The Palace Bar; The Irish Guild of Sommeliers; *The Irish Times* archives, 2015; Peter Murtagh, 'In the Editor's Chair: R.M. Smyllie's Life and Irish Times' in *The Irish Times*, 3 October 2014; Editor's Room Exhibition in the Little Museum of Dublin, 2014

51. Ian Thomson, *The Spectator*, 1 February 2014

52. James Earley, 'Liberate Ulysses', email, Dublin, 11 January 2014

53. James Joyce, *Dubliners* (London: Penguin Books, 2000), p.105

54. James Joyce, *Ulysses* (Paris: Shakespeare, 1922), pp.504–520

17. LINEN AND LIPSTICK – RESURGENCE AND RENEWAL

1. Peter Pearson, *The Heart of Dublin* (Dublin: The O'Brien Press, 2000), p.50
2. Frank McDonald, *The Destruction of Dublin* (Dublin: Gill and MacMillan, 1985), p.1
3. Frank McDonald in *The Canberra Times*, 17 March 1988
4. *The Canberra Times*, 17 March 1988
5. Frank McDonald, Open House Walking Tour of Temple Bar, 17 October 2015
6. Peter Pearson, *The Heart of Dublin* (Dublin: The O'Brien Press, 2000), p.35
7. Sean Murphy, *A Short History of Dublin's Temple Bar* (Bray: Centre for Irish Genealogical and Historical Studies, 1994)
8. Dublin City Association of An Taisce. *The Temple Area: A Policy for its Future* (Dublin: An Taisce, 1985); Sean Murphy, *A Short History of Dublin's Temple Bar* (Bray: Centre for Irish Genealogical and Historical Studies, 1994); Peter Pearson, *The Heart of Dublin* (Dublin: The O'Brien Press, 2000), pp.35–37
9. Frank McDonald, *The Construction of Dublin* (Cork: Gandon Editions, 2000), p.282
10. Dublin Corporation Planning Department, *The Temple Bar Area: Action Plan* (Dublin: Dublin Corporation Planning Department, 1990); Temple Bar Properties Ltd, *Temple Bar Guide* (Dublin: Temple Bar Properties Ltd, 1992)
11. Temple Bar Properties Ltd, *Development Programme for Temple Bar* (Dublin: Temple Bar Properties Ltd, 1992), pp.7–8, 16; Frank McDonald, *The Construction of Dublin* (Cork: Gandon Editions, 2000), pp.282–283, 290
12. MCMA/Irish Architectural Archive, 2015
13. Shane O'Toole of the original Group '91 speaking on RTÉ's *Designing Ireland*, 12 November 2015
14. Pat Liddy, *Temple Bar – Dublin: An Illustrated History* (Dublin: Temple Bar Properties Ltd, 1992), p.9; Frank McDonald, *The Construction of Dublin* (Cork: Gandon Editions, 2000, pp.283, 285, 287

FURTHER READING

Geoffrey Ashe, *The Hell-Fire Clubs: Sex, Rakes and Libertines* (London: Sutton Publishing, 2nd edition, 2005)

Jonathan Bardon, *Hallelujah* (Dublin: Gill & MacMillan, 2015)

Douglas Bennett, *Encyclopaedia of Dublin* (Dublin: Gill & MacMillan, 1991)

Charles Brooking, *A Map of the City and Suburbs of Dublin* (London, 1728) (Facsimile reproduced in 1983 by Friends of Trinity College Dublin Library)

Desmond Clarke, *Dublin* (London: B.T. Batsford, 1977)

H.B. Clarke (ed.), *Medieval Dublin: The Making of a Metropolis* (Dublin: Irish Academic Press, 1990)

S.J. Connolly (ed.), *The Oxford Companion to Irish History* (Oxford: Oxford University Press, 1998)

Peter Costello, *Dublin Churches* (Dublin: Gill & MacMillan, 1989)

Maurice Craig, *Dublin: 1660–1860* (Dublin: Allen Figgis, 1952)

Maurice Craig, *James Malton's Dublin Views* (Gerrard's Cross, Buckinghamshire: Colin Smythe, 1981)

Maurice Curtis, *A Challenge to Democracy: Militant Catholicism in Modern Ireland* (Dublin: The History Press Ireland, 2010)

Maurice Curtis, *Glasnevin* (Dublin: The History Press Ireland, 2014)

Maurice Curtis, *Portobello* (Dublin: The History Press Ireland, 2012)

Maurice Curtis, *Rathfarnham* (Dublin: The History Press Ireland, 2013)

Maurice Curtis, *Rathgar: A History* (Dublin: The History Press Ireland, 2015)

Maurice Curtis, *Rathmines* (Dublin: The History Press Ireland, 2011)

Maurice Curtis, *The Liberties: A History* (Dublin: The History Press Ireland, 2013)

Maurice Curtis, *To Hell or Monto: Dublin's Most Notorious Red-Light Districts* (Dublin: The History Press Ireland, 2015)

Margaret Anne Cusack, *An Illustrated History of Ireland* (London: MacMillan, 1868)

Mary Daly, *The Deposed Capital: A Social and Economic History, 1860–1914* (Cork: Cork University Press, 1984)

J.W. De Courcey, *The Liffey in Dublin* (Dublin: Gill & MacMillan, 1986)

David Dickson, *Dublin: The Making of a Capital City* (London: Profile Books, 2014)

David Dickson (ed.), *The Gorgeous Mask: Dublin 1700–1850* (Dublin: 1987)

Sean Duffy (ed.), *Medieval Dublin* Vol. I (Dublin: Four Courts Press, 2000)

John T. Gilbert, *A History of the City of Dublin* 3 Vols (Vol. I, 1854; Vols II & III, 1859) (reprint Dublin: Gill & Macmillan, 1972)

Desmond Guinness, *Georgian Dublin* (London: Batsford, 1979)

Stephen Gwynn, *Henry Grattan and his Times* (Westport: Greenwood Press, 1971)

Elizabeth Healy, *The Book of the Liffey* (Dublin: Wolfhound Press, 1988)

Deirdre Kelly, *Hands off Dublin* (Dublin: The O'Brien Press, 1976)

Enda MacMahon, *A Most Respectable Meeting of Merchants: A History of the Dublin Chamber of Commerce* (Dublin: Londubh Books, 2014)

James Kelly & Martyn J. Powell (eds), *Clubs and Societies in Eighteenth-Century Ireland* (Dublin: Four Courts Press, 2010)

Colm Lennon & John Montague, *John Rocque's Dublin* (Dublin: Royal Irish Academy, 2010)

Pat Liddy, *Dublin: A Celebration. From the 1st to the 21st Century* (Dublin: Dublin City Council, 2000)

Pat Liddy, *Temple Bar – Dublin: An Illustrated History* (Dublin: Temple Bar Properties, 1992)

Pat Liddy, *The Changing Landscapes of Dublin* (Dublin: City Info, Artane, 2003)

Evelyn Lord, *The Hellfire Clubs: Sex, Satanism and Secret Societies* (Yale: Yale University Press, 2008)

Marie Luddy, *Prostitution and Irish Society, 1800–1940* (Cambridge: Cambridge University Press, 2007)

Mary Lyons (ed.), *The Memoirs of Mrs Leeson, Madam, 1727–97* (Dublin: Lilliput Press, 1995)

Éamonn MacThomáis, *Janey Mack me Shirt is Black* (Dublin: The O'Brien Press, 1988)

Éamonn MacThomáis, *Me Jewel and Darling Dublin* (Dublin: The O'Brien Press, 1985)

Adrian James Malton, *A Picturesque and Descriptive View of the City of Dublin 1792–1799* (Gerrard's Cross, Buckinghamshire: Colin Smythe, 1978)

Constantia Maxwell, *Dublin Under the Georges 1714–1830* (London: George Harrap, 1946)

C.T. McCready, *Dublin Street Names Dated and Explained* (Dublin: Hodges & Figgis, 1892)

Niall McCullough, *Dublin: An Urban History* (Dublin: Ann Street Press, 1989)

Frank McDonald, *The Construction of Dublin* (Cork: Gandon Editions, 2000)

Frank McDonald, *The Destruction of Dublin* (Dublin: Gill & MacMillan, 1985)

McLoughlin, *Guide to Historic Dublin* (Dublin: Gill & Macmillan, 1979)

Flora Mitchell, *Vanishing Dublin* (Dublin: Allen & Figgis, 1966)

Sean Murphy, *A Short History of Dublin's Temple Bar* (Bray: Centre for Irish Genealogical and Historical Studies, 1994–2002)

National Library of Ireland, *Historic Dublin Maps* (Dublin: NLI, 1987)

E.E. O'Donnell, *The Annals of Dublin: Fair City* (Dublin: Wolfhound Press, 1987)

Frederick O'Dwyer, *Lost Dublin* (Dublin: Gill & MacMillan, 1981)

Diarmuid Ó Gráda, *Georgian Dublin: The Forces that Shaped the City* (Cork: Cork University Press, 2015)

Hugh Oram, *The Newspaper Book: A History of Newspapers in Ireland, 1649–1983* (Dublin: MO Books, 1983)

John O'Regan, Patricia Quinn, John Searle, Bill Hastings, Peter Barrow & Gerry Haydon. *Temple Bar: The Power of an Idea* (Dublin: Temple Bar Properties, 1996)

Peter Pearson, *The Heart of Dublin: Resurgence of an Historic City* (Dublin: The O'Brien Press, 2000)

John Rocque, *An Exact Survey of the City of and Suburbs of Dublin* (Dublin: George Faulkner, 1756)

David Ryan, *Blasphemers and Blackguards: The Irish Hellfire Clubs* (Dublin: Merrion, 2012)

Peter Somerville-Large, *Dublin* (London: Granada Publishing, 1979)

Claire L. Sweeney, *The Rivers of Dublin* (Dublin: Dublin Corporation, 1991)

J. Warburton, J. Whitelaw, & R. Walsh, *History of the City of Dublin*, 2 vols (London: Caddell, Davies and Bulmer: 1818)

J.J. Webb, *The Guilds of Dublin* (Dublin: Sign of the Three Candles, 1929)

James Whitelaw, *Essay on the Population of Dublin in 1798* (London: Graiseberry and Campbell, 1805)

Jeremy Williams, *Architecture in Ireland, 1937–1921* (Dublin: Irish Academic Press, 1994)

NEWSPAPERS AND PERIODICALS

Dublin Builder
Dublin Evening Mail
Dublin Evening Post
Dublin Gazeteer
Dublin Historical Record (the journal of the Old Dublin Society)
Dublin Journal
Dublin Penny Journal (1832–1835)
Evening Mail
Faulkner's Dublin Journal
Freeman's Journal
Irish Independent
Journal of the Royal Society of Antiquaries of Ireland
Irish Arts Review Yearbook
Quarterly Bulletin of the Irish Georgian Society
The Irish Times
Thom's Street Directories
Walker's Hibernian Journal

INDEX